The Last Word
On
MANAGEMENT

Compiled by Rolf B. White

W. *FOULSHAM & CO. LTD.*

London · New York · Toronto · Cape Town · Sydney

W. Foulsham & Company Limited
Yeovil Road, Slough, Berkshire, SL1 4JH

ISBN 0-572-01474-0

Printed in Great Britain at
St Edmundsbury Press Limited,
Bury St Edmunds.

Preface

This book is a miscellany of quotations and quips, sayings and satire, wisecracks and witticisms, proverbs and precepts, dictums and doggerel, epigrams and aphorisms, truisms and adages, axioms and maxims, poems and rhymes, limericks and graffiti arranged as an anthology.

That's what it is, but forget it!

Treat it as an interesting Management Digest and you have a unique collection of the best that has been said or written on this subject from all over the world since records began. This will benefit all those in management as a useful source of information to repeat in letters, speeches and everyday conversation. With this book you can impress others with your wit and wisdom and get the "last word" in *first*.

More than that, it is a fund of hints and useful tips, memory joggers and general guidance to help you through the management jungle. If it fails sometimes to show you how to deal with various situations, at least you can learn from the many examples of how *not* to do it.

Every time you turn to it, we hope you will find something humorous and that you will learn or be reminded of an idea for your own benefit. If this does not happen, we must assume that you are either perfect or a perfect fool. As you are reading this book, neither is likely!

Many entries accentuate the personal intrigue, backbiting and infighting that can be found in any hierarchy. I expect that many readers will recognize some of the machinations that can exist in organizations of all sorts and that are not unknown in certain business companies. Although there is a competitive element in these circumstances, it is one of the few undesirable aspects of competition and reduces effectiveness in whatever field that particular organization is engaged.

Whether this climate is present or not depends entirely on the management itself and any weakness at the top provides a fertile seedbed for the spread of personal gain at the cost of company progress. Some degree of rivalry is acceptable and a reasonable motivation to all, but if internal politics are taking up too much time and energy, the eventual future of the organization must be in doubt.

Like most things in life, some parts of this book are better than others. Old-fashioned quotations are in, because often the cleverest ideas were originally recorded back in the old days and these more literary inclusions tend to be near the end of each chapter. If you find the going a trifle heavy, you can skip these sections, but, although the language may be somewhat pedantic, the meaning still holds good today.

Entries have been selected because they meant something to me; the message may be good common sense or even something utterly ridiculous, but it is here. Wisdom and stupidity lie side by side in this book to provoke thought and provide amusement.

The difference between this work and most other management books is that the editor does not agree with everything in it. In fact, there is violent disagreement with the sentiments expressed in many of the items. It is up to the reader to interpret his or her own view, remembering always that an opposite opinion often can provoke the correct response.

One of the advantages that go with the compilation of an anthology like this is that the blame for what is said rests squarely with the author of each entry and not with the editor. This applies in particular to the anti-feminism and male/female ratio of the contents. Any objections can be countered with the indisputable fact that the vast majority of recorded sayings were expressed by men and that, until recently, "man" was a popular collective noun used to describe the human race as a whole. That's our excuse and we're sticking to it!

It has taken many years to accumulate these prime remarks about management and, before I decided to produce this collection in bookform, the source of quotations was not always recorded. The result is that a very small number can only be acknowledged as anonymous. My apologies to those who may be offended by non-recognition and to anyone whom I was unable to contact for permission to use their material. Omissions will be rectified in subsequent editions.

It is an appropriate word that describes the function of responsibility and control of assets and people. With all the emotional traumas, MAN AGES.

R. B. W.

Contents

III CONTROL

IV WORK

V PLANNING

VI OPERATIONS

X   DANGERS

I BAD MANAGEMENT

The Rat Race

If rats want to race
And outpace my jog,
They may have to face
My dog ate their dog.

In America, unhappiness about the rat race is part of the people's happiness.   RALF DAHRENDORF

I think that maybe in every company today there is always at least one person who is going crazy slowly.   JOSEPH HELLER

I don't know if I'm slowing up or they're bringing in faster rats!   ROBERT ORBEN

It's hard not to chuckle. The white man is doing to other white men what the white man once did to the Indian.   DEWITT DILLON

Dropping out gives control to those few who don't drop out.   SOLANIS

Sometimes it seems like this is the choice—either kick ass or kiss ass.   JAMES CAAN

People are not born bastards. They have to work at it. ROD McKUEN

When advised by his doctor to take a walk on an empty stomach, Sidney Smith enquired, "Whose?" LORD BIRKETT

I often feel I'll just opt out of this rat race and buy another hunk of Utah. ROBERT REDFORD

But Jesus, you can't start worrying about what's going to happen. You get spastic enough worrying about what's happening now. LAUREN BACALL

Look, we trade every day out there with hustlers, deal makers, shysters, con men... that's the way businesses get started. That's the way this country was built. HUBERT ALLEN

The trouble with the rat race is that even if you win, you're still a rat. LILY TOMLIN

Better to know everybody than everything. ANON

It is ridiculous to call this an industry. This is not. This is rat eat rat, dog eat dog. I'll kill 'em, and I'm going to kill 'em before they kill me. You're talking about the American way of survival of the fittest. RAY KROC

When they ask about Race in a questionnaire, I always put down Rat. ANON

Any idiot can face a crisis—it's this day-to-day living that wears you out. ANTON CHEKHOV

When I hear somebody sigh that "Life is hard," I am always tempted to ask, "Compared to what?" SYDNEY HARRIS

Our significance is often the cause of our safety. AESOP

Pressed into service means pressed out of shape. ROBERT FROST

I like to consume because if you don't they'll consume you. MARIAN ELLIOTT

Man is the only animal that can be skinned more than once. JIMMY DURANTE

Adherent: a follower who has yet not gotten all he expects.
                                        AMBROSE BIERCE

Why is it there are so many more horses' asses than there are horses?
                                        G. GORDON LIDDY

I like long walks, especially when they are taken by people who annoy
me.   FRED ALLEN

Include me out.   SAMUEL GOLDWYN

The same people who can deny others everything are famous for refusing
themselves nothing.   LEIGH HUNT

When smashing monuments, save the pedestals—they always come in
handy.   STANISLAW J. LEC

I am not confused. I'm just well mixed. ROBERT FROST

If you know a better 'ole, go to it.   BRUCE BAIRNSFATHER

The rat race being what it is, I could use a little more cheese each week.
                                        SALO

Those without push should hang on to their pull.   ANON

Ceux qui luttent ce sont ceux qui vivent,
And down here they luttent a very great deal indeed.
But if life be the desideratum, why grieve, ils vivent. STEVIE SMITH

There are people who must stick their nose into everybody else's
business. If you extend your little finger to such people, they will grasp
your whole hand.   BERTOLT BRECHT

It is hard for thee to kick against the pricks.   *ST. JOHN*

Democracy is the art and science of running the circus from the monkey
cage.   HENRY LOUIS MENCKEN

There is no living being that does not look for his well-being at the
expense of those he belongs to.   DENIS DIDEROT

One disadvantage of being a hog is that at any moment some blundering
fool may try to make a silk purse out of your wife's ear. J.B. MORTON

We often make people pay dearly for what we think we give them.
COMTESSE DIANE

Lots of folks don't know when they're well off, but ten times as many
don't know when they're not well off. FRANK McKINNEY HUBBARD

The dog, to gain some private ends,
Went mad and bit the man.
The man recovered of the bite,
The dog it was that died.   OLIVER GOLDSMITH

If a man once fall, all will tread upon him.   THOMAS FULLER

Modern man—whether in the womb of the masses, or with his work-
mates, or with his family, or alone—can never for one moment forget that
he is living in a world in which he is a means' and whose end is not his
business.   ALBERTO MORAVIA

It's often safer to be in chains than to be free.   FRANZ KAFKA

None are so fond of secrets as those who do not mean to keep them.
CHARLES CALEB COLTON

What destroys one man preserves another.   PIERRE CORNEILLE

Our admiration of our great organizations would soon dwindle were we to
become aware of the other side of the wonder, namely the tremendous
heaping up and accentuation of all that is primitive in man and the
unavoidable disintegration of his individuality in favour of that mon-
strosity which every great organization, on its nether side, is.
CARL GUSTAV JUNG

We grow tired of everything but turning others into ridicule, and
congratulating ourselves on their defects.   WILLIAM HAZLITT

Internal Politics

If there looking for Stability,
Then it's plain for all to see,
That a "saint" precedes ability
And that is little ol' ME.

The madness of many for the gain of a few.   JONATHAN SWIFT

Men are not against you, they are merely for themselves.
GENE FOWLER

The less important you are in the table of organization, the more you'll be missed if you don't turn up for work.   BILL VAUGHAN

While you're saving your face, you're losing your ass.
LYNDON B. JOHNSON

Those who complain the most
Usually work the least.   ANON

Going to work for a large company is like getting on a train. Are you going sixty miles an hour or is the train going sixty miles an hour and you're just sitting still?   J. PAUL GETTY

When you jump for joy beware that no one moves the ground from beneath your feet.   STANISLAW J. LEC

When we say we are certain so-and-so can't possibly have done it, what we mean is that we think he very likely did.
LOGAN PEARSALL SMITH

To Err is Human—To Forgive Is Not Company Policy.   ANON

A good deed never goes unpunished.   GORE VIDAL

University politics are vicious precisely because the stakes are so small.
HENRY KISSINGER

A former executive of a company which had been taken over in a corporate merger gave this description of what had happened to his company's executive personnel: "We got the mushroom treatment. Right after the acquisition we were kept in the dark. Then they covered us with manure. Then they cultivated us. After that they let us stew a while. Finally, they canned us."   ISADORE BARMASH

Nothing can happen but the suspicious man believes that somebody did it on purpose.   ROBERT LYND

The one that is hunting for advantages forgets there is work to do. ANON

Ability is the art of getting credit for all the home runs somebody else hits.   CASEY STENGEL

No matter how trivial the assignment, it is always possible to build it up to a major issue.   ROBERT THOMAS

No matter what occurs, there's always someone who believes it happened according to his pet theory.   J.M. MARTIN

Those who are pulling on the oars don't have much time to rock the boat.
                              ANON

The wickedness of the world is so great you have to run your legs off to avoid having them stolen from under you.   BERTOLT BRECHT

To be sure, the dog is loyal. But why, on that account, should we take him as an example? He is loyal to men, not to other dogs. KARL KRAUS

No man can serve two masters but Yes-men can serve a hundred. ANON

Many might go to heaven with half the labor they go to hell.
                              BEN JONSON

When a man has a "pet peeve" it's remarkable how often he pets it.
                              SYDNEY J. HARRIS

Madmen are people who never grow grey.   GERMAN PROVERB

We have met the enemy, and he is us.   WALT KELLY

There are no conditions to which a man cannot become accustomed, especially if he sees that all those around him live in the same way.
                              LEO TOLSTOY

In most hierarchies, super-competence is more objectionable than incompetence. Ordinary incompetence, as we have seen, is no cause for dismissal: it is simply a bar to promotion. Super-competence often leads to dismissal because it disrupts the hierarchy, and thereby violates the first commandment of hierarchial life: the hierarchy must be preserved.
                              LAURENCE J. PETER and RAYMOND HULL

Being a hypocrite has marvellous advantages!   MOLIERE

The man who sees little always sees less than there is to see, the man who hears badly always hears something more than there is to hear.
                              FRIEDRICH WILHELM NIETZSCHE

A tough lesson in life that one has to learn is that not everybody wishes you well.   DAN RATHER

Be commonplace and creeping, and you will be a success.
                              PIERRE AUGUSTIN CARON de BEAUMARCHAIS

Under this stone, Reader, Survey
Dead Sir John Vanbrugh's house of clay.
Lie heavy on him, Earth! for he
Laid many heavy loads on thee!   ABEL EVANS

One good deed has many claimants.   YIDDISH PROVERB

It is a curious fact that the worst work is always done with the best intentions, and that people are never so trivial as when they take themselves very seriously.   OSCAR WILDE

Sentimentality—that's what we call the sentiment we don't share.
                              GRAHAM GREENE

If you try to cleanse others, you will waste away in the process, like soap.   MADAGASCAN PROVERB

This struggle and scramble for office, for a way to live without work, will finally test the strength of our institutions.   ABRAHAM LINCOLN

He who puts up with insult invites injury.   JEWISH PROVERB

Whenever a man has cast a longing eye on offices, a rottenness begins in his conduct.   THOMAS JEFFERSON

A Yes-man is one who stoops to concur.   ANON

Injustice cannot reign if the community does not furnish a due supply of unjust agents.   HERBERT SPENCER

Those that have done nothing in life, are not qualified to judge of those that have done little.   SAMUEL JOHNSON

Plough deep while sluggards sleep.   BENJAMIN FRANKLIN

There are characters which are continually creating collusions and nodes for themselves in dramas which nobody is prepared to act with them.   GEORGE ELIOT

Be on the guard against the good and the just! They would fain crucify those who devise their own virtue—they hate the lonesome ones.
FRIEDRICH WILHELM NIETZSCHE

The Vicious Circle

With each pat on the back
Better watch for your life;
It's to mark out the track
Where to stick in the knife.

We're all in this together—by ourselves.   LILY TOMLIN

One of the worst things about life is not how nasty the nasty people are. You know that already. It is how nasty the nice people can be.
ANTHONY POWELL

I don't deserve this, but then, I have arthritis and I don't deserve that either.   JACK BENNY

All wrong-doing is done in the sincere belief that it is the best thing to do.   ARNOLD BENNETT

Illegitimati non carborundum—Don't let the bastards grind you down.
GENERAL JOSEPH W. STILWELL

Blessed is he who expects no gratitude, for he shall not be disappointed.
W.C. BENNETT

Anyone can do any amount of work, provided it isn't the work he is supposed to be doing at that moment. ROBERT BENCHLEY

Let's find out what everyone is doing,
And then stop everyone from doing it. SIR ALAN PATRICK HERBERT

Great fleas have little fleas
upon their backs to bite 'em.
And little fleas have lesser fleas,
and so ad infinitum.

AUGUSTUS de MORGAN

Look over your shoulder now and then to be sure someone's following you. HENRY GILMER

What they could do with round here is a good war. BERTOLT BRECHT

There are many things that we could throw away, if we were not afraid that others might pick them up. OSCAR WILDE

No one is so disappointed as the person who gets what's coming to him.
HERBERT V. PROCHNOW

When they were burning John Huss, a gentle little old lady came carrying her faggot to add it to the pile. ALBERT CAMUS

A person seldom falls sick, but the bystanders are animated with a faint hope that he will die. RALPH WALDO EMERSON

Everybody is a manipulator. ANON

Doesn't it seem some days as though other people were put in the world for no other reason than to aggravate you? EDGAR WATSON HOWE

Everybody was up to something, especially, of course, those who were up to nothing. NOEL COWARD

Life is just one damned thing after another. ELBERT HUBBARD

A great man who succeeded in being what little men desired him to be would have only one drawback—that of being like them.
ERNEST HELLO

There is no chapel on the day
On which they hang a man.   OSCAR WILDE

The men with the muck-rake are often indispensable to the well-being of
society, but only if they know when to stop raking the muck.
                                          THEODORE ROOSEVELT

I fancy that it is just as hard to do your duty when men are sneering at
you as when they are shooting at you. THOMAS WOODROW WILSON

He who can lick can bite.   FRENCH PROVERB

The ugliest of trades have their moments of pleasure. Now, if I were a
grave digger, or even a hangman, there are some people I could work for
with a great deal of enjoyment.   DOUGLAS JERROLD

Eels get used to skinning.   SIR WINSTON CHURCHILL

The tyrant grinds down his slaves and they don't turn against him, they
crush those beneath them.   EMILY BRONTE

Behold, the half was not told me.   *KINGS*

There are few men who dare publish to the world the prayers they make
to Almighty God.   MICHEL de MONTAIGNE

If a neighbor chokes, put a glass of water within reach... and do not
watch.   *Debrett's Etiquette* and *Modern Manners*

If you allow men to use you for your own purposes, they will use you for
theirs.   AESOP

The eagle suffers little birds to sing.   WILLIAM SHAKESPEARE

He that doth a good turn looketh for a good turn.   THOMAS FULLER

Live with wolves, and you will learn to howl.   SPANISH PROVERB

Now here, you see, it takes all the running you can do to keep in the
same place. If you want to get somewhere else, you must run at least
twice as fast as that!   LEWIS CARROLL

On the fall of an oak, every man gathers wood.   MENANDER

I do not know why it is that such a number of people try to make up for the virtue of their conduct by the viciousness of their beliefs.

ROBERT LYND

To the mean all becomes mean. FRIEDRICH WILHELM NIETZSCHE

The Treadmill

The way to tell you're in a rut
Is when you feel life's nothing but
The hassle that you've had today
Is just the same as yesterday.

People who bite the hand that feeds them usually lick the boot that kicks them.   ERIC HOFFER

Everything can be a deadend job if you're a deadend guy.

ANTHONY CHAFFO

It is a great shock at the age of five or six to find that in a world of Gary Coopers you are the Indian.   JAMES BALDWIN

The whole country is one vast insane asylum and they're letting the worst patients run the place.   ROBERT WELCH

The truth is there have never been very many remarkable people around at any one time. Most are always leaning on the guy next to them, asking him what to do.   WOODY ALLEN

The end may justify the means as long as there is something that justifies the end.   LEON TROTSKY

The great advantage of being in a rut is that when one is in a rut, one knows exactly where one is.   ALAN BENNETT

I never saw a Purple Cow,
I never hope to see one;
But I can tell you anyhow,
I'd rather see than be one.   GELETT BURGESS

Nothing is wonderful when you get used to it. EDGAR WATSON HOWE

If you can't stand the heat, get out of the kitchen. HARRY S. TRUMAN

The game is not about becoming somebody, it's about becoming nobody.
     BABA RAM DASS

I see the world as a football, kicked about by the higher powers, with me
clinging on by my teeth and toenails to the laces.   DAN LENO

Life is ten per cent what you make it and 90 per cent how you take it.
     IRVING BERLIN

The only difference between a rut and a grave is their dimensions.
     ELLEN GLASGOW

It is easier to get forgiveness than permission.   ARTHUR BLOCH

In the fight between you and the world, back the world.
     FRANZ KAFKA

The whole world's in a state o' chassis.   SEAN O'CASEY

I feel like a fugitive from the law of averages.   BILL MAULDIN

The supple, well-adjusted man is the one who has learned to hop into the
meat grinder while humming a hit-parade tune.
     MARSHALL MCLUHAN

People who like this sort of thing will find this is the sort of thing they
like.   ABRAHAM LINCOLN

At the age of 40 these days, an average man's alarm mechanism is shot.
     RUSSELL BAKER

There are people who, like a little bridge, exist only that others should
run over them. And the little bridge serves this, and the other, and the
third generation.   V. V. ROZINOV

Big Brother is watching you.   GEORGE ORWELL

It's always been and always will be the same in the world: The horse does the work and the coachman is tipped.   ANON

There is, of course, a certain amount of drudgery in newspaper work, just as there is in teaching classes, tunnelling into a bank, or being President of the United States.   JAMES THURBER

The manner in which one endures what must be endured is more important than the thing that must be endured.   DEAN ACHESON

Life makes no absolute statement. It is all Call and Answer.
                          DAVID HERBERT LAWRENCE

We are the products of editing, rather than authorship. GEORGE WALD

An eight-ulcer man on a four-ulcer job, and all four ulcers working.
                          HARRY S. TRUMAN

I have suffered from being misunderstood, but I would have suffered a lot more if I had been understood.   CLARENCE DARROW

The climb out of that rut can look like the highest mountain.   ANON

Every man is wanted, and no man is wanted much.
                          RALPH WALDO EMERSON

I think that cynicism is a positive value. You have to be cynical. You can't not be cynical. The more people that I have encouraged to be cynical the better job I've done.   FRANK ZAPPA

Unfortunately for us mortals and fortunately for the powers that be, it is in the nature of man that as long as he is alive there is always something which can be taken away from him. ALEXANDER SOLZHENITSYN

He has spent all his life in letting down empty buckets into empty wells; and he is frittering away his age in trying to draw them up again.
                          SYDNEY SMITH

Lifeis a grindstone whether it grinds you down or polishes you up: it depends on what you're made of.   JACOB M. BRAUDE

The truth is we are all caught in a great economic system which is heartless.   THOMAS WOODROW WILSON

All I want is a room somewhere
Far away from the cold night air
With one enormous chair
Ooh! Wouldn't it be lov-er-ly.   ALAN JAY LERNER

Modern man is born in a clinic and dies in a clinic. It is therefore not surprising that he should spend the intermediate period between these two paramount events of his life in utterly soulless clinical environments.   RICHARD ENGLAND

A man can believe a considerable deal of rubbish, and yet go about his daily work in a rational and cheerful manner.   NORMAN DOUGLAS

Americans cherish their wanderlust and constantly look forward to changes. I hear them frequently using the words—hateful to them— "stale" or "in a rut."   ERNEST DIMNET

Every base occupation makes one sharp in its practice and dull in every other.   SIR PHILIP SIDNEY

Those who complain most are most to be complained of.
                                                MATTHEW HENRY

All forms of exploitation are identical because all of them are applied against the same object—man.   FRANTZ FANON

De mortuis nil nisi bunkum.   HAROLD LASKI

Apart from blunt truth, our lives sink decadently amid the perfume of hints and suggestions.   ALFRED NORTH WHITEHEAD

Most are engaged in business the greater part of their lives, because the soul abhors a vacuum and they have not discovered any continuous employment for man's nobler faculties.   HENRY DAVID THOREAU

Bureaucracy

What takes one guy
One hour to do
Will take two guys
Two hours to do.

Bureaucracy is based on a willingness either to pass the buck or to spend it.   MRS. HENRY J. SERWAT

Men cannot live by incompetence alone.   ANON

What the world needs is some "do-give-a-damn" pills.
                                          WILLIAM MENINGER

There is nothing so permanent as a temporary job in Washington.
                                             GEORGE ALLEN

The boys are in such a mood that if someone introduced the Ten Commandments, they'd cut them down to eight.
                                   SENATOR NORRIS COTTON

Bureaucracy rules O.K.
                   O.K.
                   O.K.   ANON

Not a business brain in a bucketful.   MEGAN TERRY

There may now exist great men for things that do not exist.
                                          JAKOB BURCKHARDT

Nothing provides more leisure time than a number of capable assistants.
                                                    ANON

We also serve who only punctuate.   BRIAN MOORE

Some men are more mediocre, some men achieve mediocrity, and some men have mediocrity thrust upon them.   JOSEPH HELLER

An official man is always an official man and he has a wild belief in the value of reports.   SIR ARTHUR HELPS

Civilization declines in relation to the increase in bureaucracy.
VICTOR YANNACONE

A bureaucrat's idea of cleaning up his files is to make a copy of every paper before he destroys it.   ANON

You start by saying no to requests. Then if you have to go to yes, okay. But if you start with yes, you can't go to no.   MILDRED PERLMAN

For this real or imagined overwork there are, broadly speaking, three possible remedies. He (A) may resign; he may ask to halve the work with a colleague called B; he may demand the assistance of two subordinates, to be called C and D. There is probably no instance in history, however, of A choosing any but the third alternative.
C. NORTHCOTE PARKINSON

There is something about a bureaucrat that does not like a poem.
GORE VIDAL

There are vast realms of the bureaucracy dedicated to seeking more information, in perpetuity if need be, in order to avoid taking action.
MEG. GREENFIELD

Why don't you go down to the morgue and tell them you're ready. ANON

Guidelines for Bureaucrats:
(1) When in charge ponder.
(2) When in trouble delegate.
(3) When in doubt mumhle.   JAMES H. BOREN

I have seen it happen more often than not that when one asks for choices one is always given three: two absurd ones and the preferred one. And the experienced bureaucrat, which I am slowly becoming, can usually tell the preferred one because it is almost always the one that is typed in the middle.   HENRY A. KISSINGER

Hell hath no fury like a bureaucrat scorned.   MILTON FRIEDMAN

A man may be caught quite by chance in the wheels of the huge bureaucratic machine. He may think that only a fold of his jacket has got caught, and that everything is all right except a certain discomfort under the armpits. But all the time the slow movements of the machinery gradually pulls him in and mangles him.   ANDREI AMALRIK

Rule A: Don't.
Rule A1: Rule A does not exist.
Rule A2: Do not discuss the existence or non-existence of Rules A, A1
      or A2.   R.D. LAING

In a hierarchy every employee tends to rise to his level of incompetence. In time every post tends to be occupied by an employee who is incompetent to carry out its duties. Work is accomplished by those employees who have not yet reached their level of incompetence.
LAURENCE J. PETER

Bureaucrats speak only of parts. It's as if you decide Picasso is good at legs, so you ask him to paint your legs. And since Matisse draws lovely heads, you get him to do the head. Then when it's finished, you're astonished you've produced a mess.   HENRY A. KISSINGER

There is only one giant machine operated by pygmies, and that is bureaucracy.   HONORE de BALZAC

The perfect bureaucrat everywhere is the man who manages to make no decisions and escape all responsibility. JUSTIN BROOKS ATKINSON

Whatever was required to be done, the Circumlocution Office was beforehand with all the Public Departments in the art of perceiving—
HOW NOT TO DO IT.   CHARLES DICKENS

Where everything is done through the bureaucracy, nothing to which the bureaucracy is really adverse can be done at all. JOHN STUART MILL

A bureaucrat is a desk jockey.   DAN BENNETT

Seven officials are now doing what one did before. For these seven make so much work for each other that all are fully occupied and A. is actually working harder than ever.   C. NORTHCOTE PARKINSON

When the last trumpet sounds, *The New York Times* will want to check with Gabriel himself, and for the next edition will try to get it confirmed by even Higher Authority.   REX STOUT

That is not executive privilege. It is executive poppycock. SAM ERVIN

Creating is thinking, and thinking is dangerous for the bureaucrats who don't like to think and so dislike thinkers.   OLEG BITOV

I'm not a member of any establishment. I'm too intuitional for the intellectuals and too conservative for the way out.   EDWARD ALBEE

Bureaucratic function is sustained by fear of failure, as the church was once supported by the fear of damnation.   RICHARD N. GOODWIN

A fanatical belief in democracy makes democratic institutions impossible.   BERTRAND RUSSELL

Bureaucracy: let us treat men and women well; treat them as if they were real. Perhaps they are.   RALPH WALDO EMERSON

You may break your heart but men will still go on as before.
                                                   MARCUS AURELIUS

An efficient bureaucracy is the greatest threat to liberty.
                                                   EUGENE McCARTHY

Bureaucracy: The rule of no one has become the modern form of despotism.   MARY McCARTHY

A bureaucracy is a continuing congregation of people who must act more or less as one.   JOHN KENNETH GALBRAITH

Your levellers wish to level down as far as themselves: but they cannot bear levelling up to themselves. They would all have some people under them: why not then have some people above them? SAMUEL JOHNSON

The working of great institutions is mainly the result of a vast mass of routine, petty malice, self interest, carelessness, and sheer mistake, only a residual factor is thought.   GEORGE SANTAYANA

Bureaucracies are designed to perform public business. But as soon as a bureaucracy is established, it develops an autonomous spiritual life and comes to regard the public as its enemy. JUSTIN BROOKES ATKINSON

Bureaucracy is the antithesis of democracy.   JO GRIMOND

The age of great men is going; the epoch of the ant hill, of life in multiplicity, is beginning.   HENRY FREDERIC AMIEL

The System

A system is run by adults
So the north can monitor south;
It's there to avoid the results
Most prefer to be worK of mouth.

One man's red tape is another man's system.   DWIGHT WALDO

Nothing was ever done so systematically as nothing is being done now.
                                                   WOODROW WILSON

Mediocrity is a hand-rail. CHARLES de SECONDAT MONTESQUIEU

Galbraith's law states that anyone who says he won't resign four times,
will.   JOHN KENNETH GALBRAITH

"Esprit de Corps": embalming fluid.   R.S. MACLEOD

"Company policy" means "there is no understandable reason for this
action."   HERBERT V. PROCHNOW

There will never be a system invented which will do away with the
necessity for work.   HENRY FORD

Rules are for when brains run out.   GEORGE PAPASHVILY

I find that men talk of principles: and mean, when you come to inquire,
rules connected with certain systems.   SIR ARTHUR HELPS

All bad precedents began as justifiable measures.   JULIUS CAESAR

Build a system that even a fool can use, and only a fool will want to use
it.   ARTHUR BLOCH

The system has not failed—but some of us have failed the system.
                                                   EDMUND MUSKIE

By office boys for office boys.   ROBERT C. SALISBURY

Only mediocrities rise to the top in a system that won't tolerate wavemaking.   LAURENCE J. PETER

Stay in the system. Don't get mad, get even.   JIMMY BRESLIN

The more you let yourself go, the less others let you go.
FRIEDRICH WILHELM NIETZSCHE

If I shall be like him, who will be like me?   ANON

There's nothing the world loves more than a ready-made description which they can hang on to a man, and so save themselves all trouble in future.   WILLIAM SOMERSET MAUGHAM

The bigger the organization, the longer it takes to get a little job done.
ANON

The inevitably of gradualness.   SIDNEY WEBB

Any fool can make a rule, and every fool will mind it.
HENRY DAVID THOREAU

The last gasp of an expiring organization is to publish a new set of old rules.   *Kaiser News*

A company attitude is rarely anybody's best.   MISS WEDGWICK

If you have been put in your place long enough, you begin to act like the place.   RANDALL JARRELL

A variety of nothing is superior to a monotony of something.
JEAN PAUL RICHTER

Abandon hope, all ye who enter here.   DANTE ALIGHIERI

The more someone insists on protocol, the less his intelligence. ANON

Manic Depressive heroes pull Mankind into their cycles and carry everybody away.   SAUL BELLOW

The one thing more difficult than following a regimen is not imposing it on others.   MARCEL PROUST

Known principles are the barbed wire entanglements around the detention camps where our institutions are restrained from going into warfare.   HENRY S. HASKINS

They usually do not much care what society's rules are so long as the rules are clear.   GEORGE F. WILL

Conservatism is the maintenance of conventions already in force.
THORSTEIN VEBLEN

A man who trims himself to suit everybody will soon whittle himself away.   CHARLES SCHWAB

We are half-ruined by conformity, but we should be wholly ruined without it.   CHARLES DUDLEY WARNER

It is this everlasting mediocrity that bores me.
HARRIET BEECHER STOWE

You cannot make a man by standing a sheep on its hind legs. But by standing a flock of sheep in that position you can make a crowd of men.
MAX BEERBOHM

There's nothing like becoming established to cure one's dissatisfaction with the establishment.   HAROLD COFFIN

The security blanket of conformity is warm and comfortable—just so it doesn't cover our heads and smother us.   HERBERT HOLT

Orthodoxy: That peculiar condition where the patient can neither eliminate an old idea nor absorb a new one.   ELBERT HUBBARD

The most ingenious way of becoming foolish is by a system.
EARL of SHAFTESBURY

My soul hates the fool whose only passion is to live by rule.
GEORGE SANTAYANA

Custom reconciles us to everything.   EDMUND BURKE

Every system should allow loop holes and exceptions, for if it does not, it will in the end crush all that is best in man. BERTRAND RUSSELL

No perverseness equals that which is supported by system, no errors are so difficult to root out as those which the understanding has pledged its credit to uphold. **WILLIAM WORDSWORTH**

No written law has ever been more binding than unwritten custom supported by popular opinion. **CARRIE CHAPMAN CATT**

To be nobody but myself—in a world which is doing its best, night and day, to make you everybody else—means to fight the hardest battle which any human being can fight, and never stop fighting.
EDWARD ESTLIN CUMMINGS

If the camel once gets his nose in the tent, his body will follow.
ARABIAN PROVERB

A man must consider what a rich realm he abdicates when he becomes a conformist. **RALPH WALDO EMERSON**

If you defy the system long enough you'll be rewarded. At first life takes revenge and reduces you to a sniveling mess. But keep sniveling, have the madness, the audacity, to do what interests you, forget about your person, and eventually life will say all right, we'll let you do it.
JO COUDERT

A mouth is not always a mouth, but a bit is always a bit, and it matters little what it bridles. **SIDONIE GABRIELLE COLETTE**

I must create a system or be enslaved by another man's. **WILLIAM BLAKE**

The easiest thing to be in the world is you. The most difficult thing to be is what other people want you to be. Don't let them put you in that position. **LEO BUSCAGLIA**

There is nothing sacred about convention, there is nothing sacred about primitive passions or whims, but the fact that a convention exists indicates that a way of living has been devised capable of maintaining itself. **GEORGE SANTAYANA**

Human rights are the natural outgrowth of people becoming culturally and economically secure. As you become secure, you want to be freer.
ANDREW YOUNG

Man has such a predilection for systems and abstract deductions that he is ready to distort the truth intentionally, he is ready to deny the evidence of his senses only to justify his logic.
FYODOR MIKHAYLOVICH DOSTOYEVSKI

Our society cannot have it both ways: to maintain a conformist and ignoble system and to have skillful and spirited men to man that system with.
PAUL GOODMAN

Intrigue

Who says
I say
What they say
I say?

All business sagacity reduces itself in the last analysis to a judicious use of sabotage.
THORSTIN VEBLEN

Knowledge is power, if you know it about the right person.
ETHEL WATTS MUMFORD

How to be one up is to make the other man feel that something has gone wrong, however slightly.
STEPHEN POTTER

Clever men are the tools with which bad men work.
WILLIAM HAZLITT

When a man points a finger at someone else, he should remember that four of his fingers are pointing at himself.
LOUIS NIZER

The human mind is at its best when it is trying to cover up something.
ANON

Never murder a man who is committing suicide.
THOMAS WOODROW WILSON

Fling dirt enough, and some will stick.   PROVERB

If it has to choose who will be crucified, the crowd will always save
Barabbas.   JEAN COCTEAU

Your friend is the man who knows all about you, and still likes you.
          ELBERT HUBBARD

A smile curved like a banana.   ALBERT MORRIS

"Have a nice day."
"Thank you, but I do have other ideas."   ROBERT DUCAS

We often do good in order that we may do evil with impunity.
          FRANCOIS DUC de la ROCHEFOUCAULD

If for a tranquil mind you seek,
These things observe with care;
Of whom you speak, to whom you speak,
and how, and when, and where.   ANON

The opportunity for doing mischief is found a hundred times a day, and
of doing good, once in a year.   FRANCOIS VOLTAIRE

You can only help one of your luckless brothers by trampling down a
dozen others.   BERTOLT BRECHT

You scratch my back, and I'll scratch yours.   PROVERB

A confidence always aims at glory, scandal, excuse, propaganda.
          PAUL VALERY

As innocent as a new-laid egg.   SIR WILLIAM S. GILBERT

Nothing produces action like the opportunity to do something bad.
          ANON

It is always safe to assume that people are more subtle and less sensitive
than they seem.   ERIC HOFFER

Conspiracy: a game invented for the amusement of unoccupied men of
rank.   JOSEPH ADDISON

It is often easier to hide something than to hide the fact that you are hiding something.   GEORG CHRISTOPH LICHTENBERG

I gave 'em a sword. And they stuck it in, and they twisted it with relish. And I guess if I had been in their position, I'd have done the same thing.
RICHARD MILHOUS NIXON

Walls have ears.   PROVERB

One can be astuter than another, but not astuter than all the others.
FRANCOIS DUC de la ROCHEFOUCAULD

He who digs a pit for another will fall in it himself.
GERMAN PROVERB

Man is the only animal that can remain on friendly terms with the victims he intends to eat until he eats them.   SAMUEL BUTLER

Meekness is the mask of malice.   ROBERT G. INGERSOLL

The surest way to make a monkey of a man is to quote him.
ROBERT BENCHLEY

Don't look back, something might be gaining on you.
SATCHELL PAIGE

There are wheels within wheels.   PROVERB

If there was a trick, there must be a trickster.
DOROTHY MILLER RICHARDSON

In a devious way I am uncomplicated.   GUNTER GRASS

A bad man is worse when he pretends to be a saint. FRANCIS BACON

Confusion is mightier than the sword.   ABBIE HOFFMAN

The fox condemns the trap, not himself.   WILLIAM BLAKE

There are no secrets better kept than the secrets that everybody guesses.
GEORGE BERNARD SHAW

Without the aid of prejudice and custom, I should not be able to find my way across the room.   WILLIAM HAZLITT

Those who'll play with cats must expect to be scratched.
MIGUEL de CERVANTES

Who will free me from this turbulent priest?   HENRY II

Only one-third of the human beings are asleep at one time, and the other two-thirds are awake and up to some mischief somewhere. DEAN RUSK

When your friend holds you affectionately by both hands you are safe, for you can watch both his.   AMBROSE BIERCE

There is probably an element of malice in our readiness to over-estimate people—we are, as it were, laying up for ourselves the pleasure of cutting them down to size.   ERIC HOFFER

I admit my men made a sad mistake—they got caught.
RICHARD MILHOUS NIXON

He'd wash his hands in blood to keep them clean.
ELIZABETH BARRETT BROWNING

If you are not respected as subtle, you will be regarded as sure.
BALTASAR GRACIAN

Speak as the many, think as the few.   LATIN PROVERB

A man who keeps his shoulder to the wheel is rarely seen giving others trouble. He's like a mule in the respect that when he's pulling, he can't kick, and when he's kicking he can't pull.
REV. ARCHER E. ANDERSON

It is a trick among the dishonest to offer sacrifices that are not needed, not possible, to avoid making those that are required.
I.A. GONCHAROV

To be in the weakest camp is to be in the strongest school.
GILBERT KEITH CHESTERTON

There ain't a worm but will turn when he's trod upon.
MARGARET OLIPHANT

Let the sword decide after strategem has failed. ARABIAN PROVERB

Who sows thorns should not go barefoot.   ITALIAN PROVERB

You cannot drive straight on a twisting lane.   RUSSIAN PROVERB

He that goeth about to persuade a multitude that they are not so well governed as they ought to be, shall never want attentive and favorable hearers.   RICHARD HOOKER

He that is never suspected is either very much esteemed or very much despised.   MARQUIS of HALIFAX

Nothing so completely baffles one who is full of trick and duplicity himself, than straightforward and simple integrity in another.
CHARLES CALEB COLTON

The most subtle, the strongest and deepest art—supreme art—is the one that does not at first allow itself to be recognized.   ANDRE GIDE

Whoever battles with monsters had better see that it does not turn him into a monster. And if you gaze long into an abyss, the abyss will gaze back at you.   FRIEDRICH WILHELM NIETZSCHE

Nothing in life is so exhilarating as to be shot at without result.
SIR WINSTON CHURCHILL

Cliques

A clique is a
  Sort of society
The weak use to
  Thwart an anxiety.

Always stay in with the outs.   DAVID HALBERSTAM

A minority may be right, and a majority is always wrong.
HENRIK IBSEN

None are so brave as the anonymous.   K.K. STEINCKE

If we don't stand for something, we will fall for anything.
                                        IRENE DUNNE

A bad cause requires many words.   GERMAN PROVERB

You can always spot a well-informed man—his views are the same as
yours.   ILKA CHASE

The trouble with being "in" is that to stay there you must keep going
further out.   ANON

Do not join encounter groups. If you enjoy being made to feel
inadequate, call your mother.   LIZ SMITH

Idiot, n. A member of a large and powerful tribe whose influence in
human affairs has always been dominant and controlling.
                                        AMBROSE BIERCE

If some people got their rights, they would complain of being deprived of
their wrongs.   OLIVER HERFORD

The first duty of a revolutionary is to get away with it.
                                        ABBIE HOFFMAN

What is a rebel? A man who says no.   ALBERT CAMUS

It is always the minorities that hold the key of progress; it is always
through those who are unafraid to be different that advance comes to
human society.   RAYMOND B. FOSDICK

When you find three young cads and idiots going about together and
getting drunk together every day, you generally find that one of the three
cads and idiots is (for some extraordinary reason) not a cad and not an
idiot.   GILBERT KEITH CHESTERTON

Revolutions have never succeeded unless the establishment does three-
quarters of the work.   PETER USTINOV

When one dog barks he soon finds other dogs to bark with him.
                                        SHEMOTH RABBAH

Woe to him inside a nonconformist clique who does not conform with nonconformity.   ERIC HOFFER

It is a general error to imagine the loudest complainers for the public to be the most anxious for its welfare.   EDMUND BURKE

The man who follows the crowd will never be followed by a crowd.
JAMES DONNELL

It would be an entertaining change in human affairs to determine everything by minorities: they are almost always in the right.
SYDNEY SMITH

To betray, you must first belong.   HAROLD "KIM" PHILBY

Ten persons who speak make more noise than ten thousand who are silent.   NAPOLEON BONAPARTE

In America where movements spring up overnight like fastfood outlets, all God's children gotta have ideology.   R.D. ROSEN

All movements go too far.   BERTRAND RUSSELL

There have been quite as many martyrs for bad causes as for good ones.
HENDRIK van LOON

All courtiers gossip madly, it's part of their business.
DAPHNE du MAURIER

Insurrection, n. an unsuccessful revolution.   AMBROSE BIERCE

Minority groups impeded by discriminations usually apply themselves more diligently than the more secure dominant group. They must be "twice as good to get half as far."   JACOB M. BRAUDE

Intellectuals, like fish, often move in schools, following a leader.
ISRAEL SHENKER

The worst cliques are those which consist of one man.
GEORGE BERNARD SHAW

A minority group has "arrived" only when it has the right to produce some fools and scoundrels without the entire group paying for it.
CARL T. ROWAN

Every man becomes to a certain degree, what the people he generally converses with are.   EARL of CHESTERFIELD

In individuals insanity is rare: but in groups, parties, nations and epochs, it is the rule.   FRIEDRICH WILHELM NIETZSCHE

In weakness there is strength.   ANON

To praise oneself is considered improper, immodest; to praise one's own sect, one's own philosophy, is considered the highest duty.
                                                      LEO SHESTOV

There's something contagious about demanding freedom.
                                                  ROBIN MORGAN

The best society does not necessarily mean the "smart set."
                                      JENNIE JEROME CHURCHILL

Even weak men when united are powerful.   FREDERICK SCHILLER

Inequality is the cause of all local movements. LEONARDO da VINCI

Crowds are comforting to those who are physically dissatisfied with themselves.   MALCOLM de CHAZAL

When people are free to do as they please, they usually imitate each other.   ERIC HOFFER

Rebel, n. A proponent of a new misrule who has failed to establish it.
                                                AMBROSE BIERCE

What encourages the mocker is that he starts off with success; the punishment comes later.   EMANUEL MARBEAU

Birds of a feather flock together.   PROVERB

Take the tone of the company you are in.   EARL of CHESTERFIELD

Because half-a-dozen grasshoppers under a fern makes the field ring with their importunate chink, do not imagine that those who make the noise are the only inhabitants of the field.   EDMUND BURKE

Courtiers speak well of a man for two reasons; that he may learn they have spoken well of him, and that he may speak well of them.
                                              JEAN de la BRUYERE

The tyrant and the mob, the grandfather and the grandchild, are natural allies.   ARTHUR SCHOPENHAUER

Caged birds accept each other but flight is what they long for.
                                    TENNESSEE WILLIAMS

He who hunts two hares, leaves one and loses the other.
                                    JAPANESE PROVERB

Every man alone is sincere; at the entrance of a second person, hypocrisy begins.   RALPH WALDO EMERSON

The rebel angels fly in ranks.   HENRI PETIT

It is folly of too many to mistake the echo of a London coffee house for the voice of the kingdom.   JONATHAN SWIFT

Why did they not speak out? Because they dreaded (and could not bear) the disapproval of the people around them...The same reason has restrained me.   MARK TWAIN

Nor is the People's Judgment always true:
The Most may err as grossly as the Few.   JOHN DRYDEN

Bad Management

Bad management
Is contagious.

So much of what we call management consists in making it difficult for people to work.   PETER F. DRUCKER

In management thirty years experience does not count for much if it merely means ten times three of the same experience.
                                    NEIL J. McKINNON

Management is now where the medical profession was when it decided that working in a drug store was not sufficient training to become a doctor.   LAWRENCE APPLEY

Absentee management, no matter how honest and capable, cannot equal local management.... And it certainly does not sit well with labor, investors, consumers, and the communities back home. It is their industry and they should be in on it.   WILLIAM O. DOUGLAS

Large organization is loose organization. Nay, it would be almost as true to say that organization is always disorganization.
     GILBERT KEITH CHESTERTON

If two men on the same job agree all the time, then one is useless. If they disagree all the time, then both are useless.   DARRYL F. ZANUCK

Whenever a man's failure can be traced to management's mistakes, he has to be kept on the payroll.   ANON

The first myth of management is that it exists. The second myth of management is that success equals skill.   ROGER HELLER

What makes equality such a difficult business is that we only want it with our superiors.   HENRY BECQUE

The weakest link in a chain is its strongest because it can break it.
     STANISLAW J. LEC

Democracy is the hole in the stuffed shirt through which the sawdust slowly trickles.   ELWYN BROOKS WHITE

The first-rate man will try to surround himself with his equals, or better if possible. The second-rate man will surround himself with third-rate men. The third-rate man will surround himself with fifth-rate men.
     ANDRE WEIL

Lots of folks confuse bad management with destiny.
     FRANK McKINNEY HUBBARD

Nothing slows down action more than the belief that what was decreed today may be reversed tomorrow.   CLARENCE B. RANDALL

Popularity is a crime from the moment it is sought; it is only a virtue where men have it whether they will or no.   MARQUIS of HALIFAX

The only things that evolve by themselves in an organization are disorder, friction and malperformance.   PETER F. DRUCKER

The biggest mistake a man in management can make is to back down on a matter of principle.   CLARENCE FRANCIS

A board of directors is supposed to be a tree full of owls—hooting when management heads into the wrong part of the forest. I am still unpersuaded they even know where the forest is. ROBERT TOWNSEND

The world is disgracefully managed, one hardly knows to whom to complain.   RONALD FIRBANK

Those who cannot miss an opportunity of saying a good thing are not to be trusted with the management of any great question.
                                           WILLIAM HAZLITT

Bigness in the economy taxes the ability to manage intelligently. The growth of bigness has resulted in ruthless sacrifices of human values. The disappearance of free enterprise has submerged the individual in the impersonal corporation. When a nation of shopkeepers is transformed into a nation of clerks, enormous spiritual sacrifices are made.
                                JUSTICE WILLIAM O. DOUGLAS

The secret of the demagogue is to make himself as stupid as his audience so that they believe they are as clever as he. KARL KRAUS

II GOOD
MANAGEMENT

Good
Management

The very best link
In Management Inc.
Is to let them think.

You can handle people more successfully by enlisting their feelings than by convincing their reason.　　　　　　　　DR. PAUL P. PARKER

The great requisite for the prosperous management of ordinary business is the want of imagination.　　　　　　　　WILLIAM HAZLITT

The job of management is to get the good out of someone without letting the bad interfere.　　　　　　　　THEODORE V. HOUSER

There is a homely adage which runs 'Speak softly and carry a big stick, you will go far.'　　　　　　　　THEODORE ROOSEVELT

It's important that people know what you stand for. It's equally important that they know what you won't stand for.　　　　　　　　MARY WALDRIP

You will benefit in the long run if you give credit down the line for ideas that originated in your own mind.   PROFESSOR RAY E. BROWN

A good manager is a man who isn't worried about his own career but rather the careers of those who work for him. My advice: Don't worry about yourself. Take care of those who work for you and you'll float to greatness on their achievements.   H.S.M. BURNS

The secret of managing is to keep the guys who hate you away from the guys who are undecided.   CASEY STENGEL

The first rule a man must learn if he is to be a successful manager is that ACTION and REACTION on his part must NOT be equal and opposite.
     O.A. BATTISTA

There's a little bit of the dictator in all of us. Fortunately, I was blessed with a disproportionately generous share.   FREDERIC R. MANN

Everybody wants to be considered somebody. Make them feel important.
     ANON

The most important thing I have learned about management is that the executive must arouse the individual initiative of the men working under him.   ALFRED P. SLOAN

Healthy self-criticism and an abiding willingness to learn seem to me to be the most important requirements of any manager.
     PHILIP, DUKE of EDINBURGH

There is another trait I would like to cite that seems to me of particular importance to management success; the ability to capitalize upon criticism. It's one of the hardest things in the world to accept criticism especially when it's not presented in a constructive way, and turn it to your advantage.   J.C. PENNEY

Tradition is a guide and not a jailer.
     WILLIAM SOMERSET MAUGHAM

Two-thirds of help is to give courage.   IRISH PROVERB

Develop a willingness and ability to put yourself in other people's shoes and try to see things through their eyes—understanding their needs, wants and desires from their own point of view.
     THEODORE V. HOUSER

I love to feel events overlapping each other, crawling over one another like wet crabs in a basket.   LAURENCE DURRELL

If we believe a thing to be bad and if we have a right to prevent it, it is our duty to try to prevent it and to damn the consequences.
                                                    LORD MILNER

The nonconformist and misfit must be encouraged.   ANON

If things happen all the time you are never nervous. It is when they are not happening that you are nervous.   GERTRUDE STEIN

Men who pass most comfortably through the world are those who possess good digestions and hard hearts.   HARRIET MARTINEAU

To know just what has to be done, then to do it comprises the whole philosophy of practical life.   SIR WILLIAM OSLER

Strengthen me by sympathizing with my strength, not my weakness.
                                                    BRONSON ALCOTT

Believe not your own brother—believe, instead, your own blind eye.
                                                    RUSSIAN PROVERB

To manage men, one ought to have a sharp mind in a velvet sheath.
                                                    GEORGE ELIOT

The secret of managing a man is to let him have his way in little things. He will change his life when he won't change his bootmaker.
                                                    JOHN OLIVER HOBBS

Five things are requisite to a good officer—ability, clean hands, despatch, patience, and impartiality.   WILLIAM PENN

Use the memory of thy predecessors fairly and tenderly; for if thou dost not, it is a debt will surely be paid when thou art gone.
                                                    FRANCIS BACON

Think nothing done while aught remains to do.   SAMUEL ROGERS

Leadership

To succeed a
Good leader
Must get folk
At a stroke
Not to shirk
From more work
Than they thought
That they ought.

True leadership must be for the benefit of the followers, not the enrichment of the leaders.   ROBERT TOWNSEND

American people have always yearned mightily for leadership and have consistently mistrusted and maligned it when it appeared.
                                                    SAMUEL B. GOULD

It is time for a new generation of leadership, to cope with new problems and new opportunities. For there is a new world to be won.
                                                    JOHN F. KENNEDY

There are plenty of people willing to give directions but most of them don't know how to get there either.   ANON

You do not lead by hitting people over the head—that's assault, not leadership.   DWIGHT D. EISENHOWER

The executive is exhorted to serve as leader but to let the group command.   PROFESSOR RAY E. BROWN

The trouble with being a leader today is that you can't be sure whether people are following you or chasing you.   ANON

A mean streak is a very important quality of leadership.
                                                    CHARLES E. GOODELL

Everybody's friend is nobody's.   ARTHUR SCHOPENHAUER

In enterprise of martial kind,
    When there was any fighting,

He led his regiment from behind—
   He found it less exciting.   SIR WILLIAM GILBERT

I suppose that leadership at one time meant muscle; but today it means getting along with people.   INDIRA GANDHI

I've got to follow them—I am their leader.
                              ALEXANDRE LEDRU-ROLLIN

Don't do for others what you wouldn't think of asking them to do for you.
                              JOSH BILLINGS

A leader is a dealer in hope.   NAPOLEON BONAPARTE

A bad leader wants to share the credit for the work of other people.
                              ANON

No person can be a great leader unless he takes genuine joy in the successes of those under him.   W.A. NANCE

He who has always been a subordinate will make a bad leader.
                              PIERRE CORNEILLE

He lacks only one thing as a natural leader—natural followers. ANON

The art of leadership consists in consolidating the attention of the people against a single adversary and taking care that nothing will split that attention.   ADOLF HITLER

The weaknesses of the many make the leader possible.
                              ELBERT HUBBLE

If the blind lead the blind, both shall fall into the ditch. *ST. MATTHEW*

No man is good enough to govern another man without the other's consent.   ABRAHAM LINCOLN

Out of 25 guys there should be 15 who would run through a wall for you, two or three who don't like you at all, five who are indifferent and maybe three undecided. My job is to keep the last two groups from going the wrong way.   BILLY MARTIN

Leadership should be born out of the understanding of the needs of those who would be affected by it.   MARTIN ANDERSON

You take people as far as they will go, not as far as you would like them to go. JEANNETTE RANKIN

Any leader worth following gives credit easily where credit is due. He does not take someone's ideas, dress it up and offer it as his own. He offers it as theirs. Otherwise, ideas will soon cease to flow his way. He plays fair with everyone and recognizes the strong points in people as well as the weak ones. He never takes advantage for his own selfish purposes. FRANKLIN J. LUNDLING

Never discourage anyone who continually makes progress, no matter how slow. PLATO

The best way to insure support is to involve others. ANON

I would rather try to persuade a man to go along, because once I have persuaded him he will stick. If I scare him, he will stay just as long as he is scared, and then he is gone. DWIGHT D. EISENHOWER

A manager can either act as a judge or leader. In the former case, he sits and waits until subordinates bring to him problems for solution, or alternatives for choice. In the latter case, he immerses himself in the operations of the business, examines the problems, the objectives, the alternative courses of action, chooses among them, and leads the organization to their accomplishment. In the one case it's a passive role; in the other case, an active role. I've always believed in and endeavoured to follow the active leadership role as opposed to the passive judicial role. ROBERT S. McNAMARA

Fear and hope are the two great instruments for the governance of men. JEAN JACQUES ROUSSEAU

Remember that it is far better to follow well than to lead indifferently. JOHN G. VANCE

To lead the people, walk behind them. LAO-TZU

A man may lead a horse to the water, but he cannot make it drink. PROVERB

Nothing does so much honour to a newly-risen leader than the new laws and measures that he introduces. NICCOLO MACHIAVELLI

When we think we lead we most are led. ROBERT BROWNING

The height of ability in the least able consists in knowing how to submit to the good leadership of others.

FRANCOIS DUC de la ROCHEFOUCAULD

Let us not look back in anger or forward in fear, but around in awareness.
JAMES THURBER

To be in hell is to drift; to be in heaven is to steer.
GEORGE BERNARD SHAW

No amount of study or learning will make a man a leader unless he has the natural qualities of one.
SIR ARCHIBALD WAVELL

The trouble in modern democracy is that men do not approach to leadership until they have lost the desire to lead anyone.
LORD BEVERIDGE

If you cry "Forward!" you must without fail make plain in what direction to go. Don't you see that if, without doing so, you call out the word to both a monk and revolutionary, they will go in directions precisely opposite?
ANTON CHEKHOV

Conspired leadership is the most adhesive of all.
ANON

The true leader is always led.
CARL GUSTAV JUNG

To be a leader of men one must turn one's back on men.
HENRY HAVELOCK ELLIS

Even though counting heads is not an ideal way to govern, it's better than breaking them.
ANON

There is no necessary connection between the desire to lead and the ability to lead, and even less to the ability to lead somewhere that will be to the advantage of the led. Leadership is more likely to be assumed by the aggressive than by the able, and those who scramble to the top are more often motivated by their own inner torments than by any demand for their guidance.
BERGEN EVANS

Leadership, like everything else in life that is vital, finds its source in understanding. To be worthy of management responsibility today, a man must have insight into the human heart, for unless he has an awareness of human problems, a sensitivity towards the hopes and aspirations of those whom he supervises, and a capacity for analysis of the emotional

forces that motivate their conduct, the projects entrusted to him will not get ahead no matter how often wages are raised.
CLARENCE B. RANDALL

Discipline is then not the end, but a means to an end—the end that each man shall be imbued with a spirit of loyalty to leader and to organization, which will result in unity and promptness of action in instant response to the will of the leader. CAPTAIN L.C. ANDREWS

As for the best leaders, the people do not notice their existence. The next best, the people honour and praise. The next, the people fear, and the next the people hate. When the best leader's work is done, the people say, "we did it ourselves!"
LAO-TZU

To lead means to direct and to exact, and no man dare do either. He might be unpopular. What authority we are given is a trinity: the grin, the generality, and God (the word).
MARYA MANNES

Don't be too sweet, lest you be eaten up; don't be too bitter, lest you be spewed out.
JEWISH PROVERB

Charlatanism of some degree is indispensable to effective leadership.
ERIC HOFFER

The first duty of a leader is to make himself be loved without courting love. To be loved without 'playing up' to anyone—even to himself.
ANDRE MALRAUX

Competition

What you do,
When they do,
What you do.

Competition brings out the best in products and the worst in people.
DAVID SARNOFF

Remember that your competitor does give a damn about getting ahead of you!
ANON

There is no resting place for an enterprise in a competitive economy.
ALFRED P. SLOAN

An economic struggle for survival among businessmen in which the consumer benefits the most.   ANON

I don't meet competition, I crush it.   CHARLES REVSON

America's competitive spirit, the work ethic of this people, is alive and well. The dignity of work, the value of achievement, the morality of self-reliance—none of these is going out of style.   RICHARD M. NIXON

A company is known by the competition it creates.   ANON

Of all human powers operating on the affairs of mankind, none is greater than that of competition.   HENRY CLAY

The biggest things are always the easiest to do because there is no competition.   WILLIAM Van HORNE

Competition is the keen cutting edge of business, always shaving away at costs.   HENRY FORD

Blowing out the other fellow's candle won't make yours shine any brighter.   ANON

A fairly decent man does not need laws to keep him straight; his competitors and patrons usually tend to do that.
EDGAR WATSON HOWE

Competition is the life of trade and the death of the trader.
ELBERT HUBBARD

The person who is not bothered who gets the credit, never has to worry about competition.   ANON

When Ty Cobb got on first base he had an apparently nervous habit of kicking the bag. It wasn't until he retired from the game that the secret came out. By kicking the bag hard enough Cobb could move it a full two inches closer to second base. He figured that this improved his chances for a steal or for reaching second base safely on a hit. Compete, compete, compete—this is the keep-it-going spirit by which the person who tries will ultimately make records. NORMAN VINCENT PEALE

Never get into a squirting match with a skunk! AMERICAN PROVERB

You can't fart against thunder. ANON

The weakest goes to the wall. PROVERB

It isn't likely that we'll win, but we can give 'em something to beat.
JOSEPHINE DODGE BACON

America is the land of opportunity—for the businessman in Japan.
ANON

Fear of losing is what makes competitors so great. Show me a gracious
loser and I'll show you a perennial loser. O.J. SIMPSON

A strong position creates strong opposition. ANON

Man eats the big fish
The big fish eat the
little fish
the little fish
eat insects
in the water
the water insects
eat the water plants
the water plants
eat mud
mud eats man. DONALD ROBERT PERRY MARQUIS

A horse never runs so fast as when he has other horses to catch up and
outpace. PUBLIUS OVID

In business, the competition will bite you if you keep running; if you
stand still, they will swallow you. WILLIAM S. KNUDSEN

If I seem to be running, it's because I'm pursued. MIA FARROW

In the management of a business the sharp bite of honest, aggressive
competition is the automatic corrective that safeguards the public from
extortion. CLARENCE B. RANDALL

Our competitors always write for our catalog. ANON

Thou shalt not covet, but tradition approves all forms of competition.
ARTHUR HUGH CLOUGH

We believe in competition, in the excitement of conflict and the testing of man against man in a fair fight.   FELIX FRANKFURTER

There is no substitute for personal contact to strengthen a company's cooperative effort and sharpen its competitive spirit.   E.J. THOMAS

Good will is the one and only asset that competition cannot undersell or destroy.   MARSHALL FIELD

Survival of the fittest.   HERBERT SPENCER

David Sarnoff, reminiscing about his early years in the radio industry, mentioned the strong competition he has had to face. "But I'm grateful to my enemies," he said. "In the long-range movement toward progress, a kick in the pants sends you further along than a friendly handshake."
LEONARD LYONS

The purpose of our competitive system is to maintain that degree of competition which induces progress and protects the consumer.
HERBERT HOOVER

The mountain sheep are sweeter,
But the valley sheep are fatter;
We therefore deemed it meeter
To carry off the latter.   THOMAS PEACOCK

And while the law of competition may be sometimes hard for the individual it is best for the race, because it ensures the survival of the fittest in every department. We accept and welcome, therefore, as conditions to which we must accommodate ourselves, great inequality of environment, the concentration of business, industrial and commercial, in the hands of a few, and the law of competition between these, as being not only beneficial but essential for the future progress of the race.
ANDREW CARNEGIE

'Tis better to have fought and lost,
Than never to have fought at all.   ARTHUR HUGH CLOUGH

Never contend with a man who has nothing to lose.
BALTASAR GRACIAN

My centre is giving way, my right is retreating. Situation excellent. Shall attack. FERDINAND MARSHAL FOCH

If a man would cross a business that he doubts some other would handsomely and effectively move, let him, pretend to wish it well, and move it himself in such sort as may foil it. FRANCIS BACON

Every sect is a moral check on its neighbor. Competition is as wholesome in religion as in commerce. WALTER SAVAGE LANDOR

The only competition worthy of a wise man is with himself.
WASHINGTON ALLSTON

The best of truth is the power of the thought to get itself accepted in the competition of the market. OLIVER WENDELL HOLMES

We might as well urge the destruction of the highest existing type of man, because he failed to reach our ideal as to favor the destruction of individualism, Private Property, the Law of Accumulation of Wealth, and the Law of Competition; for these are the highest results of human experience, the soil in which society has so far produced the best fruit.
ANDREW CARNEGIE

Competitiveness pervades everything we do and is taught from the time we are small children. Work and play are conceived of as contest and race. We seize the half-truth that competition forces everyone to do his best (half-truth because his best is by no means always the best in human terms) and completely ignore what this does to human meeting. Our fundamental stance is not to respond to others, but to outdo them, vie with them, beat them. GEORGE W. MORGAN

Those who pursue him hotly have many points of attack—quality, design, service, and above all price—and he re-doubles his effort as they approach because he knows that today's profit may be tomorrow's loss. He is spurred both by hope of gain and fear of loss, and never for a moment can he relax his effort. He spends his life actually producing the most that he can for the common good. CLARENCE B. RANDALL

Delegation

Use other brains
For your own gains.

If you want a crop for one year, grow millet.
If you want a crop for ten years, grow a tree.
If you want a crop for one hundred years, grow men.
CHINESE PROVERB

You understand delegation if you can turn over a job to a subordinate and then support him if he does it in a manner quite different from that which he himself would have chosen. CLARENCE FRANCIS

There's a longer lease for the old gang in letting the youngsters in than in keeping them out, isn't there? GRANVILLE H. BARKER

Delegate to the one with the most to lose
And not to the one with the most to gain. ANON

You can delegate authority, but you can never delegate responsibility for delegating a task to someone else. If you picked the right man, fine, but if you picked the wrong man, the responsibility is yours—not his.
RICHARD E. KRAFVE

If he works for you, you work for him. JAPANESE PROVERB

The most difficult thing in the world is to know how to do a thing and to watch somebody else doing it wrong, without comment. T.H. WHITE

When you delegate don't shift the blame or take the credit. ANON

The price of an affluent society may be that by the time one is well enough off to turn the dirty work over to someone else, there will be no one willing to do it. W. WILLARD WIRTZ

One chops the wood, the other does the grunting. YIDDISH PROVERB

Robinson had a servant who was even better than Friday—his name was Crusoe. FRIEDRICH WILHELM NIETZSCHE

One can pass on responsibility, but not the discretion that goes with it.
BENVENUTO CELLINI

For the best results, choose a busy man; the others have no time. ANON

Nothing is impossible for the man who does not have to do it himself.
A.H. WIELER

Four eyes see more than two.   PROVERB

It is those underneath who can hold you up.   ANON

Do not keep a dog and bark yourself.   PROVERB

A fellow's usefulness frequently ends when he gets an assistant.
FRANK McKINNEY HUBBARD

Few people willingly accept as an assistant a man who they feel would be superior to them in capabilities.   H.B. MAYNARD

When in doubt, mumble; when in trouble, delegate; when in charge, ponder.   JAMES H. BOREN

I don't never have any trouble in regulating my own conduct, but to keep other folks' straight is what bothers me.   JOSH BILLINGS

You take a chance when you put your stakes on somebody else; like a horse race, it often pays, but sooner or later you're gonna be left standing in the rain.   PATTI SMITH

Clever men are the tools with which bad men work.
WILLIAM HAZLITT

The surest way for an executive to kill himself is to refuse to learn how, and when, and to whom to delegate work.   J.C. PENNEY

The inability to delegate properly is the main reason that executives fail.
ANON

A strong leader knows that if he develops his associates he will be ever stronger.   JAMES F. LINCOLN

Sooner or later, everything becomes too important for someone else to handle.   RICHARD WEST

The most successful managers aim at making themselves unnecessary to their staff. ANON

There's no one like a disciple to expose our faults. JULES RENARD

Now the only decent way to get something done is to get it done by somebody who quite likes doing it. DAVID HERBERT LAWRENCE

Do pleasant things yourself, but unpleasant things through others. BALTASAR GRACIAN

They will never let you down if they understand that your destiny is in their hands, and vice versa. ANON

The manager is always a busy man. He cannot personally hire every individual who is brought into the company. Yet if he wishes his company to grow, he must be careful when delegating authority to hire a key man. H.B. MAYNARD

Send a fool to the market, and a fool he'll return. PROVERB

In the discharge of the duties of the office, there is one rule of action more important than all others. It consists in never doing anything that someone else can do for you. CALVIN COOLIDGE

4 Reasons to Delegate:

1. To give you an opportunity to take on additional work yourself; to expand your department or division.

2. To relieve you of petty, routine details that are not part of your executive job and which can probably be done just as efficiently by someone else.

3. To help keep your department from becoming a bottleneck, which is very apt to happen when the executive insists on doing everything himself.

4. To improve the morale of your employees by giving them a feeling of sharing responsibility. J.C. PENNEY

No man can serve two masters. *ST. MATTHEW*

Don't underestimate the capacity of youth. ANON

Unless the executive establishes priorities for the things he is to do himself, he will not delegate responsibility properly, because he will never know what to delegate.   PROFESSOR RAY E. BROWN

Don't make use of another's mouth unless it has been lent to you.
BELGIAN PROVERB

We sin grievously against ourselves when we get somebody to do something for us which we could do.   HENRY S. HASKINS

He who makes great demands upon himself is naturally inclined to make great demands on others.   ANDRE GIDE

Some men owe most of their greatness to the ability of detecting in those they destine for their tools the exact quality of strength that matters for their work.   JOSEPH CONRAD

Divided duties are seldom split in the middle.   HENRY S. HASKINS

What is worth doing is worth the trouble of asking somebody to do it.
AMBROSE BIERCE

The great trouble today is that there are too many people looking for someone else to do something for them. The solution of most of our troubles is to be found in everyone doing something for himself.
HENRY FORD

You can get almost everything accomplished if you don't mind who gets the credit.   NED HAY

Choose none for thy servant who have served thy betters.
GEORGE HERBERT

Men cease to interest us when we find their limitations.
RALPH WALDO EMERSON

Let the boy win his spurs.   EDWARD III

The great thing in life is not to be able to do things, because then they are always done for you.   ANGELA THIRKELL

Life is too short to do anything for oneself that one can pay others to do for one.   WILLIAM SOMERSET MAUGHAM

The ability to allow others to serve him is not the least of the talents that produce a great ruler.   CARDINAL ARMAND-JEAN RICHELIEU

It's the folks that depend on us for this and for the other that we most do miss.   MARY WEBB

The first impression one gets of a ruler and of his brains is from seeing the men that he has about him.   HENRY KISSINGER

It is never a sign of weakness when a man in high position delegates authority: on the contrary, it is a sign of his strength and of his capacity to deserve success.   WALTER LIPPMAN

Next to doing a job yourself the greatest joy is in having someone else do a first-class job under your direction.   WILLIAM FEATHER

Two heads are better than one.   PROVERB

One cannot make oneself, but one can sometimes help a little in the making of somebody else.   DINAH MULOCK CRAIK

I always suspect a director who says he can afford to be away from the office only for a week at a time. This generally means either that he is a frightened man or else he is thoroughly inefficient and incapable of delegation.   SIR RICHARD POWELL

Cooperation

They are always up
In this world,
Who are never down
On people.

No rewards are handed out for cooperating merely with people we like. It's cooperating with the stinkers that counts.   J.C. PENNEY

See what the boys in the back room will have,
And tell them I'll have the same.   FRANK LOESSER

There is little chance for people to get together as long as most of us want to be in the front of the bus, the back of the church and the middle of the road.
                                                                          ANON

We're not primarily put on this earth to see through one another, but to see one another through.
                                                          PETER de VRIES

It is almost as great a misfortune to be of use to everybody as to be of use to nobody.
                                                      BALTASAR GRACIAN

I have noticed that when chickens quit quarrelling over their food they often find that there is enough for all of them. I wonder if it might not be the same way with the human race.
                              DONALD ROBERT PERRY MARQUIS

The true definition of a snob is one who craves for what separates men rather than for what unites them.
                                                          JOHN BUCHAN

There's as much danger in doing a good turn to a bad man, as in doing a bad turn to a good man.
                                          TITUS MACCIUS PLAUTUS

I might give my life for my friend, but he had better not ask me to do up a parcel.
                                          LOGAN PEARSALL SMITH

One man will carry two buckets of water for his own use,
Two men will carry one for their joint use;
Three men will carry none for anybody's use.   CONFUCIUS

The French will only be united under the threat of danger. Nobody can simply bring together a country that has 265 kinds of cheese.
                                                      CHARLES de GAULLE

"Let us agree not to step on each other's feet," said the cock to the horse.
                                                      ENGLISH PROVERB

There are only two forces that unite men—fear and interest.
                                              NAPOLEON BONAPARTE

He who boasts of a favor bestowed, would like it back again.
                                                          PUBLIUS SYRUS

I don't know why in the West, 13 is considered an unlucky number, but in the East, 2 is considered the unlucky number because it marks the first departure from 1, unity.
                                                          JOE FRANKEL

The hands of one person may express more than the face of another.
NATHANIEL HAWTHORNE

When spider webs unite, they can tie up a lion. ETHIOPIAN PROVERB

The obsession to win at all costs is one of the biggest deterrents to full participation by colleagues and subordinates.
PROFESSOR RAY E. BROWN

The ass that is common property is always the worst saddled.
ENGLISH PROVERB

Cooperation is not so much learning how to get along with others as taking the kinks out of yourself so that others can get along with you.
IAN FERGUSON

You can employ men and hire hands to work for you, but you must win their hearts to have them work with you.   TIORIO

Never give a man up until he has failed at something he likes.
LEWIS E. LAWES

The wise man would rather see men needing him than thanking him.
BALTASAR GRACIAN

People who have given us their complete confidence believe that they have a right to ours. The inference is false: a gift confers no rights.
FRIEDRICH WILHELM NIETZSCHE

Help thy brother's boat across, and Lo! thine own has reached the shore.
HINDU PROVERB

From someone else's cart you have to get off halfway.
POLISH PROVERB

If you aspire to anything better than politics, expect no cooperation from men. They will not further anything good. You must prevail of your own force, as a plant springs and grows by its own vitality.
HENRY DAVID THOREAU

Influence

The best way to influence guys
Is always be their guide;
Let them see through your own eyes
And get them on your side.

Influence is like a savings account. The less you use it, the more you've got.   ANDREW YOUNG

The ability to influence people is a foremost requirement for every executive.   WILLIAM L. BATT

I should always prefer influence to power.   KINGSLEY MARTIN

The real power is to make people say yes to you when they want to say no.
JULIAN BOND

A cock has great influence on his own dunghill. PUBLILIUS SYRUS

No man ever quite believes in any other man. One may believe in an idea absolutely, but not in a man.   HENRY LOUIS MENCKEN

I sit here all day trying to persuade people to do the things they ought to have sense enough to do without my persuading them.
HARRY S. TRUMAN

You can handle people more successfully by enlisting their feelings than by convincing their reason.   THEODORE V. HOUSER

Influence is not government.   GEORGE WASHINGTON

Influence those who influence others.   JOHN FAIRCHILD

If you can make an issue really complicated, most people will say they understand.   ANON

I am certainly not one of those who need to be prodded: in fact, if anything, I am the prod.   SIR WINSTON CHURCHILL

What convinces is conviction.   LYNDON BAINES JOHNSON

All influence ceases when the person receiving it becomes aware of it.
ALAIN RESNAIS

He has one of those terribly weak natures that are not susceptible to influence.
OSCAR WILDE

To please people is a great step towards persuading them.
LORD CHESTERFIELD

The people may be made to follow a path of action, but they may not be made to understand it.
CONFUCIUS

Few are open to conviction, but the majority of men are open to persuasion.
JOHANN WOLFGANG von GOETHE

If you would win a man to your cause, first convince him that you are his sincere friend.
ABRAHAM LINCOLN

Subtlety is better than force.
PROVERB

The finger that turns the dial rules the air.
WILL DURANT

When are men most useless, would you say?
When they can't command and can't obey.
JOHANN WOLFGANG von GOETHE

By persuading others we convince ourselves.
JUNIUS

The secret of getting others to do as you want them to do lies in your ability to penetrate and understand this hidden world of self-interest that each of us carries around within himself.
THEODORE V. HOUSER

Men become attached to us not by reason of the services we render them, but by reason of the services they render us.
EUGENE LABICHE

None but a fool worries about things he cannot influence.
SAMUEL JOHNSON

You can exert no influence if you are not susceptible to influence.
CARL GUSTAV JUNG

To succeed in chaining the crowd you must seem to wear the same fetters.
FRANCOIS VOLTAIRE

Do as we say, and not as we do.   GIOVANNI BOCCACCIO

The superior man is easy to serve and difficult to please. CONFUCIUS

There is little influence where there is not great sympathy.
SAMUEL J. PRIME

A word or a nod from the good, has more weight than the eloquent
speeches of others.   PLUTARCH

The very essence of all power to influence lies in getting the other
person to participate. The mind that can do that has a powerful leverage
on this human world.   HARRY A. OVERSTREET

Never has there been one possessed of complete sincerity who did not
move others. Never has there been one who had not sincerity who was
able to move others.   MENCIUS

He who wants to persuade should put his trust not in the right argument
but in the right word. The power of sound has always been greater than
the power of sense.   JOSEPH CONRAD

Others are affected by what I am and say and do. And these others have
also these spheres of influence. So that a single act of mine may spread
in widening circles through a nation of humanity. WILLIAM ELLERY

The most dangerous follower is he whose defection would destroy the
whole party; that is to say, the best follower.
FRIEDRICH WILHELM NIETZSCHE

Let no man imagine that he has no influence. Whoever he may be, and
wherever he may be placed, the man who thinks becomes a light and a
power.   HENRY GEORGE

Each and every one of us has one obligation, during the bewildered days
of our pilgrimage here: the saving of his own soul, and secondarily and
incidentally thereby affecting for good such other souls as come under
our influence.   KATHLEEN NORRIS

Training

With training you learn
You're the one gainer,
Because you can earn
More than the trainer.

Give a man a fish, and you feed him for a day. Teach a man to fish and you feed him for a lifetime.   CHINESE PROVERB

Lessons are not given, they are taken.   CESARE PAVESE

It's what you learn after you know it all that counts. JOHN WOODEN

A man who has never gone to school may steal from a freight car but if he has a university education he may steal the whole railroad.
FRANKLIN D. ROOSEVELT

I am of the opinion that had your father spent more of your mother's immoral earnings on your education you would not even then have been a gentleman.   FRANK OTTER

I would suggest that the B.A. be issued on paper which deteriorates in five years.   WILLIAM HABER

We receive three educations, one from our parents, one from our schoolmasters, and one from the world. The third contradicts all that the first two teach us.   CHARLES de MONTESQUIEU

Personally I am always ready to learn, although I do not always like being taught.   SIR WINSTON CHURCHILL

He who can does. He who can't, teaches. GEORGE BERNARD SHAW

Education is an admirable thing, but it is well to remember from time to time that nothing that is worth knowing can be taught. OSCAR WILDE

For every person wishing to teach there are thirty not wanting to be taught.   W.C. SELLAR

The secret of teaching is to appear to have known all your life what you learned this afternoon.   ANON

My degree was a kind of inoculation. I got just enough education to make me immune from it for the rest of my life.   ALAN BENNETT

Mediocre men often have the most acquired knowledge.
                                     CLAUDE BERNARD

In life it is training rather than birth which counts. IHARA SAIKUKU

You know more than you think you do.   DR. BENJAMIN SPOCK

The first problem for all of us, men and women, is not to learn, but to unlearn.   GLORIA STEINEM

Creative minds always have been known to survive any kind of bad training.   ANNA FREUD

To teach is to learn twice.   JOSEPH JOUBERT

It is nothing short of a miracle that modern methods of instruction have not yet strangled the holy curiosity of enquiry.   ALBERT EINSTEIN

When a man teaches something he does not know to somebody else who has no aptitude for it, and gives him a certificate of proficiency, the latter has undergone the education of a gentleman.
                                     GEORGE BERNARD SHAW

I had, out of my sixty teachers, a scant half dozen who couldn't have been supplanted by phonographs.   DON HEROLD

The first duty of a lecturer—to hand up after an hour's discourse a nugget of pure truth to wrap up between the pages of your notebooks and keep on the mantelpiece for ever.   VIRGINIA WOOLF

An ounce of discretion is worth a pound of learning.   PROVERB

The vanity of teaching often tempts a man to forget he is a blockhead.
                                     GEORGE SAVILE

A teacher affects eternity, he can never tell where his influence stops.
                                     HENRY ADAMS

The first thing education teaches you to do is walk alone.
ALFRED ALOYSIUS HERN

He not only overflowed with learning, but stood in the slop.
SYDNEY SMITH

To teach a man how he may learn to grow independently, and for himself, is perhaps the greatest service that one man can do to another.
BENJAMIN JOWETT

The human mind is full of curiosity but it don't love to be taught.   JOSH BILLINGS

See and do all you can; never miss a new experience. That is education, and something no one can rob you of however poor you might become.
ANON

Few people of attainments take easily to a plan of self-improvement. Some discover very early their perfection cannot endure the insult. Others find their intellectual pleasure lies in the theory, not in the practice. Only a few stubborn ones will blunder on, painfully, out of the luxuriant world of their pretensions into the desert of mortification and reward.   PATRICK WHITE

No man is the wiser for his learning.   JOHN SELDEN

Example

Those who cannot lead
And hate to obey
Will often impede
And stand in the way.

Watch what we do, not what we say.   JOHN MITCHELL

Example is not the main thing in influencing others, it's the only thing.
ALBERT SCHWEITZER

You don't lead by pointing and telling people some place to go. You lead by going to that place and making a case.   KEN KESEY

No people do so much harm as those who go about doing good.
MANDELL CREIGHTON

An ounce of example is worth a pound of advice.   ANON

Positive anything is better than negative nothing.
ELBERT HUBBARD

But those behind cried "Forward!"
And those before cried "Back!"
LORD THOMAS BABINGTON MACAULAY

You can preach a better sermon with your life than with your lips.
OLIVER GOLDSMITH

Never try to make anyone like yourself—you know, and God knows, that one of you is enough.   RALPH WALDO EMERSON

A frightened captain makes a frightened crew.   LISTER SINCLAIR

It is a safer thing any time to follow a man's advice rather than his example.   JOSH BILLINGS

Few things are harder to put up with than the annoyance of a good example.   MARK TWAIN

The hands that help are holier than the lips that pray.
ROBERT GREEN INGERSOLL

It is easier to appear worthy of a position one does not hold, than of the office which one fills.   FRANCOIS Duc de la ROCHEFOUCAULD

It is hard to look up to a leader who keeps his ear to the ground.
JAMES H. BOREN

It is better to have a lion at the head of an army of sheep, than a sheep at the head of an army of lions.   DANIEL DEFOE

The final test of a leader is that he leaves behind him in other men the conviction and the will to carry on.   WALTER LIPPMAN

Example is the school of mankind, and they will learn at no other.
EDMUND BURKE

Example is not only the best way of propagating an opinion, but it is the only way worth taking into account. SAMUEL BUTLER

Example is better than precept. PROVERB

He cures most in whom most have faith. GALEN

If you would convince a man that he does wrong, do right. Men will believe what they see. HENRY DAVID THOREAU

Example moves the world more than doctrine. HENRY MILLER

Never promise more than you can perform. PUBLILIUS SYRUS

When people are free to do as they please, they usually imitate each other. ERIC HOFFER

Example is often but a lying mirror. PIERRE CORNEILLE

Through obedience learn to command. PLATO

No man regards himself as in all ways inferior to the man he most admires. FRANCOIS DUC de la ROCHEFOUCAULD

He that would govern others, first should be
The master of himself. PHILIP MASSINGER

No man is so insignificant as to be sure his example can do no hurt.
LORD CLARENDON

The blossom cannot tell what becomes of its odor, and no man can tell what becomes of his influence and example, that roll away from him, and go beyond his ken on their perilous mission.
HENRY WARD BEECHER

My advice is to consult the lives of other men, as one would a looking-glass, and from thence fetch examples for imitation.
PUBLIUS TERENCE

Efficiency

High efficiency
Somehow implies
Low morality.

There is nothing so useless as doing efficiently that which should not be done at all.   PETER F. DRUCKER

It's pretty hard to be efficient without being obnoxious.
                                    FRANK McKINNEY HUBBARD

Why is it that there is never enough time to do a job right, but always time enough to do it over?   ANON

Don't put off for tomorrow what you can do today, because if you enjoy it today you can do it again tomorrow.   JAMES A MICHENER

Most of us would rather risk catastrophe than read the directions.
                                    MIGNON McLAUGHLIN

Going along the street of mañana, bye and bye one arrives at the house never.   MIGUEL de CERVANTES

Efficiency is intelligent laziness.   ARNOLD GLASGOW

Efficiency experts—
At least those I've known—
Can cope with my troubles
But not with their own.   ANON

The world has moved from the wire to the wireless, the track to the trackless, the visible to the invisible. More and more can be done with less and less.   R. BUCKMINSTER FULLER

When I makes tea, I makes tea, as old Mother Grogan said, and when I makes water, I makes water.   JAMES JOYCE

How can you be in two places at once when you're not supposed to be anywhere at all?   THEATER FIRESIGN

Waste of time is the most extravagant and costly of all expenses.
                                                    THEOPHRASTUS

We all find time to do what we really want to do. WILLIAM FEATHER

The difference between rising at five and seven o'clock in the morning,
for forty years, supposing a man to go to bed at the same hour at night, is
nearly equivalent to the addition of ten years to a man's life.
                                                    PHILIP DODDRIDGE

I haven't had time to work in weeks.   JACK KEROUAC

Lost time was like a run in a stocking. It always got worse.
                                          ANNE MORROW LINDBERGH

Procrastination—a fault that most people put off trying to correct.
                                                    Indianapolis News

Waste not, want not.   PROVERB

The less one has to do, the less time one finds to do it in.
                                                    LORD CHESTERFIELD

A practical man is a man who practices the errors of his forefathers.
                                                    BENJAMIN DISRAELI

When the cat's away,
The mice will play.   PROVERB

One of the greatest labor-saving inventions of today is tomorrow.
                                                    VINCENT T. FOSS

It takes time to save time.   SIR THEODORE FOX

Delays are dangerous.   PROVERB

More free time means more time to waste. The worker who used to have
only a little time in which to get drunk and beat his wife now has time to
get drunk, beat his wife—and watch T.V.   ROBERT M. HUTCHINS

The best carpenters make the fewest chips.   GERMAN PROVERB

Ask yourself always: how can this be done better?
                                          GEORG CHRISTOPH LICHTENBERG

It is more than probable that the average man could, with no injury to his health, increase his efficiency fifty percent. WALTER DILL SCOTT

Never get up with the lark. Get up only for a lark. LORD BOYD-ORR

You will never "find" time for anything. If you want time, you must make it. CHARLES BIXTON

If the boss quits early, so will the staff. ANON

It is not half as important to burn the midnight oil as it is to be awake in the daytime. E. W. ELMORE

Tomorrow is two days late for yesterday's job. ANON

Procrastination is the thief of time. EDWARD YOUNG

Time is the measure of business. FRANCIS BACON

There are only two qualities in the world: efficiency and inefficiency: and only two sorts of people: the efficient and the inefficient.
GEORGE BERNARD SHAW

Those who make the worst use of their time are the first to complain of its brevity. JEAN de la BRUYERE

Nine times out of ten the inefficient manager becomes so, not because of lack of training or lack of information, but because of evading hard decisions. GENERAL LUCIUS D. CLAY

The efficient man is the man who thinks for himself, and is capable of thinking hard and long. CHARLES W. ELIOT

Time is like an enterprising manager always bent on staging some new and surprising production, without knowing very well what it will be.
GEORGE SANTAYANA

Time is really the only capital that any human being has, and the one thing that he can't afford to lose. THOMAS EDISON

Everyone has time if he likes. Business runs after nobody; people cling to it of their own free will and think that to be busy is a proof of happiness. LUCIUS ANNAEUS SENECA

Extravagance is the luxury of the poor, penury the luxury of the rich.
OSCAR WILDE

There is no royal road to anything. One thing at a time, and all things in succession. That which grows slowly endures.   J.G. HOLLAND

Arrears of small things to be attended to, if allowed to accumulate, worry and depress like unpaid debts. The main work should always stand aside for these, not these for the main work, as large debts should stand aside for small ones, or truth for common charity and good feeling. If we attend continually and promptly to the little that we can do, we shall ere long be surprised to find how little remains that we cannot do.   SAMUEL BUTLER

Procrastination is the art of keeping up with yesterday.
DONALD ROBERT PERRY MARQUIS

Character

We are born with
Most of our personality
But we acquire
Nearly all of our character.

Every man has three characters: that which he exhibits, that which he has, and that which he thinks he has.   ALPHONSE KARR

The shell is America's most active contribution to the formation of character. A tough hide. Grow it early.   ANAIS NIN

When some moralists write about the importance of having character, they appear to mean only the importance of having a dull character.
GILBERT KEITH CHESTERTON

I'd always assumed I was the central character in my own story but now it occurred to me I might in fact be only a minor character in someone else's.   RUSSELL HOBAN

Just be yourself.   HUGHES RUDD

It doesn't matter if you're a nice guy or a bastard. What matters is you won't bend.   KIRK DOUGLAS

Many people have character who have nothing else.   DON HEROLD

Underneath this flabby exterior is an enormous lack of character.
OSCAR LEVANT

Character building begins in our infancy, and continues until death.
ELEANOR ROOSEVELT

The measure of a man's real character is what he would do if he knew he would never be found out.   THOMAS B. MACAULAY

There is nothing so fatal to character as half-finished tasks.
DAVID LLOYD GEORGE

When wealth is lost, nothing is lost;
When health is lost, something is lost;
When character is lost, all is lost!   ANON

Character is much easier kept than recovered.   THOMAS PAINE

To judge a man's character by only one of its manifestations is like judging the sea by a jugful of its water.   PAUL ELDRIDGE

Nearly all men can stand adversity, but if you want to test a man's character give him power.   ABRAHAM LINCOLN

Character is perfectly educated will.   NOVALIS

You cannot dream yourself into a character: you must hammer and forge yourself one.   JAMES A. FROUDE

When a man thinks he is reading the character of another, he is often unconsciously betraying his own.   JOSEPH FARRELL

Nothing is more characteristic of a man than the manner in which he behaves toward fools.   HENRI FREDERIC AMIEL

The more peculiarly his own a man's character is, the better it fits him.
CICERO

As William James said of the boarder: "It is much more important for the landlady to know his philosophy than his income."
HARRY SCHERMAN

Simplicity of character is the natural result of profound thought.
WILLIAM HAZLITT

Character is long-standing habit.   PLUTARCH

As much character as a china shepherdess.   ANON

The universe seems bankrupt as soon as we begin to discuss the characters of individuals.   HENRY DAVID THOREAU

It is with trifles, and when he is off guard, that a man best reveals his character.   ARTHUR SCHOPENHAUER

A man is not determined by what he does and still less by what he says. But in the deepest part of himself a being is determined solely by what he is.   CHARLES PEGUY

If a man has character, he also has his typical experience, which always recurs.   FRIEDRICH WILHELM NIETZSCHE

Get to know two things about a man—how he earns his money and how he spends it—and you have the clue to his character, for you have a search light that shows up the inmost recesses of his soul. You know all you need to know about his standards, his motives, his driving desires, and his real religion.   ROBERT J. McCRACKEN

Character, in great and little things, means carrying through what you feel able to do.   JOHANN WOLFGANG von GOETHE

No man can climb out beyond the limitations of his own character.
JOHN MORLEY

When a person lacks character, he is badly in need of a method.
ALBERT CAMUS

He is a hard man who is only just, and a sad one who is only wise.
FRANCOIS VOLTAIRE

Moderation is an ostentatious proof of our strength of character.
FRANCOIS DUC de la ROCHEFOUCAULD

I have discovered that we may be in some degree whatever character we choose. Besides, practice forms a man to anything. JAMES BOSWELL

Personality is more important than surroundings. SENECA

To enjoy the things we ought, and to hate the things we ought, has the greatest bearing on excellence of character. ARISTOTLE

Fame is what you have taken,
  Character's what you give;
When to this truth you waken,
  Then you begin to live. BAYARD TAYLOR

The wise man, the true friend, the finished character, we seek everywhere, and only find in fragments. RALPH WALDO EMERSON

No matter how full a reservoir of maxims one may possess, and no matter how good one's sentiments may be, if one has not taken advantage of every concrete opportunity to act, one's character may remain entirely unaffected for the better. WILLIAM JAMES

The palm-tree grows best beneath a ponderous weight, and even so the character of man. The petty pangs of small daily cares have often bent the character of men, but great misfortune seldom. LOUIS KOSSUTH

Talents are best nurtured in solitude: character is best formed in the stormy billows of the world. JOHANN WOLFGANG von GOETHE

III CONTROL

Control

Just to have
The right to do it
Does not mean
It's right to do it.

Holding office is like trying to dance in a Night Club. No matter what you do, you rub somebody the wrong way.   ANON

It is the anonymous "they," the enigmatic "they" who are in charge. Who is "they"? I don't know. Nobody knows. Not even "they" themselves.
JOSEPH HELLER

Discipline is like cabbage. We may not care for it ourselves, but feel sure it would be good for somebody else.   BILL VAUGHAN

The inevitable end of multiple chiefs is that they fade and disappear for lack of unity.   NAPOLEON BONAPARTE

He is a giant who has many dwarfs about him.   YIDDISH PROVERB

Nothing appears more surprising to those who consider human affairs with a philosophical eye than the ease with which the many are governed by the few.   DAVID HUME

Suited for office if only he had not had to hold it. CORNELIUS TACITUS

If you wish to succeed in managing and controlling others learn to manage and control yourself.   WILLIAM J.H. BOETCKER

Invoking the artistic prerogative clause in my contract, a clause that gives me total control over what necktie I can wear while rewriting, I insisted that I go forward with the project.   WOODY ALLEN

The urge to save humanity is almost always only a false-face for the urge to rule it.   HENRY LOUIS MENCKEN

Men will let you abuse them if only you will make them laugh.
HENRY WARD BEECHER

It is the old practice of despots to use a part of the people to keep the rest in order.   THOMAS JEFFERSON

If one word does not succeed, ten thousand are of no avail.
CHINESE PROVERB

He who has never learned to obey cannot be a good commander.
ARISTOTLE

How shall I be able to rule over others, that have not full power and command of myself?   FRANCOIS RABELAIS

Divide and rule.   PROVERB

A resolution that is communicated is no longer within your power; your intentions become now the plaything of chance; he who would have his commands certainly carried out must take men by surprise.
JOHANN WOLFGANG von GOETHE

The officer and the office, the doer and the thing done, seldom fit so exactly that we can say they were almost made for each other.
SYDNEY SMITH

He that fears you present will hate you absent.   THOMAS FULLER

The insolence of office.   WILLIAM SHAKESPEARE

It is one thing to praise discipline, and another to submit to it.
MIGUEL de CERVANTES

Admissions are mostly made by those who do not know their importance
                                      MR. JUSTICE DARLING

The man who commands efficiently must have obeyed others in the past,
and the man who obeys dutifully is worthy of being some day a
commander.   MARCUS TULLIUS

Should anyone become the ruler either of a city or of a state, especially if
he has no sure footing in it . . . the best thing he can do in order to retain
such a principality, is to organise everything in that state afresh; e.g. in
its cities to appoint new governors, with new titles and new authority, the
governors themselves being new men; to make the rich poor and the poor
rich . . . as well as to build new cities, to destroy those already built, and
to move the inhabitants from one place to another far distant from it; in
short, to leave nothing of that province intact, and nothing in it, neither
rank, nor institution, nor form of government, nor wealth, except that it
be held by such as recognise that it comes from you.
                                      NICCOLO MACHIAVELLI

He who governs should possess energy without fanaticism, principles
without demagogy, severity without cruelty; he must neither be weak,
nor vacillating, nor, so to express it, must he be ashamed to do his duty.
                                      NAPOLEON BONAPARTE

Responsibility

*They may know how
But that's one half;
Who bulls the cow
Must keep the calf.*

I had a great deal of responsibility and damn all authority.
                                      PETER TEBBIT

I am responsible for my actions, but who is responsible for those of
General Motors?   RALPH NADER

If one defines the term "Dropout" to mean a person who has given up
serious effort to meet his responsibilities, then every business office,

government agency, golf club and university faculty would yield its quota.   JOHN W. GARDNER

The buck stops with the guy who signs the checks.
RUPERT MURDOCH

It's a pity to shoot the pianist when the piano is out of tune. RENE COTY

You can dodge your responsibilities but not the consequences. ANON

If men did not put their responsibilities above everything else, the bulk of lovemaking would not be done at night.   HENRY S. HASKINS

There is no room for a chip on the shoulders of responsibility. ANON

No matter how lofty you are in your department, the responsibility for what your lowliest assistant is doing is yours.
BESSIE R. JAMES and MARY WATERSTREET

A chief is a man who assumes responsibility. He says, "I was beaten," he does not say "My men were beaten." ANTOINE de SAINT-EXUPERY

Why did the Lord give us so much quickness of movement unless it was to avoid responsibility?   OGDEN NASH

A man who enjoys responsibility usually gets it. A man who merely likes exercising authority usually loses it.   MALCOLM FORBES

Everybody threw the blame on me. I have noticed that they nearly always do. I suppose it is because they think I shall be able to bear it best.
SIR WINSTON CHURCHILL

It is our responsibilities, not ourselves, that we should take seriously.
PETER USTINOV

Responsibility, n. A detachable burden easily shifted to the shoulders of God, Fate, Fortune, Luck or one's neighbor. In the days of astrology it was customary to unload it upon a star.   AMBROSE BIERCE

The organization needs the obedient rebel who thinks on his own, but it cannot function on efficiency and tolerate rebels who have no sense of the responsibilities to which they must be obedient.
PROFESSOR RAY E. BROWN

To leave positions of great responsibility and authority is to die a little.
DEAN ACHESON

The best way to cure an associate who shirks responsibility is to give him more responsibility.   J.C. PENNEY

Action springs not from thought, but from a readiness for responsibility.
DIETRICH BONHOEFFER

To act responsibly you have to take leaps without being sure.
DANIEL ELLSBERG

Liberty means responsibility. That is why most men dread it.
GEORGE BERNARD SHAW

Adversity attracts the man of character. He seeks out the bitter joy of responsibility.   CHARLES de GAULLE

Responsibility's like a string we can only see the middle of. Both ends are out of sight.   WILLIAM McFEE

Responsibility educates.   WENDELL PHILLIPS

The price of greatness is responsibility. SIR WINSTON CHURCHILL

A prig always finds a last refuge in responsibility.   JEAN COCTEAU

A new position of responsibility will usually show a man to be a far stronger creature than was supposed.   WILLIAM JAMES

The great thought, the great concern, the great anxiety of men is to restrict, as much as possible, the limits of their own responsibility.
GIOSUE BORSI

There may be responsible persons, but there are no guilty ones.
ALBERT CAMUS

Few things help an individual more than to place responsibility upon him and to let him know that you trust him. BOOKER WASHINGTON

Responsibility is to keep the ability to respond.   ROBERT DUNCAN

Do not fear responsibility for what you decide.
New York Adult Education Council

It seems to me that any full grown, mature adult would have a desire to be responsible, to help where he can in a world that needs so very much, that threatens us so very much. NORMAN LEAR

Genuine responsibility exists only where there is real responding. MARTIN BUBER

If it's going to be responsible, it has to be insecure. It has to have something to lose. RALPH NADER

To gain one's way is no escape from the responsibility for an inferior solution. SIR WINSTON CHURCHILL

Our privileges can be no greater than our obligations. The protection of our rights can endure no longer than the performance of our responsibilities. JOHN F. KENNEDY

Absence of responsibility, an automatic and stereotyped rhythm is what men most desire for themselves. All struggle has for its end relief or repose. PERCY WYNDHAM LEWIS

Administration

The origination
Of administration
Is good defense
And common sense.

If people always did naturally what was best for the enterprise, then there would be no need for administration. ANON

The trouble with having a place for everything is how often it gets filled up with everything else. DON FRASER

I don't particularly mind waste, but I think it's a pity not to know what one is wasting. PETER BROOK

Without a doubt, there is such a thing as too much order. ARNOLD LOBEL

Bad administration, to be sure, can destroy good policy; but good administration can never save bad policy.   ADLAI STEVENSON

The man of narrower mind is often the better administrator.
JOSEPH RICKABY

The welfare of the common man is more deeply affected by the administrator than the legislator.   STANLEY BALDWIN

Perfect order is the forerunner of perfect horror. CARLOS FUENTES

Order leads to all the virtues, but what leads to order?
GEORG CHRISTOPH LICHTENBERG

An established form of expression is also a form of oppression.
EUGENE IONESCO

Order and harmony arise as an accidental byproduct of individuals pursuing their own self-interests.   STEPHEN JAY GOULD

He becomes fussy about filing, keen on seeing that pencils are sharpened, eager to ensure that the windows are open (or shut) and apt to use two or three different coloured inks. C. NORTHCOTE PARKINSON

Madness is often the logic of an accurate mind overtaxed.
OLIVER WENDELL HOLMES

Good order is the foundation of all good things.   EDMUND BURKE

Organizationally, we must provide for a system of sequential controls, which will make certain that ideas are brought forward, evaluated and carried through.   WILLIAM T. BRADY

An administration, like a machine, does not create. It carries on.
ANTOINE de SAINT-EXUPERY

He thinks that to say something is to do something, which is an imperfect view of administration.   HENRY CABOT LODGE

If you think you came into being for the purpose of taking an important part in the administration of events, to guard a province of the moral creation from ruin, and that its salvation hangs on the success of your single arm, you have wholly mistaken your business.
RALPH WALDO EMERSON

There is no course of life so weak and sottish as that which is managed by order, method and discipline.   MICHEL de MONTAIGNE

It is best to do things systematically, since we are only human, and disorder is our worst enemy.   HESIOD

Have a time and place for everything, and do everything in its time and place, and you will not only accomplish more, but have far more leisure than those who are always hurrying, as if vainly attempting to overtake time that had been lost.   TYRON EDWARDS

Chaos often breeds life, when order breeds habit.
                                              HENRY BROOKS ADAMS

Those who would administer wisely must, indeed, be wise; for one of the serious obstacles to improvement of our race is indiscriminate charity.
                                                    ANDREW CARNEGIE

Forms are for mediocrity, and it is fortunate that mediocrity can act only according to routine. Ability takes its flight unhindered.
                                                  NAPOLEON BONAPARTE

Let all things be done decently and in order.   *CORINTHIANS*

The purpose of administration is to influence human behavior, both internal and external to the organization, through modifying the causes by some system of inducements so as to accomplish the objectives and ends of the particular organization.   PROFESSOR RAY E. BROWN

It is meritorious to insist on forms, religion and all else naturally clothes itself in forms. Everywhere the formed world is the only habitable one.
                                                     THOMAS CARLYLE

Symmetry is ennui, and ennui is the very essence of grief and melancholy. Despair yawns.   VICTOR HUGO

When liberty destroys order, the hunger for order will destroy liberty.
                                                       WILL DURANT

The virtue of the soul does not consist in flying high, but in walking orderly.   MICHEL de MONTAIGNE

Set all things in their own peculiar place, and know that order is the greatest grace.   JOHN DRYDEN

Authority

Withholding information
To increase authority
Is only confirmation
Of inferiority.

In the Far East the master is considered a living Buddha, but in Minneapolis they wonder why he doesn't have a job.
ROBERT M. BIERCE

There would be no great ones if there were no little ones. PROVERB

My sole inspiration is a telephone call from a director. COLE PORTER

The stronger never treat, they dictate the terms which the weak obey.
NAPOLEON BONAPARTE

It is my theory that if you have authority, know your business and know you have authority, you have the authority. DOROTHY ARZNER

Whenever you're sitting across from some important person, always picture him sitting there in a suit of long red underwear. That's the way I always operated in business. JOSEPH P. KENNEDY

When I say "everybody says so," I mean I say so.
EDGAR WATSON HOWE

Many organizations are straight-line authoritarian in character. The top executive or department head consciously or unconsciously wants only a group of rubber stamps who agree with him. PIERRE MARTINEAU

The man who bows before the ruler, shows his behind to the courtiers.
STANISLAW J. LEC

The weaker a man in authority the stronger his insistence that all his privileges be acknowledged. AUSTIN O'MALLEY

The boss's secretary can wield great power, like the king's mistress, without any authority at all.
ANTHONY JAY

It's a clever man who can throw his weight around without losing his balance.
ANON

The slavery of being waited upon that is more deadening than the slavery of waiting upon other people.
SIR COMPTON MACKENZIE

The only gracious way to accept an insult is to ignore it; if you can't ignore it, top it; if you can't top it, laugh at it; if you can't laugh at it, it's probably deserved.
RUSSELL LYNES

One of the surest signs of the Philistine is his reverence for the superior tastes of those who put him down.
PAULINE KAEL

Almost all absurdity of conduct arises from the imitation of those whom we can not resemble.
SAMUEL JOHNSON

When too much emphasis is placed on job definition, one is apt to think more about the limits of authority than upon the opportunities.
CLARENCE FRANCIS

Distrust all in whom the impulse to punish is strong.
FRIEDRICH WILHELM NIETZSCHE

When they were going to be flagrantly, brutally selfish, how men did love to talk of being fair!
KATHLEEN NORRIS

Alas, it seems that for all time the Small have suffered from the folly of the Great.
JEAN de la FONTAINE

To be a complete victim may be another source of power.
IRIS MURDOCH

Among those who dislike oppression are many who like to oppress.
NAPOLEON BONAPARTE

If you wish to know what a man is, place him in authority.
YUGOSLAV PROVERB

I think it is not well for any of us to allow another personality to submerge in any way your own.
OLIVE SCHREINER

When you make your peace with authority you become authority.
JIM MORRISON

Golden fetters hurt as cruelly as iron ones.   MINNA ANTRIM

The tyrant dies and his rule is over; the martyr dies and his rule begins.
                                                SOREN KIERKEGAARD

Every despotism has a specially keen and hostile instinct for whatever
keeps up human dignity and independence.
                                          HENRI FREDERIC AMIEL

It is an observation no less just than common, that there is no stronger
test of a man's real character than power and authority, exciting as they
do every passion, and discovering every latest vice.   PLUTARCH

Nothing destroys authority so much as the unequal and untimely
interchange of power pressed too far and relaxed too much.
                                                   FRANCIS BACON

Authority forgets a dying king.   ALFRED LORD TENNYSON

Learn to obey before you command.   SOLON

Power

Power's like a penny
To give it its due;
It passes the many,
To stay with a few.

Power! What do we know about it? We don't know anything about it. We
have sex education. Why don't we have power education?
                                          REV. JOHN J. McLAUGHLIN

Being powerful is like being a lady. If you have to tell people you are,
you ain't.   JESSE CARR

The wrong sort of people are always in power because they would not be
in power if they were not the wrong sort of people. JON WYNNE-TYSON

And not
to spot
the purer
Fuhrer.

ANON

So long as men worship the Caesars and Napoleons, Caesars and Napoleons will duly rise and make them miserable.

ALDOUS LEONARD HUXLEY

Power can be built more easily on lies than on truth. ANON

If you would be powerful, pretend to be powerful. HORNE TOOKE

Power only tires those who don't exercise it.

PIERRE ELLIOTT TRUDEAU

Being a great power is no longer much fun. DAVID SCHOENBRUN

Knowledge itself is power. FRANCIS BACON

He who has his thumb on the purse has the power.

OTTO von BISMARCK

Life is not easy...but it's easier with power. ANON

The qualities that get a man into power are not those that lead him, once established, to use power wisely. LYMAN BRYSON

Responsibilities gravitate to the person who can shoulder them; power flows to the man who knows how. ELBERT HUBBARD

In the past, those who foolishly sought power by riding the back of the tiger ended up inside. JOHN F. KENNEDY

The more you are talked about the less powerful you are.

BENJAMIN DISRAELI

People who obtain power do so because it delights them for its own sake and for no other reason. GORE VIDAL

Power? It's like a Dead Sea fruit. When you achieve it, there is nothing there. HAROLD MACMILLAN

No influence so quickly converts a radical into a reactionary as does his election to power.   ELIZABETH MARBURY

A friend in power is a friend lost.   HENRY BROOKS ADAMS

Unused power slips imperceptibly into the hands of another.
                                          KONRAD HEIDEN

If you have no power, then having right on your side is useless.
                                          ADOLF HITLER

Make the best use of what is in your power, and take the rest as it happens.   EPICTETUS

For the mighty even to give way is grace.   AESCHYLUS

It is a strange desire to seek power and to lose liberty.
                                          FRANCIS BACON

Assuming that none of us was born to make life easy for his rulers, the first law of power is its desire to continue.   LUDVIK VACULIK

A smile like a happy crocodile's.   G. MACDONALD FRASER

Those in power want only to perpetuate it.
                                    JUSTICE WILLIAM O. DOUGLAS

The sudden acquisition of power by those who have never had it before can be intoxicating, and we run the risk of becoming absorbed in petty power games with our organization that in the last analysis can only be self-defeating.   TONI CARABILLO

If a man can accept a situation in a place of power with the thought that it's only temporary, he comes out all right. But when he thinks that he is the cause of the power, that can be his ruination. HARRY S. TRUMAN

It is when power is wedded to chronic fear that it becomes formidable.
                                          ERIC HOFFER

He was one of those men who possess almost every gift, except the gift of the power to use them.   CHARLES KINGSLEY

Power does not corrupt men; fools, however, if they get into a position of power, corrupt power.   GEORGE BERNARD SHAW

The lust for power is not rooted in strength but weakness.
ERICH FROMM

Power will intoxicate the best hearts, as wine the strongest heads.
CHARLES CALEB COLTON

Let not thy will roar, when thy power can but whisper.
THOMAS FULLER

Our sense of power is more vivid whenever we break a man's spirit than when we win his heart.   ERIC HOFFER

As for the men in power, they are so anxious to establish the myth of infallibility that they do their utmost to ignore truth.
BORIS PASTERNAK

Mankind is safer when men seek pleasure than when they seek the power and the glory.   GEOFFREY GORER

The destruction of the personality is the great evil of the time.
ELLEN KEY

Ideals are the noble toga that political gentlemen drape over their will to power.   ALDOUS LEONARD HUXLEY

It is certainly more agreeable to have power than to receive.
SIR WINSTON CHURCHILL

There is a universal need to exercise some kind of power, or to create for one's self the appearance of some power, if only temporarily, in the form of intoxication.   FRIEDRICH WILHELM NIETZSCHE

To know the pains of power, we must go to those who have it; to know its pleasures, we must go to those who are seeking it. The pains of power are real; its pleasures imaginary.   CHARLES CALEB COLTON

It reproduces itself in evermore faithful copies...power prefers people of the same inner constitution as itself, but since these are in short supply, it has to make use of other people too and adjust them to its needs.   LUDVIK VACULIK

He who has the greatest power put into his hands will only become the more impatient of any restraint in the use of it. WILLIAM HAZLITT

Power is not a means, it is an end. One does not establish a dictatorship in order to safeguard a revolution, one makes the revolution in order to establish the dictatorship.   GEORGE ORWELL

Anyone who by his nature is not his own man, but is another's, is by nature a slave.   ARISTOTLE

Those who deny freedom to others, deserve it not for themselves.
ABRAHAM LINCOLN

Better to have a handful of might than a sack of justice.
CZECH PROVERB

I believe there are more instances of the abridgment of the freedom of the people by gradual and silent encroachments of those in power than by violent and sudden usurpations.   JAMES MADISON

The wise become as the unwise in the exchanged chambers of Power, whose lamps make every face the same colour.
WALTER SAVAGE LANDOR

In this world no one rules by love; if you are but amiable, you are no hero; to be powerful, you must be strong, and to have dominion you must have a genius for organizing.   JOHN HENRY CARDINAL NEWMAN

Supervision

Good sense about actualities
Is more important than
Nonsense about unrealities.

Grow antennae, not horns.   JAMES B. ANGELL

A nose that can see is worth two that sniff.   EUGENE IONESCO

An old poacher makes a good game-keeper.   PROVERB

He regretted that he was not a bird, and could not be in two places at once. SIR BOYLE ROCHE

The wrong way to make your way is to insist on having it. ANON

I'm like an orchestra conductor. I don't write the music, I just make sure it comes out right. CHRISTOPHER KRAFT

Never claim as a right what you can ask as a favour. JOHN CHURTON COLLINS

See everything, overlook a great deal, correct a little. POPE JOHN XXIII

Stand tall with your shoulders back and your head high but don't turn up your nose. ANON

He's invented a most marvellous gadget for speeding up production in all kinds of factories. He's calling it a whip. PETER CAGNEY

The machine, yes, the machine, never wastes anybody's time, never watches the foreman, never talks back. CARL SANDBURG

You must always appear right as well as be right. STROM THURMOND

Be neither too remote nor too familiar. CHARLES, PRINCE OF WALES

You can observe a lot by just watching. YOGI BERRA

Nothing is harder than to make people think about what they're going to do. ANDRE MALRAUX

That weakness in human nature which goes by the name of strength. PETER USTINOV

He hurts the good who spares the bad. PUBLILIUS SYRUS

There are two kinds of men who never amount to much—those who cannot do what they are told and those who can do nothing else. CYRUS H.K. CURTIS

A little uncertainty is good for everyone. HENRY KISSINGER

Men are never attached to you by favors.   NAPOLEON BONAPARTE

Forgive many things in others, nothing in yourself.   AUSONIUS

A watched pot never boils.   PROVERB

He who refuses nothing will soon have nothing to refuse.
MARCUS VALERIUS MARTIAL

There are some acts of justice which corrupt those who perform them.
JOSEPH JOUBERT

He who is only just is cruel. LORD GEORGE GORDON NOEL BYRON

Those who believe that they are exclusively in the right are generally those who achieve something.   ALDOUS LEONARD HUXLEY

If thou art a master, be sometimes blind, if a servant, sometimes deaf.
THOMAS FULLER

Lookers-on see most of the game.   PROVERB

The best way to get things done is to allow your subordinates to formulate their own methods of operation.   THEODORE V. HOUSER

Be sincere. Be simple in words, manners and gestures. Amuse as well as instruct. If you can make a man laugh, you can make him think and make him like and believe you.   ALFRED EMANUEL SMITH

To get the best out of a man go to what is best in him.
DANIEL CONSIDINE

A man who cannot tolerate small ills can never accomplish great things.
CHINESE PROVERB

One should oblige everyone to the extent of one's ability. One often needs someone smaller than oneself.   JEAN de la FONTAINE

He is the rich man who can avail himself of all men's faculties.
RALPH WALDO EMERSON

Tzu-lu asked how to serve the King. The Master said: 'Never cheat him: withstand him to the face.'   CONFUCIUS

Dealing with Superiors

Never take out of
Your inferiors
What you have to take from
Your superiors.

Never fall out with your bread and butter.   ENGLISH PROVERB

The Fuhrer is always right.   JOACHIM von RIBBENTROP

The defect of equality is that we only desire it with our superiors.
HENRY BECQUE

Though familiarity may not breed contempt, it takes the edge off
admiration.   WILLIAM HAZLITT

Make sure to be in with your equals if you're going to fall out with your
superiors.   JEWISH PROVERB

People who bite the hand that feeds them usually lick the boot that kicks
them.   ERIC HOFFER

Never stand begging for that which you have the power to earn.
MIGUEL de CERVANTES

I've met a few people in my time who were enthusiastic about hard work,
and it was just my luck that all of them happened to be men I was
working for at the time.   BILL GOLD

Whose bread I eat, whose wine I drink, his songs I sing.
DAMON RUNYON

The one virtue most often respected by your superiors is brevity. ANON

To feel themselves in the presence of true greatness many men find it
necessary only to be alone.   TOM MASSON

If you bow at all, bow low.   CHINESE PROVERB

You cannot do a kindness too soon, for you never know how soon it will be too late.   RALPH WALDO EMERSON

We are almost always bored by just those whom we must not find boring.
FRANCOIS DUC de la ROCHEFOUCAULD

Never descend to the ways of those above you.   GEORGE MALLABY

He's fair. He treats us all the same—like dogs.   HENRY JORDAN

To oblige persons often costs little and helps much.
BALTASAR GRACIAN

A man is very apt to complain of the ingratitude of those who have risen far above him.   SAMUEL JOHNSON

A great man does enough for us when he refrains from doing us harm.
PIERRE AUGUSTIN CARON de BEAUMARCHAIS

One could not even dignify him with the name of stuffed shirt. He was simply a hole in the air.   GEORGE ORWELL

Familiarity in one's superiors causes bitterness, for it may not be returned.   FRIEDRICH WILHELM NIETZSCHE

No sadder proof can be given by a man of his own littleness than disbelief in great men.   THOMAS CARLYLE

The pleasure we derive from doing favors is partly in the feeling it gives us that we are not altogether worthless.   ERIC HOFFER

The Americans burn incense before it (democracy), but they are themselves ruled by the Boss and the Trust.
DEAN WILLIAM RALPH INGE

Great men with great truths have seldom had much support from their associates.   PHILIP WYLIE

He merits no thanks that does a kindness for his own end.
THOMAS FULLER

He is a man whom it is impossible to please because he is never pleased with himself.   JOHANN WOLFGANG von GOETHE

I have learned the truth of the observation that the more one approaches great men the more one finds that they are men.
BERNARD M. BARUCH

We rarely confide in those who are better than we are. ALBERT CAMUS

Never sit in the place of a man who can say to you, "Rise."
ARAB PROVERB

If you would stand well with a great mind, leave him with a favourable impression of yourself; if with a little mind, leave him a favourable impression of himself. SAMUEL TAYLOR COLERIDGE

Superior people never make long visits. MARIANNE MOORE

What really flatters a man is that you think him worth flattering.
GEORGE BERNARD SHAW

To have a great man for a friend seems pleasant to those who have never tried it; those who have, fear it. QUINTUS HORACE

A man can't ride your back unless it's bent. MARTIN LUTHER KING

He who forgets his own friends merely to follow after those of a higher degree is a snob. WILLIAM MAKEPEACE THACKERAY

The parson knows enough who knows a duke. WILLIAM COWPER

One-way first-name calling always means inequality—witness servants, children and dogs. MARJORIE KARMEL

Though men in great positions are easily flattered, we are still more easily flattered when in their company.
MARQUIS de VAUVENARGUES

Complain to one who can help you. YUGOSLAV PROVERB

There is no need to fear the strong. All one needs is to know the method of overcoming them. There is a special jujitsu for every strong man.
YEVGENY YEVTUSHENKO

We are much harder on people who betray us in small ways than on people who betray others in great ones.
FRANCOIS DUC de la ROCHEFOUCAULD

So far is it from being true that men are naturally equal, that no two people can be half an hour together, but one shall acquire an evident superiority over the other.   SAMUEL JOHNSON

The value of a man, however, should be seen in what he gives and not in what he is able to receive.   ALBERT EINSTEIN

Injustice is relatively easy to bear; it is justice that hurts.
HENRY LOUIS MENCKEN

We cannot work for others without working for ourselves.
JEAN-JACQUES ROUSSEAU

No one can make you feel inferior without your consent.
ELEANOR ROOSEVELT

I think it is not well for any of us to allow another personality to submerge in any way our own.   OLIVE SCHREINER

Neither beg of him who has been a beggar, nor serve him who has been a servant.   PROVERB

We cannot render benefits to those from whom we receive them, or only seldom. But the benefits we receive must be rendered again line for line, deed for deed, to somebody.

RALPH WALDO EMERSON

The true way to be humble is not to stoop till you are smaller than yourself, but to stand at your real height against some higher nature that shall show you what the real smallness of your greatest greatness is.
PHILLIPS BROOKS

The great are only great because we are on our knees; let us arise.
PIERRE JOSEPH

Dealing with Subordinates

When you treat 'em mean
To keep 'em keen,
Will they rebel
If you give 'em hell?

Men in business are in as much danger from those at work under them as from those that work against them. MARQUESS of HALIFAX

Never let your inferiors do you a favor—it will be extremely costly.
HENRY LOUIS MENCKEN

More have been ruined by their servants, than by their masters.
CHARLES CALEB COLTON

Mistrust a subordinate who never finds fault with his superior.
JOHN CHURTON COLLINS

The only real equality is in the cemetery. GERMAN PROVERB

We often need someone smaller than ourselves. JEAN de la FONTAINE

Many a man would rather you heard his story than granted his request.
EARL of CHESTERFIELD

After the verb "To Love," "To Help" is the most beautiful verb in the world! BERTHA von SUTTNER

You cannot make a crab walk straight. ARISTOPHANES

They can't see eye to eye with you, when you're looking down on them.
ANON

The people cannot see, but they can feel. JAMES HARRINGTON

Flattery is all right—if you don't inhale. ADLAI STEVENSON

All men are born free and unequal. GRANT ALLEN

The four letter word for psychotherapy is Talk. ERIC HODGINS

Those who object when they miss out on a favor, wouldn't appreciate it if they got it.   ANON

Watch the faces of those who bow low.   POLISH PROVERB

Servants sometimes don't see what we show them, but they always see what we hide from them.   LOUIS DEPRET

A sheep in sheep's clothing.   SIR WINSTON CHURCHILL

If someone below us does not treat us politely, we don't like anything he does. If, instead, we take a liking to someone, we forgive him anything he does.   ST. FRANCIS de SALES

There is the great man who makes every man feel small, but the really great man is the man who makes every man feel great.
                                        GILBERT KEITH CHESTERTON

By far the most effective method by which executives can tap ideas of subordinates is sympathetic listening in day-to-day informal contacts within and outside the workplace.   DR. EARL PLANTY

Treat 'em like dogs, and you'll have dogs' works and dogs' actions.
Treat 'em like men, and you'll have men's works.
                                        HARRIET BEECHER STOWE

Men want recognition of their work, to help them to believe in themselves.   DOROTHY MILLER RICHARDSON

The little stations are very proud because the expresses have to pass them by.   KARL KRAUS

Inferiors revolt in order that they may be equal, and equals that they may be superior. Such is the state of mind which creates revolutions.
                                                        ARISTOTLE

The stupider the peasant, the better the horse understands.
                                                    ANTON CHEKHOV

There is no one so radical as a manservant whose freedom of the champagne bin has been interfered with.   TOM STOPPARD

If you treat a man as he is, he will become worse, but if you treat him as if he were what he ought to be he will become what he ought to be.
                                        JOHANN WOLFGANG von GOETHE

A successful man is he who received a great deal more from his fellow men, usually incomparably more than corresponds to his service to them.   ALBERT EINSTEIN

Don't put no constrictions on de people. Leave 'em ta hell alone.
                                                                JIMMY DURANTE

Pity costs nothing, and ain't worth nothing.   JOSH BILLINGS

The time to stop a revolution is at the beginning, not the end.
                                                                ADLAI STEVENSON

As to abuse—I thrive on it. Abuse, hearty abuse, is a tonic to all save men of indifferent health.   NORMAN DOUGLAS

Men may be convinced, but they cannot be pleased, against their will.
                                                                SAMUEL JOHNSON

People hate those who make them feel their own inferiority.
                                                                EARL of CHESTERFIELD

To ease another's heartache is to forget one's own.
                                                                ABRAHAM LINCOLN

We appreciate frankness from those who like us, frankness from others is called insolence.   ANON

If you ride a horse, sit close and tight. If you ride a man, sit easy and light.   BENJAMIN FRANKLIN

We are always much better pleased to see those whom we have obliged, than those who have obliged us.
                                                FRANCOIS DUC de la ROCHEFOUCAULD

Shifts in prejudice can work both ways.   MIDGE DECTER

Tread on a worm and it will turn.   PROVERB

No man can serve two masters: for either he will hate the one, and love the other; or else he will hold to the one, and despise the other.
                                                                St. Matthew

If you will please people, you must please them in their own way, and as you cannot make them what they should be, you must take them as they are.   EARL of CHESTERFIELD

Words of comfort, skillfully administered, are the oldest therapy known.
LOUIS NIZER

An injury is much sooner forgotten than an insult.
EARL of CHESTERFIELD

One despairs of others so as not to despair too much of oneself.
HENRI PETIT

He that complies against his will,
Is of his own opinion still.   SAMUEL BUTLER

Most men cry better than they speak. You get more nature out of them by
pinching than addressing them.   HENRY DAVID THOREAU

He who has suffered you to impose on him, knows you.
WILLIAM BLAKE

Great indebtedness does not make men grateful, but vengeful.
FRIEDRICH WILHELM NIETZSCHE

The world's idea of greatness has been that he is greatest who best
succeeds in using his fellow-men for the furtherance of his own ends.
Christianity holds him the greatest who is himself most useful to others.
P.H. HOGE

Subordination tends greatly to human happiness. Were we all upon an
equality, we should have no other enjoyment than mere animal pleasure.
SAMUEL JOHNSON

Respect

You cannot command
Or even demand
Respect from the rest,
Unless you are best.

The defeats and victories of the fellows at the top aren't always defeats
and victories for the fellows at the bottom.   BERTOLT BRECHT

I think you're a son of a bitch and I respect you.   ANON

I have found some of the best reasons I ever had for remaining at the bottom simply by looking at the men at the top.
                              FRANK MOORE COLBY

The amount of respect from your superiors will affect the amount of respect from your inferiors—and vice versa.   ANON

An employer who is strict, but fair, is usually respected by his workers.
                              ROBERT WOOD JOHNSON

The Ford car is Henry Ford done in steel, and other things.
                              SAMUEL S. MARQUIS

Man is still a savage to the extent that he has little respect for anything that cannot hurt him.   EDGAR WATSON HOWE

The cobra will bite you whether you call it cobra or Mr. Cobra.
                              INDIAN PROVERB

He respects nothing and nobody. Why, I once heard him speak disrespectfully of the equator.   SYDNEY SMITH

You've got a fine personality, sir—but not for a human being.   ANON

Admiration: Our polite recognition of another man's resemblance to ourselves.   AMBROSE BIERCE

Young people are always more given to admiring what is gigantic than what is reasonable.   EUGENE DELACROIX

Money is the only substance which can keep a cold world from nicknaming a citizen 'Hey, you!'   WILSON MIZNER

It is the master who makes the house respected, not the house the master.   SPANISH PROVERB

People like admiration more than anything.   MARGARET DRABBLE

Render unto Caesar the things that are Caesar's, and unto God the things that are God's, and unto human beings, what?   STANISLAW J. LEC

Even workhouses have their aristocracy.   ENGLISH PROVERB

A man is not as big as his belief in himself; he is as big as the number of persons who believe in him.   THOMAS WOODROW WILSON

A fly, sir, may sting a stately horse and make him wince but one is but an insect and the other is a horse still.   SAMUEL JOHNSON

Look down if you would know how high you stand. YIDDISH PROVERB

Man is great only when he is kneeling.   POPE PIUS XII

I don't mind when a private fails to salute me, but he must never forget to salute a second lieutenant.   GENERAL JOHN J. PERSHING

There is a vast difference in one's respect for the man who has made himself, and the man who has only made his money.
                                        DINAH MARIA MULOCK

If you want to be respected, you must respect yourself.
                                        SPANISH PROVERB

I respect only those who resist me, but I cannot tolerate them.
                                        CHARLES de GAULLE

No man who is occupied in doing a very difficult thing, and doing it very well, ever loses his self-respect.   GEORGE BERNARD SHAW

Poor men's words have little weight.   GREEK PROVERB

The prestige you acquire by being able to tell your friends that you know famous men proves only that you are yourself of small account.
                                        WILLIAM SOMERSET MAUGHAM

The superiority of some men is merely local. They are great because their associates are little.   SAMUEL JOHNSON

Better in the dust than crawl near the throne.   GERMAN PROVERB

Goose pimples rose all over me, my hair stood on end, my eyes filled with tears of love and gratitude for this greatest of all conquerors of human misery and shame, and my breath came in little gasps. If I had not known that the Leader would have scorned such adulation, I might have fallen to my knees in unashamed worship, but instead I drew myself to attention, raised my arm in the eternal salute of the ancient Roman Legions and repeated the holy words, "Heil Hitler!"
                                        GEORGE LINCOLN ROCKWELL

Men naturally despise those who court them but respect those who do not give way to them. THUCYDIDES

We seldom respect ourselves enough. MARCUS FABIUS QUINTILIAN

Men are like the stars; some generate their own light while others reflect the brilliance they receive. JOSE MARTI

Respect yourself if you would have others respect you.
BALTASAR GRACIAN

A man known to us only as a celebrity in politics or in trade, gains largely in our esteem if we discover that he has some intellectual taste or skill. RALPH WALDO EMERSON

When you come into the presence of a leader of men, you know that you have come into the presence of fire—that it is best not uncautiously to touch that man—that there is something that makes it dangerous to cross him. THOMAS WOODROW WILSON

Never respect men merely for their riches, but rather for their philanthropy; we do not value the sun for its height; but for its use.
GAMALIEL BAILEY

Respect is often paid in proportion as it is claimed.
SAMUEL JOHNSON

It is difficult to like those whom we do not esteem, but it is no less so to like those whom we esteem more than ourselves.
FRANCOIS DUC de la ROCHEFOUCAULD

The honor paid to a wise man is a great good for those who honor him.
EPICURUS

Render therefore to all their dues: tribute to whom tribute is due; custom to whom custom; fear to whom fear; honour to whom honour. *Romans*

If you have some respect for people as they are, you can be more effective in helping them to become better than they are.
JOHN W. GARDNER

The good Lord sees your heart, not the braid on your jacket, before Him we are all in our birthday suits, generals and common men alike.
THOMAS MANN

When fortune surprises us by giving us an important position, without having led us to it by degrees, or without our being elevated to it by our hopes, it is almost impossible for us to maintain ourselves suitably in it, and appear worthy of possessing it.

FRANCOIS DUC de la ROCHEFOUCAULD

Respect a man, he will do the more. JAMES HOWELL

We can always make ourselves liked provided we act likable, but we cannot always make ourselves esteemed, no matter what our merits are.

NICHOLAS MALEBRANCHE

It is difficult to esteem a man as he desires to be esteemed.

MARQUIS de VAUVENARGUES

IV WORK

Work

If your work is just a joke,
That may not last, it's true:
Just remember that the oak
Was once a nut like you.

Work smarter, not harder.   RON CARSWELL

My father taught me to work, he did not teach me how to love it.
                                ABRAHAM LINCOLN

Nothing is really work unless you would rather be doing something else.
                                JAMES M. BARRIE

I've met a few people in my time who were enthusiastic about hard work.
And it was just my luck that all of them happened to be men I worked for
at the time.   BILL GOLD

Half a loaf is better than no time off.   ANON

Many might go to Heaven with half the labor they go to Hell.
                                BEN JONSON

The wicked often work harder to go to hell than the righteous do to enter
heaven.   JOSH BILLINGS

Work is what you do so that sometime you won't have to do it any more.
ALFRED POLGAR

Work is the curse of the drinking classes.   MIKE ROMANOFF

All work and no play makes Jack's wife a wealthy widow.
T. McDERMOTT

Whenever you look at a piece of work and you think the fellow was crazy,
then you want to pay some attention to that. One of you is likely to be,
and you better find out which one it is. It makes an awful lot of
difference.   CHARLES F. KETTERING

If you stop and think about it, you'll realize that three out of four persons
do not know exactly what they're doing a large part of the time.
GELETT BURGESS

The best thing to go with hard work is enthusiasm.   ANON

Never work before breakfast; if you have to work before breakfast, get
your breakfast first.   JOSH BILLINGS

We have too many people who live without working, and we have
altogether too many who work without living.   CHARLES R. BROWN

Don't condescend to unskilled labor. Try it for half a day first.
BROOKS ATKINSON

Everybody is overworked. Now the main occupation of the educated man
is not his job, but helping his wife at home.   MARGARET MEAD

It is easier to admire hard work if you don't do it. HENRY S. HASKINS

I go on working for the same reason that a hen goes on laying eggs.
HENRY LOUIS MENCKEN

Never complain about any job, unless it's too easy.   ANON

I hold that if the Almighty had ever made a set of men that should do all
the eating and none of the work, He would have made them with mouths
only and no hands; and if He had ever made another class that He
intended should do all the work and no eating, He would have made
them with hands only and no mouths.   ABRAHAM LINCOLN

The only kind of pride that is never criticized is pride in one's work.
ANON

If people knew how hard I work to get my mastery, it wouldn't seem so wonderful after all. MICHELANGELO

Any work looks wonderful to me except the one which I can do.
RALPH WALDO EMERSON

It appears on close examination, that work is less boring than amusing oneself. CHARLES BAUDELAIRE

The power to work hard may not be a talent, but it is the best possible substitute for it. ANON

The man who does not work for the love of work but only for money is not likely to make money nor to find much fun in life.
CHARLES M. SCHWAB

He that can work is born a king of something. THOMAS CARLYLE

Work is work if you're paid to do it,
and it's pleasure if you pay to be allowed to do it.
FINLEY PETER DUNNE

Work is less boring than pleasure. J. PIEPER

We work to become, not to acquire. ELBERT HUBBARD

If any would not work, neither should he eat. *THESSALONIANS*

How many years of fatigue and punishment it takes to learn the simple truth that work, that disagreeable thing, is the only way of not suffering in life, or at all events, of suffering less. CHARLES BAUDELAIRE

Work with some men is as besetting a sin as idleness with others.
SAMUEL BUTLER

Far and away the best prize that life offers is the chance to work hard at work worth doing. THEODORE ROOSEVELT

Perfect freedom is reserved for the man who lives by his own work, and in that work does what he wants to do. ROBIN G. COLLINGWOOD

Remember, you have to work. Whether you handle a pick or a pen, digging ditches or editing a paper, ringing an auction bell or writing funny things—you must work. If you look around, you will see the men who are the most able to live the rest of their days without work are the men who work the hardest. Don't be afraid of killing yourself with overwork. It is beyond your power to do that on the sunny side of thirty. So find out what you want to be, and do, and take off your coat, and make a dust in the world.   CHARLES READE

Work is the inevitable condition of human life, the true source of human welfare.   LEO TOLSTOY

There is no short cut to fame and comfort and all there is is to bore into it as hard as you can.   OLIVER WENDELL HOLMES

If you cannot work with love but only with distaste, it is better that you should leave your work and sit at the gate of the temple and take alms of those who work with joy.   KAHLIL GIBRAN

One must work, nothing but work.
And one must have patience.   AUGUSTE RODIN

No man is born into the world whose work is not born with him. There is always work, and tools to work with, for those who will; and blessed are the horny hands of toil.   JAMES RUSSELL LOWELL

The moment a man can really do his work, he becomes speechless about it: all words are idle to him: all theories. Does a bird need to theorize about building its nest or boast of it when built? All good work is essentially done that way without hesitation: without difficulty: without boasting.   JOHN RUSKIN

God gave man work, not to burden him, but to bless him, and useful work, willingly, cheerfully, effectively done, has always been the finest expression of the human spirit.   WALTER R. COURTENAY

If a man loves the labor of his trade, apart from any questions of success or fame, the gods have called him.   ROBERT LOUIS STEVENSON

Career

For women it's justice miscarriage,
That more people ought to disparage;
When a man's not asked how
He can combine now
His full-time career with his marriage.

There is always room at the top.   DANIEL WEBSTER

A man with a career can have no time to waste upon his wife and friends, he has to devote it wholly to his enemies.
JOHN OLIVER HOBBES

The difference between a job and a career is the difference between 40 and 60 hours a week.   ROBERT FROST

The passion to get ahead is sometimes born of the fear lest we be left behind.   ERIC HOFFER

His was the sort of career that made the Recording Angel think seriously about taking up shorthand.   NICHOLAS BENTLEY

You can tell the people who are in your class: they are the ones you hate to see get ahead of you.   CAREY WILLIAMS

It is a fact of history that, almost without exception, every great contributor to world society from Jesus Christ to Einstein to Alexander Calder in modern times was accused openly early in their respective careers of being either crackpots or crazy.   O.A. BATTISTA

I started at the top and worked my way down.   ORSON WELLES

You can't hold a man down without staying down with him.
BOOKER T. WASHINGTON

A corporal is as high as you can go and still have friends.
ANON

Always take a job that is too big for you. HARRY EMERSON FOSDICK

If a man will not work, he shall not eat.   *THESSALONIANS*

Youth is glorious, but it isn't a career.   ANON

The progress of women in the working world is not unlike a bath filling
with the outflow left open.   LYNNE EDMUNDS

You've forgotten the grandest moral attribute of a Scotsman, Maggie,
that he'll do nothing which might damage his career.
                                        SIR JAMES BARRIE

Total commitment to family and total commitment to career is possible,
but fatiguing.   MURIEL FOX

A caress is better than a career.   ELISABETH MARBURY

A career is born in public, talent in private.   MARILYN MONROE

A man finds he has been wrong at every preceding stage of his career,
only to deduce the astonishing conclusion that he is at last entirely right.
                                      ROBERT LOUIS STEVENSON

It is a most mortifying reflection for a man to consider what he has done,
compared to what he might have done.   SAMUEL JOHNSON

It is equally a mistake to hold one's self too high, or to rate one's self too
cheap.   JOHANN WOLFGANG von GOETHE

How many "coming men" has one known? Where on earth do they all go
to?   SIR ARTHUR WING PINERO

The best careers advice given to the young is, "Find out what you like
doing best and get someone to pay you for doing it."
                                      KATHERINE WHITEHORN

It is better to die on your feet than to live on your knees!
                                        DOLORES IBARRURI

The failure is to be 40 and not to have tried.   BEATRICE COLEN

The career of every individual man or woman is essentially non-
progressive.   ALDOUS LEONARD HUXLEY

A plant that is transplanted too often seldom prospers.   ANON

The very first step towards success in any occupation is to become interested in it. SIR WILLIAM OSLER

There are those who consider business dull, monotonous, and unrewarding. Many of our young people give a low rating to business as a career. Yet I look back on my business life with a mixture of wonder, amounting almost to disbelief, and gratitude for my good fortune. CLARENCE FRANCIS

A man must love a thing very much if he not only practises it without any hope of fame and money, but even practises it without any hope of doing it well. GILBERT KEITH CHESTERTON

What young people should do to avoid temptation: get a job and work at it so hard that temptation would not exist. THOMAS EDISON

Our language is full of suggestions that it is a privilege to work sitting down. We respect our chairman, we honor the throne, we speak of a professor's chair, a seat in Parliament. The lawyer looks to the judge's bench, and the Turks speak of their divan, and the Hebrews of the Sanhedrin, all in the same sense. Even the word "president" means the man in the best seat. All this betokens a habit of mind, respecting the man who does his work sitting down. PROFESSOR DAVID L. THOMPSON

He who shuns the millstone, shuns the meal. DESIDERIUS ERASMUS

From thirty to forty-five runs the stage in which a man normally finds all his ideas, the first principles, at least, of that ideology of which he is to make his own. After forty-five he devotes himself to the full development of the inspirations he has had between thirty and forty-five. ORTEGA Y GASSET

One of the saddest experiences which can come to a human being is to awaken gray-haired and wrinkled, near the close of an unproductive career, to the fact that all through the years he has been using only a small part of himself. V.W. BURROWS

It is only God and a few rare spirits for whom their careers extend as they advance. DENIS DIDEROT

In the hope of bettering themselves, men willingly change masters. NICCOLO MACHIAVELLI

Employment is nature's physician, and is essential to human happiness.
GALEN

Better to be a minor lord than an important menial.
GERMAN PROVERB

The career of a great man remains an enduring monument of human energy. The man dies and disappears, but his thoughts and acts survive and leave an indelible stamp upon his race.   SAMUEL SMILES

The men of real skill are almost always men who earn their living by their skill.   PHILIP G. HAMERTON

Selecting jobs for the pseudo independence that higher pay seems to offer, instead of for autonomous reasons—i.e., the job offering deepest satisfaction because it has intrinsic meaning for the person and adds to his self respect—is likewise due to neurotic tendencies, namely the unrecognized equation of money with true status. Here, too, the outer security (what money can buy) is accepted in lieu of inner security, the impersonal coin of exchange is given more relevance than the particular product of one's labor.   BRUNO BETTELHEIM

Out of the best and most productive years of each man's life, he should carve a segment in which he puts his private career aside to serve his community and his country, and thereby serve his children, his neighbours, his fellow men, and the cause of freedom.
DAVID LILIENTHAL

Duty

It's easy to be dutiful,
Referring to one's brothers,
'Cos duty is more beautiful,
When carried out by others.

When a stupid man is doing something he is ashamed of, he always declares that it is his duty.   GEORGE BERNARD SHAW

In practice it is seldom very hard to do one's duty when one knows what it is, but it is sometimes exceedingly difficult to find this out.

SAMUEL BUTLER

The worst of doing one's duty was that it apparently unfitted one for doing anything else.   EDITH WHARTON

My duty is a thing I never do, on principle.   OSCAR WILDE

What's a man's first duty? The answer's brief: To be himself.

HENRIK IBSEN

Duty largely consists of pretending that the trivial is critical.

JOHN FOWLES

If you assign people duties without granting them any rights, you must pay them well.   JOHANN WOLFGANG von GOETHE

Those who know the least obey the best.   GEORGE FARQUHAR

Always obey your superiors—if you have any.   MARK TWAIN

The man who obeys is nearly always better than the man who commands.

JOSEPH ERNEST RENAN

Obedience is the sensible alternative for those who cannot lead.

EUGENE E. BRUSSELL

I was only following orders.   ADOLF EICHMANN

Duty implies obedience.   ANON

Any employee wishing to attend the funeral of a relative must notify management before 10 a.m. on the day of the same.

Unknown Company Notice

Duty. That which sternly impels us in the direction of profit, along the line of desire.   AMBROSE BIERCE

Where it is a duty to worship the sun it is pretty sure to be a crime to examine the laws of heat.   JOHN MORLEY

The association of duty and claptrap is what really dehumanizes man.

THEODORE HAECKER

This free will business is a bit terrifying anyway. It's almost pleasanter to obey, and make the most of it. UGO BETT

The first duty in life is to be as artificial as possible. What the second duty is no one has yet discovered. OSCAR WILDE

The great highway men call "I ought." ELLEN S. HOOPER

O Duty
Why hast thou not the visage of a sweetie or a cutie?
Why glitter thy spectacles so ominously?
Why art thou clad so abominously?
Why art thou so different from Venus?
And why do you and I have so few interests in common between us?
OSCAR WILDE

It is much safer to obey than to rule. THOMAS KEMPIS

Learn to obey before you command. PERCY BYSSHE SHELLEY

Make it a point to do something every day that you don't want to do. This is the golden rule for acquiring the habit of doing your duty without pain. MARK TWAIN

There are a lot of things in life which need doing which you may not like the idea of doing. This is the whole idea of duty.
CHARLES, PRINCE OF WALES

When you have a number of disagreeable duties to perform, always do the most disagreeable first. JOSIAH QUINCY

A sense of duty is useful in work, but offensive in personal relations. People wish to be liked, not to be endured with patient resignation.
BERTRAND RUSSELL

Once a rigid idea of duty has got inside a narrow mind, it can never again get out. JOSEPH JOUBERT

There is no duty we so much underrate as the duty of being happy.
ROBERT LOUIS STEVENSON

Perhaps one never seems so much at one's ease as when one has to play a part. OSCAR WILDE

The best security for people doing their duty is, that they should not have anything else to do.   WALTER BAGEHOT

All the time that he can spare from the adornment of his person he devoted to the neglect of his duties.   PROFESSOR SIDGWICK

Every duty which is bidden to wait returns with seven fresh duties at its back.   CHARLES KINGSLEY

When a duty ceases to be a pleasure then it ceases to exist.
                                                         NORMAN DOUGLAS

If the prior plays cards, what will the monks get up to?
                                                          SPANISH PROVERB

When men get by pleasing and lose by serving, the choice is so easy that nobody can miss it.   MARQUESS of HALIFAX

Do your duty and leave the rest to the Gods.   PIERRE CORNEILLE

I know better than to argue when the English talk about their duty.
                                                         RUDYARD KIPLING

The reward of one duty done is the power to fulfill another.
                                                             GEORGE ELIOT

Justice is the insurance we have on our lives, and obedience is the premium we pay for it.   WILLIAM PENN

Never mind your happiness; do your duty.   WILL DURANT

Only he who is uncompromising as to his rights maintains the sense of duty.   ALBERT CAMUS

A man born to obey will obey even on a throne.
                                            MARQUIS de VAUVENARGUES

When duty comes a-knocking at your gate,
Welcome him in; for if you bid him wait,
He will depart only to come once more
And bring seven other duties to your door.   EDWIN MARKHAM

A task becomes a duty from the moment you suspect it to be an essential part of that integrity which alone entitles a man to assume responsibility.   DAG HAMMARSKJOLD

Duty is the sublimest word in the language; you can never do more than your duty; you should never wish to do less.   ROBERT E. LEE

Duties are not performed for duty's sake, but because their neglect would make the man uncomfortable. A man performs but one duty—the duty of contenting his spirit, the duty of making himself agreeable to himself.   MARK TWAIN

Knowledge of your duties is the most essential part of the philosophy of life. If you avoid duty, you avoid action. The world demands results.
GEORGE W. GOETHALS

Laws are not masters, but servants, and he rules them who obey them.
HENRY WARD BEECHER

That which is common to the greatest number has the least care bestowed upon it.   ARISTOTLE

Obedience is much more seen in little things than in great. PROVERB

This is the sum of duty: Do naught unto others which would cause you pain if done to you.   MAHABHARATA

New occasions teach new duties.   JAMES RUSSELL LOWELL

He who yields a prudent obedience exercises a partial control.
PUBLILIUS SYRUS

Render therefore unto Caesar the things which are Caesar's; and unto God the things that are God's.   *St. Matthew*

It is right that what is just should be obeyed; it is necessary that what is strongest should be obeyed.   BLAISE PASCAL

Power, to its last particle, is duty.   JOHN FOSTER

Keeping Busy

One saying that I think is untrue
Concerns the work of the bee and his crew;
I want to know is he
So very busy,
Because he only has one job to do?

You can't imagine the extra work I had when I was a god.
HIROHITO, EMPEROR OF JAPAN

The hardest job of all is trying to look busy when you're not.
WILLIAM FEATHER

Tell him I've been too fucking busy—or vice versa.
DOROTHY PARKER

As busy as a one-armed billsticker in a gale. ANON

Busier than a man with four hundred dollars and a thirst.
DAMON RUNYON

The best thing about being busy is that you never have to think of what to do next. ANON

It's not enough to be busy... the question is: What are we busy about?
HENRY DAVID THOREAU

It is the busiest man who has time to spare.
CYRIL NORTHCOTE PARKINSON

He works all the time. He's a picket. GERALD F. LIEBERMAN

There are people who want to be everywhere at once and they seem to get nowhere. CARL SANDBURG

The busiest people are often those trying to make a living without working for it. ANON

You have to keep busy. After all, a dog's never pissed on a moving car. Know what I mean. TOM WAITS

Some folks can look so busy doing nothin' that they seem indispensable.
FRANK McKINNEY HUBBARD

Never get sick, Hubert; there isn't time.
HUBERT H. HUMPHREY'S FATHER

A really busy person never knows how much he weighs.
EDGAR WATSON HOWE

The formula for complete happiness is to be very busy with the unimportant.   A. EDWARD NEWTON

There's a big difference between busy and real work. TOM McGREAL

What's the good of a home, if you are never in it?
GEORGE and WALTER CROSSMITH

A bee is never as busy as it seems: it's just that it can't buzz any slower.
FRANK McKINNEY HUBBARD

I have so much to do that I am going to bed.   SAVOYARD PROVERB

As busy as a one-legged man in a forest fire.   ANON

All men have the idea that they are always busy, and if they are not, a woman can soon persuade them that they are. Just say, "I don't see how you do it all," without saying what all is.   STEPHEN LEACOCK

I work my head to the bone.   ANON

Those who work much do not work hard.   HENRY DAVID THOREAU

The busy have no time for tears.
LORD GEORGE GORDON NOEL BYRON

Busy souls have no time to be busybodies.   AUSTIN O'MALLEY

While I am busy with little things, I am not required to do greater things.   ST. FRANCIS de SALES

Industry keeps the body healthy, the mind clear, the heart whole, and the purse full.   CHARLES SIMMONS

Love of bustle is not industry.   SENECA

A busy fool is fitter to be shut up than a downwright madman.
LORD HALIFAX

No man ever worked his way anywhere in a dead calm; kites rise against, not with, the wind.   JOHN NEAL

It always does seem to me that I am doing more work than I should do. It is not that I object to the work, mind you; I like work; it fascinates me, I can sit and look at it for hours. I love to keep it by me; the idea of getting rid of it nearly breaks my heart.   JEROME K. JEROME

As peace is the end of war, so to be idle is the ultimate purpose of the busy.   SAMUEL JOHNSON

The more we do, the more we can do; the more busy we are, the more leisure we have.   WILLIAM HAZLITT

The majority prove their worth by keeping busy. A busy life is the nearest thing to a purposeful life.   ERIC HOFFER

In every rank, both great and small, it is industry that supports us all.
JOHN GAY

Who is more busy, than he that hath least to do?   PROVERB

The veriest nobodies are the greatest busybodies.
BENJAMIN WHICHCOTE

Tell me what you are busy about, and I will tell you what you are.
JOHANN WOLFGANG von GOETHE

You will soon break the bow if you keep it always stretched.
PHAEDRUS

If it be difficult to persuade the idle to be busy, it is likewise not easy to convince the busy that it is better to be idle.   SAMUEL JOHNSON

I sometimes try to be miserable that I may do more work.
WILLIAM BLAKE

Punctuality

*Better never late
is better than
Better late than never.*

I'd rather be late for supper in this world tonight than be in some other world on time for breakfast in the morning.   IRVING S. COBB

The trouble with being punctual is that nobody's there to appreciate it.
FRANKLIN P. JONES

Nothing, of course, begins at the time you think it did.
LILLIAN HELLMAN

If you're there before it's over, you're on time.
MAYOR JIMMY J. WALKER

The early worm should read the proverbs.   EDMUND FULLER

The habitually punctual make all their mistakes right on time.
LAURENCE J. PETER

Showing up is 80 per cent of life.   WOODY ALLEN

Punctuality is the art of keeping an appointment in time to object at the lateness of the other party.   ANON

What is time but the stuff delay is made of? HENRY DAVID THOREAU

I've been on a calendar, but never on time.   MARILYN MONROE

The early worm—has to get his own breakfast.   PETER CAGNEY

If a thing's worth doing, it's worth doing late.   FREDERICK OLIVER

A punctual person is patient, because he gets that way waiting for those who are not punctual.   HERBERT V. PROCHNOW

The habitual latecomer was asked if he knew what time they started work and admitted that he did not because they were always at it when he arrived.   ANON

There are two kinds of people in one's life—people whom one keeps waiting—and the people for whom one waits. S.N. BEHRAM

Nothing helps one to reach the first destination more than knowing exactly what time one is due at the second. ANON

People count up the faults of those who are keeping them waiting. PROVERB

Three o'clock is always too late or too early for anything you want to do. JEAN-PAUL SARTRE

Solitude is the reward for being punctual. ANON

We haven't the time to take our time. EUGENE IONESCO

Punctuality is one of the cardinal virtues. Always insist on it in your subordinates and dependents. DONALD ROBERT PERRY MARQUIS

When a secretary of Washington, excusing himself for being late, said that his watch was too slow, the reply of Washington was, "You must get a new watch or I must get a new secretary." ANON

I have noticed that the people who are late are often so much jollier than the people who have to wait for them. EDWARD VERRAL LUCAS

Gioacchino Rossini was born in 1892, five months after his parents got married and it taught him a lesson. He was never early for another appointment in his life. VICTOR BORGE

No one goes early unless the boss leaves before. ANON

He's a real eager-beaver. Why, he gets up at six o'clock in the morning no matter what time it is. HYMAN KAPLAN

Punctuality is something that, if you have it, there's often no one around to share it with you. ANON

Delay is preferable to error. THOMAS JEFFERSON

Be early which, if you are not, you will, when it is too late. EARL of CHESTERFIELD

I am a believer in punctuality, though it makes me very lonely. EDWARD VERRALL LUCAS

He was always late on principle, his principle being that punctuality is the thief of time.   OSCAR WILDE

In telephoning for a taxicab to meet a specific engagement, such as a train or a dinner, it is better to ask that the cab call at 6:55 rather than at 7 p.m. An even hour is vague, but an odd hour is specific.
                                                    WILLIAM FEATHER

Time and tide wait for no man.   PROVERB

Promptness is the soul of business.   EARL of CHESTERFIELD

Better three hours too soon, than one minute late.
                                            WILLIAM SHAKESPEARE

I have always been a quarter of an hour before my time, and it has made a man of me.   HORATIO NELSON

He who is late may gnaw the bones.   YUGOSLAV PROVERB

In spite of all our speeding it's still the fashion to be late.
                                        FRANK McKINNEY HUBBARD

Want of punctuality is a want of virtue.   JOHN M. MASON

Punctuality is the stern virtue of men of business, and the graceful courtesy of princes.   EDWARD GEORGE BULWER-LYTTON

I would never think well of a man's intellectual or moral character, if he was habitually unfaithful to his appointments. NATHANIEL EMMONS

I give it as my deliberate and solemn conviction that the individual who is habitually tardy in meeting an appointment, will never be respected or successful in life.   WILBUR FISK

They get up early because they have so much to do and go to bed early because they have so little to think about.   OSCAR WILDE

Punctuality is the virtue of the bored.   EVELYN WAUGH

It is of no use running: to set out betimes is the main point.
                                                CHARLES FONTAINE

One watch set right will do to set many by, one that goes wrong may be the means of misleading a whole neighborhood; and the same may be said of example. LEWIS W. DILWYN

Being early is an unpardonable sin. If you are early, you'll witness the last-minute confusion and panic that always attend making anything seem effortlessly gracious. Looking in on this scene is almost as rude as asking someone where he got his face-lift. P. J. O'ROURKE

Time Off

Unless I rest,
I bust.
But when I rest,
I rust.

Nearly everybody underestimates the price of a vacation.
WILLIAM FEATHER

The most important thing about a vacation for many people is the fact that they can brag about having been on one. BRENDAN FRANCIS

A vacation is when you need half the clothes and twice the money that you took with you. ANON

A good rest is half the work. YUGOSLAV PROVERB

One cannot rest except after steady practice. GEORGE ADE

A vacation is what you take when you can no longer take what you've been taking. EARL WILSON

The ant is knowing and wise, but he doesn't know enough to take a vacation. CLARENCE DAY

A holiday is when father works twice as hard as he does at the office.
ANON

Leisure is time at personal risk.   A.M. SULLIVAN

A good vacation is over when you begin to yearn for your work.
                                              DR. MORRIS FISHBEIN

Holidays are often overrated disturbances of routine, costly and uncomfortable, and they usually need another holiday to correct their ravages.
                                              EDWARD VERRALL LUCAS

There is less leisure now than in the Middle Ages, when one third of the year consisted of holidays and festivals.   RALPH BORSODI

A good holiday is one spent among people whose notions of time are vaguer than yours.   JOHN BOYNTON PRIESTLEY

Rest is the sweet sauce of labour.   PLUTARCH

To those who sweat for their daily bread leisure is a longed-for sweet until they get it.   JOHN MAYNARD KEYNES

Alternate rest and labor long endure.   OVID

All work and no rest takes the spring and bound out of the most vigorous life. Time spent in judicious resting is not time wasted, but time gained.
                                                    M.B. GRIER

Leisure only means a chance to do other jobs that demand attention.
                                        OLIVER WENDELL HOLMES

To work is simple enough: but to rest, there is the difficulty.
                                              ERNEST HELLO

Sit in reverie, and watch the changing color of the waves that break upon the idle seashore of the mind. HENRY WADSWORTH LONGFELLOW

Retirement

It took me all my life to make it
And when I go, I'll never take it;
At last there's not one debt I owe
But will it last until I go?

Don't rejoice over him that goes, before you see him that comes.
JAPANESE PROVERB

When a man retires and time is no longer a matter of urgent importance, his colleagues generally present him with a watch.   R.C. SHERRIFF

First you forget names, then you forget faces, then you forget to pull your zipper up, then you forget to pull your zipper down. LEO ROSENBERG

There are plenty of managers who have retired on the job.   ANON

It takes a man a lifetime to work himself up from the country to the country club and back again.   HERBERT V. PROCHNOW

Retirement is when you settle back and see which gets collected first— pensions, annuities, Social Securities, or you.   ROBERT ORBEN

The question isn't at what age I want to retire, it's at what income.
GEORGE FOREMAN

Old age is not so bad when you consider the alternatives.
MAURICE CHEVALIER

Retirement at sixty-five is ridiculous. When I was sixty-five, I still had pimples.   GEORGE BURNS

I married him for better or worse, but not for lunch.   HAZEL WEISS

Retirement takes all the fun out of Saturdays.   ANON

Yes, I'm 68, but when I was a boy I was too poor to smoke, so knock off ten years. That makes me 58. And since I never developed the drinking habit, you can knock off ten more years. So I'm 48—in the prime of my life. Retire? Retire to what?   W.A.C. BENNETT

To a wife retirement means twice as much husband on half as much income.   ANON

Senescence begins
And middle age ends,
The day your descendants
Outnumber your friends.   OGDEN NASH

Life would be wonderful if a man could retire without telling his wife.
                                                              EVAN ESAR

They tell you that you'll lose your mind when you grow older. What they don't tell you is that you won't miss it very much. MALCOLM COWLEY

Sit on your arse for fifty years and hang your hat on a pension.
                                                         LOUIS MacNEICE

To me, old age is always fifteen years older than I am.
                                                         BERNARD BARUCH

If life had a second edition, how would I correct the proofs.
                                                              JOHN CLARE

Retirement is one sure way of shortening life.   FRANK CONKLIN

One trouble with growing older is that it gets progressively tougher to find a famous historical figure who didn't amount to much when he was your age.   BILL VAUGHAN

Few men of action have been able to make a graceful exit at the appropriate time.   MALCOLM MUGGERIDGE

Growing old—it's not nice but it's interesting. AUGUST STRINDBERG

There comes a time in every man's life when he must make way for an older man.   REGINALD MAUDLING

The great man is he who leaves his successors in difficulties.
                                                              PAUL VALERY

Sooner or later I'm going to die, but I'm not going to retire.
                                                          MARGARET MEAD

You can get very hungry while waiting, if your livelihood depends on someone's decease.   JEAN BAPTISTE MOLIERE

Well enough for old folks to rise early, because they have done so many mean things all their lives they can't sleep anyhow.   MARK TWAIN

Many a man that couldn't direct ye to th' drug store on th' corner when he was thirty will get a respectful hearin' when age has further impaired his mind.   FINLEY PETER DUNNE

When I am dead, you'll find it hard, says he,
To ever find another man like me,
What makes you think, as I suppose you do,
I'll ever want another man like you?   EUGENE F. WARE

Last month I bought a retirement policy. All I've got to do is keep up the payments for 20 years and my salesman can retire.
                    LEOPOLD FECHTNER

Age has a good mind and sorry shanks.   PIETRO ARETINO

Growing old is no more than a bad habit which a busy man has no time to form.   ANDRE MAUROIS

Dismiss the old horse in good time, lest he fail in the lists and the spectators laugh.   HORACE

What a man in the street wants is not a big debate on fundamental issues; he wants a little medical care, a rug on the floor, a picture on the wall, a little music in the house, and a place to take Molly and the grandchildren when he retires.   LYNDON BAINES JOHNSON

In the last few years everything I'd done up to sixty or so has seemed very childish.   THOMAS STEARNS ELIOT

Don't simply retire from something, have something to retire to.
                    HARRY EMERSON FOSDICK

The end of ambition comes as a great relief.
                    MALCOLM MUGGERIDGE

To an old man any place that's warm is homeland.   MAXIM GORKY

Retirement, we understand, is great if you are busy, rich and healthy. But then, under those conditions, work is great too. BILL VAUGHAN

I felt after reaching ninety-two it was time to sleep in the morning if I chose to do so, and I have a lot of projects of my own to work on.
                                        JUDGE HAROLD R. MEDINA

Be honest with yourself until the end of your life. Then listen to the slow movement of the Schubert Quintet and kick the bucket.
                                        NATHAN MILSTEIN

When a man dies he clutches in his hands only that which he has given away during his lifetime. JEAN-JACQUES ROUSSEAU

Death is the next step after the pension—it's perpetual retirement without pay.   JEAN GIRAUDOUX

Retiring must not mean just vegetatinig. I don't think anybody can do that.   EDWARD STEICHEN

Don't think of retiring from the world until the world will be sorry that you retire. I hate a fellow whom pride or cowardice or laziness drives into a corner, and who does nothing when he is there but sit and growl. Let him come out as I do, and bark. SAMUEL JOHNSON

Old age is a time of humiliations, the most disagreeable of which, for me, is that I cannot work long at sustained high pressure with no leaks in concentration.   IGOR STRAVINSKY

On retirement: My advice is: If at all possible, don't cut your bridges to what you've done and where you've been. LUCILLE T. WESSMANN

I advise you to go on living solely to enrage those who are paying your annuities. It is the only pleasure I have left. FRANCOIS VOLTAIRE

Know when your time is over. It's the only advice I have. Hell, I knew twenty five years ago it wasn't going to last. Sooner or later, the demand won't be there, and you better get ready for it. I know actresses who go ape if they're not invited to a party. What the hell is that? I am content. Happiness is within yourself. Get ready for the dream to fade. So I'm no longer in demand, but so what? I see no reason to go into a decline or hit the bottle or sink into a melancholy depression. I've had my time and it was lovely. And I'm very grateful for it. But now I move over and make room for somebody else.... What the hell. Whatever I had, it worked, didn't it?   BARBARA STANWYCK

I will be more than delighted when the time comes that I can retire to a cabin somewhere and take it easy and let others worry about budgets and all the other things that are constantly on my desk.
                                    DWIGHT D. EISENHOWER

It is very grand to "die in harness," but it is very pleasant to have the tight straps unbuckled and the heavy collar lifted from the neck and shoulders.   OLIVER WENDELL HOLMES

The importance of an individual thinker owes something to chance. For it depends upon the fate of his ideas in the minds of his successors.
                                    ALFRED NORTH WHITEHEAD

When you reach your sixties, you have to decide whether you're going to be a sot or an ascetic. In other words if you want to go on working after you're sixty, some degree of ascetism is inevitable.
                                    MALCOLM MUGGERIDGE

Train up a fig tree in the way it should go, and when you are old sit under the shade of it.   CHARLES DICKENS

Dignity, high station, or great riches, are in some sort necessary to old men, in order to keep the younger at a distance, who are otherwise too apt to insult them upon the score of their age.   JONATHAN SWIFT

Few people know how to be old.
                                    FRANCOIS DUC de la ROCHEFOUCAULD

Individuality

For each individual
There's one thought residual;
Is he the true center
Of his life's adventure.

Men are born equal but they are also born different. ERICH FROMM

The personal pronoun "I" might well be the coat of arms of some individuals.   ANTOINE RIVAROL

He may well win the race that runs by himself. BENJAMIN FRANKLIN

I may not amount to much, but at least I am unique.
                                    JEAN JACQUES ROUSSEAU

It's pretty damn hard to bring your uniqueness into actual being if you're always doing the same things as a lot of other people.
                                    BRENDAN FRANCIS

Most people—one may say the best sort of people—greatly prefer to do things for themselves, however badly, than to have things done for them, however well.   ARTHUR PONSONBY

Individualism is the death of individuality... if only because it is an ism.   GILBERT KEITH CHESTERTON

Certain defects are necessary for the existence of individuality.
                                    JOHANN WOLFGANG von GOETHE

If I had not been born Peron, I would have liked to be Peron.
                                    JUAN PERON

Individualism may be regarded as the system in which human stupidity can do the least harm.   JAMES BEAUCHAMP CLARK

On Western individualism... It is a race of wolves. He who arrives does so only at the expense of the failure of others.
                                    ERNESTO "CHE" GUEVARA

No man can, for any considerable time, wear one face to himself and another to the multitude without finally getting bewildered as to which is the true one.   NATHANIEL HAWTHORNE

The liberty of the individual must thus far be limited: he must not make himself a nuisance to other people.   JOHN STUART MILL

What we suffer, what we endure, what we muff, what we kill, what we miss, what we are guilty of, is done by us, as individuals, in private.
                                    LOUISE ROGAN

Individualism is rather like innocence; there must be something unconscious about it.   LOUIS KRONENBERGER

If you wish to understand others you must intensify your own individualism.   OSCAR WILDE

Every now and then we discover in the seething mass of humanity round us a person who does not seem to need anybody else, and the contrast with ourselves is stinging.   ERNEST DIMNET

Individuality is acquiring a particular quality by acting in a particular way.   ARISTOTLE

Meeting people unlike oneself does not enlarge one's outlook; it only confirms one's idea that one is unique.   ELIZABETH BOWEN

It is perfectly consistent to want to be part of a way of life but to regard yourself as superior to it if it rejects you.   STEPHEN SPENDER

A people, it appears, may be progressive for a certain length of time, and then stop. When does it stop? When it ceases to possess individuality.   JOHN STUART MILL

I'm afraid of losing my obscurity. Genuineness only thrives in the dark.
                                    ALDOUS LEONARD HUXLEY

The individual never asserts himself more than when he forgets himself.
                                            ANDRE GIDE

We are all exceptional cases...each man insists on being innocent, even if it means accusing the whole human race and heaven.
                                          ALBERT CAMUS

None but himself can be his parallel.   LEWIS THEOBALD

The man whom God wills to slay in the struggle of life He first individualizes.   HENRIK IBSEN

Every forward step we take we leave some phantom of ourselves behind.
                                JOHN LANCASTER SPALDING

Avoid the reeking herd,
Shun the polluted flock,
Live like that stoic bird,
The eagle of the rock.

                                          ELINOR WYLIE

Who is the Potter, pray, and who the Pot?   EDWARD FITZGERALD

Whatever crushes individuality is despotism, by whatever name it may be called.   JOHN STUART MILL

It is in part the very uniqueness of every individual that makes him, not only a member of a family, race, nation, or class, but a human being.
HELEN MERRELL LYND

What's the good of winning honors and the good opinion of the world if you can't live on good terms with yourself?   ROBERTSON DAVIES

We live too much in platoons; we march by sections; we do not live in our individuality enough; we are slaves to fashion in mind and heart, if not to our passions and appetite.   EDWARD HUBBELL CHAPIN

If a man does not keep pace with his companions, perhaps it is because he hears a different drummer. Let him step to the music which he hears, however measured or far away.   HENRY DAVID THOREAU

The real man is a maze of a million notes: the label is all one note.
HILAIRE BELLOC

We require individualism which does not wall man off from community: we require community which sustains but does not suffocate the individual.   ARTHUR M. SCHLESINGER

V   PLANNING

Planning

We had only two alternatives,
*   Either one of which was great.*
We eliminated negatives
*   And ended up with eight.*

The probability of anything happening is in inverse ratio to its desirability.   JOHN W. HAZARD

(1) It is very difficult to forecast, especially about the future.
(2) He who lives by the crystal ball soon learns to eat ground glass.
(3) The moment you forecast, you know you're going to be wrong— you just don't know when and in which direction.
(4) If you're ever right, never let them forget it.   EDGAR FIEDLER

A theory has only the alternative of being right or wrong. A model has a third possibility—it may be right but irrelevant.   MANFRED EIGEN

Planned obsolescence is not really a new concept. God used it with people.   ROBERT ORBEN

The truth is too simple. One must always get there by a complicated route.   GEORGE SAND

World ain't going to be saved by nobody's scheme. It's fellows with schemes that got us into this mess. Plans get you into things but you got to work your way out.   **WILL ROGERS**

The executive who has seen his carefully laid plans go up in smoke, because of certain changes that could not have been anticipated, is outnumbered 12 to 1 by the executive who has himself gone down the drain, swept along by conditions for which he was totally unprepared simply because he has failed to plan at all.   **JESSE WERNER**

We often discover what will do, by finding out what will not do; and probably he who never made a mistake never made a discovery.
SAMUEL SMILES

The whole is simpler than the sum of its parts.   **WILLARD GIBBS**

Management are invariably making policies on the basis of what somebody else told them about the employees and the customers. And this 'somebody else' is changing the communication so that it will fit what the middle man has figured out to be what management wants to think.   **PIERRE MARTINEAU**

It takes a nonentity to think of everything.   **HONORE de BALZAC**

The superfluous, a very necessary thing.   **FRANCOIS VOLTAIRE**

It is more important to select one of half-a-dozen possible plans and get on with the job than it is to prolong the debate until the last shred of doubt as to which is the perfect best can be removed.
CLARENCE B. RANDALL

I always avoid prophesying beforehand because it is much better to prophesy after the event has already taken place.
SIR WINSTON CHURCHILL

A prophet is a man that foresees trouble.   **FINLEY PETER DUNNE**

The chief phenomenon in our days is the sense of the provisional.
JAKOB BURCKHARDT

Last night I thought over a thousand plans, but this morning I went my old way.   **CHINESE PROVERB**

You can't hope to be lucky. You have to prepare to be lucky.
TIMOTHY DOWD

I have observed, in the course of a dishonest life, that when a rogue is outlining a treacherous plan, he works harder to convince himself than to move his hearers. GEORGE MACDONALD FRASER

I don't give a shit what happens. I want you all to stonewall it. Let them plead the Fifth Amendment, cover up, or anything else if it'll save the plan. RICHARD MILHOUSE NIXON

Plans are more likely to be modified by the preconceived notions of others than for any other reason. PROFESSOR RAY E. BROWN

The finest plans are often spoilt through the pettiness of those who are supposed to carry them out, since even emperors can do nothing without the support of their soldiers and hangers-on. BERTOLT BRECHT

Long-range planning is a top-management responsibility. Staff functions may assist but decisions must be made by line management who will put their plans into action. IAN FERGUSON

The existence of a long-range plan which all departments, functions and specialists have helped to create can often be an important means of creating and maintaining greater harmony and cooperation.
JESSE WERNER

Objectives

The objective was very profound,
As long as they all were not drowned,
When they set out to sail
For that Holy Grail;
But what to do with it, once it was found?

Management by objectives works if you know the objectives. Ninety percent of the time you don't. LAURENCE J. PETER

The world turns aside to let any man pass who knows whither he is going.
DAVID STARR JORDAN

The great thing in this world is not so much where we stand, as in what direction we are moving. OLIVER WENDELL HOLMES

You must have long-range goals to keep you from being frustrated by short-range failures.   CHARLES C. NOBLE

You've got a goal, I've got a goal. Now all we need is a football team.
GROUCHO MARX

The trouble is, Mr. Goldwyn, that you are only interested in art, and I am only interested in money.   GEORGE BERNARD SHAW

The trouble with our age is that it is all signpost and no destination.
LOUIS KRONENBERGER

You've got to be very careful if you don't know where you are going, because you might not get there.   YOGI BERRA

He that is not handsome at twenty, nor strong at thirty, nor rich at forty, nor wise at fifty, will never be handsome, strong, rich or wise.
PROVERB

When you get there, there isn't any there.   GERTRUDE STEIN

Those who stand for nothing fall for anything.   ALEX HAMILTON

To me sophistication and goal have a lot in common.
JONATHAN RICHMAN

Show me a man who claims he is objective and I'll show you a man with illusions.   HENRY R. LUCE

It is a paradoxical but profoundly true and important principle of life that the most likely way to reach a goal is to be aiming not at that goal itself but at some more ambitious goal beyond it.
ARNOLD TOYNBEE

When a thing is done, it's done. Don't look back. Look forward to your next objective.   GEORGE C. MARSHALL

If you don't know where you are going, you will probably end up somewhere else.

A thing long expected takes the form of the unexpected when at last it comes.   MARK TWAIN

Remember that happiness is a way of travel—not a destination.

ROY M. GOODMAN

If I were objective or if you were objective or if anyone was, he would have to be put away somewhere in an institution because he'd be some sort of vegetable.   DAVID BRINKLEY

A man watched two masons working on a building. One frowned, groaned, and cursed over his labors. Asked what he was doing, he replied, "Just piling one stone on top of another all day long until my back is about to break." The other mason whistled at his work. His movements were swift and sure, and his face wore a glow of satisfaction. Asked what he was doing, he replied, "Sir, I'm not just making a stone wall—I'm helping to build a cathedral."   CLARENCE FRANCIS

A straight path never leads anywhere except the objective.

ANDRE GIDE

If you know where you're heading, you'll always make headway. ANON

There is one thing certain, namely, that we can have nothing certain, therefore it is not certain that we can have nothing certain.

SAMUEL BUTLER

We need objectives. We need focus and direction. Most of all, we need the sense of accomplishment that comes from achieving what we set out to do... it's important to make plans, even if we decide to change them, so that at least for the moment we know where we're going and we can have a sense of progress. In the long run, it's frustrating, not liberating, to be like the airplane pilot who radios, "I have good news and bad news. The good news is that I'm making excellent time. The bad news is that I'm lost!" Or, putting it another way, a sailor without a destination cannot hope for a favorable wind.   DR. LEON TEC

As a general rule, the shorter the interval that separates us from our planned objective the longer it seems to us, because we apply to it a more minute scale of measurement, or simply because it occurs to us to measure it.   MARCEL PROUST

Men, like snails, lose their usefulness when they lose direction and begin to bend.   WALTER SAVAGE LANDOR

It's never too late to reach your destination. You should never doubt what is in front of your eyes. WILLIE 'THE LION' SMITH

We all live under the same sky, but we don't all have the same horizon. KONRAD ADENAUER

A widely prevalent notion today seems to demand instant achievement of goals, without any of the wearying, frustrating preparation that is indispensable to any task. As the exemplar of a way of life, the professional—that man or woman who invests every new task or duty, no matter how small, with discipline of mind and spirit—is a vanishing American, particularly among those who too often believe that dreams come true because they ought to and not because they are caused to materialize. JACK VALENTI

The Facts

To make up
What lacks
Just break up
The facts.

Get the facts first. You can distort them later. MARK TWAIN

"As a matter of fact" is an expression that precedes many an expression that isn't. LAURENCE J. PETER

The trouble with facts is that there are so many of them. SAMUEL McCORD CROTHERS

She always says, that facts are like cows. If you look at them in the face hard enough they generally run away. DOROTHY L. SAYERS

Comment is free but facts are sacred. C. P. SCOTT

There are men who can think no deeper than a fact. FRANCOIS VOLTAIRE

The likelihood of what appears to be a wise and impressive statement of fact being reversed by nature almost immediately it is made, is enhanced by the importance of the speaker.   N. STACEY

The lazy deal in generalizations.   ANON

Reporting facts is the refuge of those who have no imagination.
MARQUIS de VAUVENARGUES

The inescapable though often dodged fact is that anything, absolutely anything, which may be used to do good may be used to do harm, or worse.   J. W. LAMBERT

Don't tell me, I never believe facts; you know Canning said nothing was so fallacious as facts, except figures.   SYDNEY SMITH

A fact is like a sack which won't stand up when it is empty. In order that it may stand up, one has to put into it the reason and sentiment which have caused it to exist.   LUIGI PIRANDELLO

I think there is one smashing rule. Never face the facts.
RUTH GORDON

Facts that are not frankly faced have a habit of stabbing us in the back.
SIR HAROLD BOWDEN

Variables won't, constants aren't.   DON OSBORN

There is nothing stubborn about a fact; whenever it meets a fool it is ready to lay down its life for him.   FRANK MOORE COLBY

A wise man recognizes the convenience of a general statement, but he bows to the authority of a particular fact.
OLIVER WENDELL HOLMES

Knowledge is power; but only if a man knows what facts not to bother about.   ROBERT LYND

He wasn't exactly hostile to facts, but he was apathetic about them.
WOLCOTT GIBBS

Any fact is better established by two or three good testimonies than by a thousand arguments.   NATHANIEL EMMONS

Facts as facts do not always create a spirit of reality, because reality is a
spirit.   GILBERT KEITH CHESTERTON

All generous minds have a horror of what are commonly called 'facts'.
They are the brute beasts of the intellectual domain.
                                     OLIVER WENDELL HOLMES

The facts are to blame, my friend. We are all imprisoned by facts.
                                     LUIGI PIRANDELLO

Information

Information's just a guide
But there's one thing to decide;
Did they take away or add
Something to the good or bad?

Drowning problems in an ocean of information is not the same as solving
them.   PROFESSOR RAY E. BROWN

Information means money.   B. C. FORBES

Information equals power.   IRWIN BLYE

Relying too much on current statistics and internal management
information is but a continuation of today into tomorrow.
                                     JESSE WERNER

History is bunk.   HENRY FORD

It is a very sad thing that nowadays there is so little useless information.
                                     OSCAR WILDE

Every general wishes he had more information before he goes into battle,
but each crisis you get into is on insufficient information.
                                     ROBERT FROST

An oil company executive once complained to me that the only close
confidante he could discuss policy with were simply playing back to him

his own ideas. He said he wished it were possible for him to find out what the younger people in his company were thinking. But this was impossible because his company's whole system was operating to shield the man at the top from information and communication trying to figure out what "they thought he wanted to hear."   PIERRE MARTINEAU

He had never outgrown the feeling that a quest for information was a series of maneuvers in a game of espionage.   MARY McCARTHY

The two words "information" and "communication" are often used interchangeably, but they signify quite different things. Information is giving out; communication is getting through.   SIDNEY J. HARRIS

A great part of the information I have was acquired by looking up something and finding something else on the way.
FRANKLIN P. ADAMS

When numbered pieces of toast and marmalade were dropped on various samples of carpet arranged in quality, from coir matting to the finest Kirman rugs, the marmalade-downwards-incidence varied indirectly with the quality of the carpet.   PAUL JENNINGS

Some men will never ask for information, because it implies that they do not know.   HENRY CARDINAL MANNING

Today's "fact" becomes tomorrow's "misinformation." ALVIN TOFFLER

I've told you for the fifty-thousandth time, stop exaggerating.
GRAFFITO

Life is the art of drawing sufficient conclusions from insufficient premises.   SAMUEL BUTLER

I usually get my stuff from people who promised somebody else that they would keep it a secret.   WALTER WINCHELL

We tend to accept data in the light of our personal drives and wishes, giving greater emphasis to factual information that is in accord with our individual feelings and less importance to equally objective evidence that is not in line with what we are seeking to accomplish.
HARRY A. BULLIS

It is a little hard to believe but the Oxford Dictionary carries 14,070 different definitions for the 500 most used words in English. This is an average of 28 separate definitions per word.   JOHN O'HAYRE

The best way to become acquainted with a subject is to write a book about it.   BENJAMIN DISRAELI

When action grows profitable, gather information; when information grows unprofitable, sleep.   URSULA K. Le GUIN

It is completely unimportant. That is why it is so interesting.
                                                AGATHA CHRISTIE

Look into almost any field of practical endeavour and we will find accurate data going back only a century or two. Civilization has just begun.   ARTHUR E. MORGAN

Information is the currency of democracy.   RALPH NADER

With a knowledge of the name comes a distinctive recognition and knowledge of the thing.   HENRY DAVID THOREAU

We know too much for one man to know much.
                                          J. ROBERT OPPENHEIMER

I attribute the little I know to my not having been ashamed to ask for information and to my rule of conversing with all descriptions of men on those topics that form their own peculiar professions and pursuits.
                                                      JOHN LOCKE

We live by information, not by sight.   BALTASAR GRACIAN

Enthusiasm is not always the companion of total ignorance, it is often that of erroneous information.   FRANCOIS VOLTAIRE

Progress

The most disappointed,
When change comes at last,
Are those self-appointed
To look after the past.

Somewhere between the extremes of procrastination and those of abortive change the executive finds the path of consistent progress.
PROFESSOR RAY E. BROWN

The world hates change, yet it is the only thing that has brought progress.
CHARLES F. KETTERING

Those who speak most of progress measure it by quantity and not quality.
GEORGE SANTAYANA

What we call "Progress" is the exchange of one nuisance for another nuisance.
HENRY HAVELOCK ELLIS

Progress was all right. Only it went on too long.
JAMES THURBER

I have always considered that the substitution of the internal combustion engine for the horse marked a very gloomy milestone in the progress of mankind.
SIR WINSTON CHURCHILL

A thousand things advance; nine hundred and ninety-nine retreat: that is progress.
HENRI FREDERIC AMIEL

In the number of lives taken and lands laid waste America's score is unhappily far higher than any other country's since the end of World War Two.
ARNOLD TOYNBEE

Progress imposes not only new possibilities for the future but new restrictions.
NORBERT WIENER

The marvels of modern technology include the development of a soda can which, when discarded, will last forever—and a $7000 car, which, when properly cared for, will rust out in two or three years.
PAUL HARWITZ

Irreproducible research too often leads to great discoveries.   ANON

We owe a lot to Thomas Edison—if it wasn't for him, we'd be watching television by candlelight.   MILTON BERLE

The era of low cost energy is almost dead. Popeye has run out of cheap spinach.   PETER PATERSON

Not blind opposition to progress, but opposition to blind progress.
Sierra Club

Progress is the activity of today and the assurance of tomorrow.
RALPH WALDO EMERSON

Consider the wheelbarrow. It may lack the grace of an airplane, the speed of an automobile, the initial capacity of a freight car, but its humble wheel marked out the path of what civilization we still have.
HAL BORLAND

Old methods must relentlessly be weeded out if they are now wrong, not because they are old but only because they are wrong.
ARTHUR B. DOUGALL

The art of progress is to preserve order amid change, and to preserve change amid order.   ALFRED NORTH WHITEHEAD

True progress quietly and persistently moves along without notice.
ST. FRANCIS de SALES

Obsolescence is a factor which says that the new thing I bring you is worth more than the unused value of the old thing.
CHARLES F. KETTERING

"Creative Destruction" describes the incessant change both in the structure and in the product of our economy.
PROFESSOR JOSEPH A. SCHUMPETER

I can't help thinking that science would be more appealing if it had no practical use. In what we call progress. 90 per cent of our efforts go into finding a cure for the harms linked to the advantage brought by the remaining 10 per cent.   CLAUDE LEVI-STRAUSS

Progress is a comfortable disease.   EDWARD ESTLIN CUMMINGS

It takes only a year or two for the exaggerations to come true. Nothing will remain in the next ten years. Or there will be twice as much of it.
WARREN G. BENNIS

The further back one goes, the science one does encounter is of a consistently higher quality. For example, in studying the science of yesteryear one comes upon such interesting notions as gravity, electricity, and the roundness of the earth—while an examination of more recent phenomena shows a strong trend toward spray cheese, stretch denim, and the Moog synthesizer.   FRAN LEBOWITZ

Carnation Milk is the best in the land;
Here I sit with a can in my hand—
No tits to pull, no hay to pitch,
You just punch a hole in the son of a bitch.   ANON

People are the common denominator of progress. No improvement is possible with unimproved people, and advance is certain when people are liberated and educated. It would be wrong to dismiss the importance of roads, railroads, power plants, mills, and other familiar furniture of economic development... but we are coming to realize... that there is a certain sterility in economic monuments that stand alone in a sea of illiteracy. Conquest of illiteracy comes first.
JOHN KENNETH GALBRAITH

So long as all the increased wealth which modern progress brings, goes but to build up great fortunes, to increase luxury, and make sharper the contest between the House of Have and the House of Want, progress is not real and cannot be permanent.   HENRY GEORGE

"Change" is scientific, "progress" is ethical. Change is indubitable, whereas progress is a matter of controversy.   BERTRAND RUSSELL

Obsolescence is a fact and not a theory... old communities will modernize or die. So will our industries.   BERNARD KILGORE

The highest function of conservatism is to keep what progressiveness has accomplished.   ROBERT H. FULTON

I have tried at various times in my life to grasp the rudiments of such inventions as the telephone, the camera, wireless telegraphy and even the ordinary motorcar, but without success. Television, of course, and radar and atomic energy are so far beyond my comprehension that my brain shudders at the thought of them and scurries for cover like a primitive tribesman confronted for the first time with a Dunhill cigarette lighter.   NOEL COWARD

Conformity is the jailer of freedom and the enemy of growth.
                                           JOHN F. KENNEDY

The reasonable man adapts himself to the world: the unreasonable one persists in trying to adapt the world to himself. Therefore all progress depends on the unreasonable man.   GEORGE BERNARD SHAW

By his very success in inventing labor-saving devices, modern man has manufactured an abyss of boredom that only the privileged classes have ever fathomed.   LEWIS MUMFORD

Change

The words you arrange
  To get the right rhyming
Are just like all change;
  The best thing is timing.

If you have always done it that way, it is probably wrong.
                                        CHARLES F. KETTERING

The one thing that does not change is that at any and every time it appears that there have been "great changes."   MARCEL PROUST

How come nothing's like it was until it's gone?   WILL MASTIN

Come, come, my conservative friend, wipe the dew off your spectacles, and see that the world is moving.   ELIZABETH CADY STANTON

There is in all change something at once sordid and agreeable, smacking of infidelity and household removals.
                                        CHARLES BAUDELAIRE

One-fifth of the people are against everything all the time.
                                           ROBERT F. KENNEDY

Most of the change we think we see in life is due to truths being in and out of favour.   ROBERT FROST

When our first parents were driven out of Paradise, Adam is believed to have remarked to Eve: "My dear, we live in an age of transition."
DEAN WILLIAM RALPH INGE

God grant me the serenity to accept the things I cannot change, courage to change things I can, and wisdom to know the difference.
REINHOLD NIEBUHR

Want to have some fun? Walk into an antique shop and say, "What's new?"   HENNY YOUNGMAN

Hovering around the status quo like a sick kitten around a hot brick.
WILLIAM ALLEN WHITE

People are very open-minded about new things as long as they're exactly like the old ones.   CHARLES F. KETTERING

Only that which is provisional endures.   FRENCH PROVERB

Once in Persia reigned a king
Who upon his signet ring
Graved a maxim true and wise,
Solemn words, and these are they,
"Even this shall pass away."   THEODORE TILTON

Management of change and innovation is probably the most critical and pervasive task facing business and industry today.
WILLIAM T. BRADY

Planning for change must be the ever-present concern of every single executive.   JESSE WERNER

I think anything you try to do to change anything, even if you explain it to them, the majority of people object.   PHILIP K. WRIGLEY

One can hope that our habit of equating 'old' with obsolete and 'new' with best will in time disappear.   VICE ADM. HYMAN RICKOVER

When you start dealing with real change you are talking about interfering with those who are in possession of something.
CARL B. STOKES

All conservatism is based upon the idea that if you leave things alone you leave them as they are. But you do not. If you leave a thing alone you leave it to a torrent of change.   GILBERT KEITH CHESTERTON

Young people reflect social change most radically because they are partly its products.   HERBERT HENDIN

Human creatures have a marvellous power of adapting themselves to necessity.   GEORGE GISSING

Never throw away hastily any old faith, tradition or convention. They may require modification, but they are the result of the experience of many generations.   OLIVER LODGE

Every new adjustment is a crisis in self-esteem.   ERIC HOFFER

Reminds me of nothing so much as a dead fish before it has time to stiffen.   GEORGE ORWELL

Automized and computerized industry requires more and more young men and women who have white collar skills but behave with the docility expected of blue-collar workers.   STAUGHTON LYND

Someday perhaps change will occur when times are ready for it instead of always when it is too late. Someday change will be accepted as life itself.   SHIRLEY MACLAINE

What is actual is actual only for one time. And only for one place.   THOMAS STEARNS ELIOT

The calamity of modern existence is that the world changes so fast that there is little likelihood that the old will continue to remain very much wiser than the young.   SEYMOUR L. HALLECK

Haut et bas, gauche et droite,
Avenirs et passés,
Sont dans la même boite
L'un sur l'autre entassés.   JEAN COCTEAU

I see great changes takin' place ivry day, but no change at all ivry fifty years.   FINLEY PETER DUNNE

Men are conservative when they are least vigorous, or when they are most luxurious.   RALPH WALDO EMERSON

Keep constantly in mind in how many things you yourself have witnessed changes already. The universe is change, life is understanding.

MARCUS AURELIUS

The interval between the decay of the old and the formation and the establishment of the new, constitutes a period of transition, which must always necessarily be one of uncertainty, confusion, error and wild and fierce fanaticism.   JOHN C. CALHOUN

What a deal of talking there would be in the world if we desired at all costs to change the names of things into definitions.

GEORGE CHRISTOPH LICHTENBERG

We cannot change anything unless we accept it. Condemnation does not liberate, it oppresses.   CARL GUSTAV JUNG

The dogmas of the quiet past are inadequate to the stormy present. The occasion is piled high with difficulty, and we must rise with the occasion. As our case is new, so we must think anew and act anew. We must disenthrall ourselves.   ABRAHAM LINCOLN

Reform

Isn't it strange,
We welcome change
But few conform,
If called 'reform'.

Reform always comes from below. No man with four aces asks for a new deal.   *The Irish Digest*

Old reformers never die. They get thrown out.   HERBERT HOOVER

A reformer is one who, when he smells a rat, is eager to let the cat out of the bag.

ANON

A reformer is one who sets forth cheerfully toward sure defeat.

RICHARD S. CHILDS

Nothing so needs reforming as other people's habits.   MARK TWAIN

An indefinable something to be done, in a way nobody knows how, at a time nobody knows when, that will accomplish nobody knows what.
THOMAS B. REES

Reformers have the idea that change can be achieved by brute sanity.
GEORGE BERNARD SHAW

I think I am better than the people who are trying to reform me.
EDGAR WATSON HOWE

Reform is the utopium of the people.   ARTHUR CASE

A reformer is one who does not realize how much worse things can be made.   ANON

The trouble is that everyone talks about reforming others, and no one thinks about reforming himself.   SAINT PETER of ALCANTARA

Every reform was once a private opinion.
RALPH WALDO EMERSON

All reformers, however strict their social conscience live in houses just as big as they can pay for.   LOGAN PEARSALL SMITH

A reformer is a virtuous person with a mean mind.
WALTER BAGEHOT

Like all other zealous reformers, we do what we do because we like doing it better than anything else.   DONALD ROBERT PERRY MARQUIS

A reformer is a guy who rides through a sewer in a glass-bottomed boat.
JAMES J. WALKER

To innovate is not to reform.   EDMUND BURKE

It is essential to the triumph of reform that it shall never succeed.
WILLIAM HAZLITT

Unless the reformer can invent something which substitutes attractive virtue for attractive vices, he will fail.   WALTER LIPPMANN

Reformers are nine parts of self-interest with one part philanthrophy.
HERBERT SPENCER

All reformism is characterized by utopian strategy and tactical opportunism.
                                                                GRAFFITO

Nobody expects to find comfort and companionability in reformers.
                                                    HEYWOOD BROUN

Every man is a reformer until reform tramps on his toes.
                                              EDGAR WATSON HOWE

When A. annoys or injures B. on the pretense of improving B., A. is a scoundrel.
                                          HENRY LOUIS MENCKEN

There was the don who, whenever any reform was proposed, made exactly the same speech. He would say: "Whenever a measure of this kind is suggested, I ask myself two questions: 'Has the old system worked badly?' 'Is the new system likely to work better?' I see no reason to answer either question in the affirmative, and I shall therefore vote against the proposal."
                                                BERTRAND RUSSELL

Every reform, however necessary, will by weak minds be carried to an excess which will itself need reforming.
                                      SAMUEL TAYLOR COLERIDGE

Reforms are less to be dreaded than revolutions, for they cause less reaction.
                                          MR. JUSTICE DARLING

Reformers, as a group, are not a very attractive group of people. As you get older you recognize that. They are too self-righteous. They feel that they have the call.
                                                    ROBERT MOSES

Every reform is only a mask under cover of which a more terrible reform, which dares not yet name itself, advances.
                                            RALPH WALDO EMERSON

Reforming is a trade—with some a swindling trade—with others an honest but yet a lucrative trade.
                                            JOHN QUINCY ADAMS

Attempts at reform, when they fail, strengthen despotism, as he that struggles tightens those cords he does not succeed in breaking.
                                        CHARLES CALEB COLTON

Men reform a thing by removing the reality from it, and then do not know what to do with the unreality that is left.
                                      GILBERT KEITH CHESTERTON

Decisions

The cruelest phrase
I'll ever know
Is when one says
"I told you so."

A decision is the action an executive must take when he has information so incomplete that the answer does not suggest itself.

ARTHUR WILLIAM RADFORD

An amazing number of executives regard the outcome of their decisions as a certainty.

Fortune

A decision is what a man makes when he can't get anyone to serve on a committee.

FLETCHER KNEBEL

The decision is maybe and that's final.

ANON

The most common source of mistakes in management decisions is the emphasis on finding the right answer rather than the right question.

PETER F. DRUCKER

Extremely few executives can point to a record as good as four out of five correct decisions.

HARRY A. BULLIS

Conclusions are usually consolidated guesses.   HENRY S. HASKINS

If I could but spot a conclusion, I should race to it.   OGDEN NASH

The results of the decisions you have made and will make are the most important factors in your future career and earning capacity.

HERMAN W. STEINKRAUS

All our final decisions are made in a state of mind that is not going to last.

MARCEL PROUST

Academic staff rather enjoy coming to a conclusion but they don't like coming to decisions at all.

LORD ANNAN

Jumping to conclusions is an occupational hazard.   ANON

Yielding to the pressures of the moment is an open invitation for a raid by the most aggressive and most vocal members of the organization.
PROFESSOR RAY E. BROWN

A successful man generally has a wife who saves his time by making the decisions.
HERBERT V. PROCHNOW

In too many organizations the power of decision is restricted to the top. Empire-building by yes-men becomes the main preoccupation and in this struggle for status, the creative thoughts of people all along the line are stifled.
WILLIAM T. BRADY

1. Get the facts straight.
2. Arrange them in logical order.
3. Convey them clearly and concisely.
E. J. THOMAS

We make our decisions conform with what we would like them to be, rather than what they necessarily should be.
DR. HERBERT A. SIMON

There is a fatality about all good resolutions. They are invariably made too soon.
OSCAR WILDE

Merely making proposals takes only a typewriter; making workable proposals takes time.
RICHARD MILHOUS NIXON

It is a capital mistake to theorize before one has data.
SIR ARTHUR CONAN DOYLE

The weak are always forced to decide between alternatives they have not chosen themselves.
DIETRICH BONHOEFFER

In industry, the harder the decisions to be made, the better an executive must be to make them right.
O. A. BATTISTA

It does not take much strength to do things but it requires great strength to decide on what to do.
FREDERICH B. WILCOX

The chief end of man is to frame general propositions, and no general proposition is worth a damn.
OLIVER WENDELL HOLMES

Permitting colleagues to participate in decision-making is not so much a favour to the participants as it is to the executive.
PROFESSOR RAY E. BROWN

Too much agreement, from too narrow a group, makes for decisions that don't work.   HARLAN CLEVELAND

It is well known that we are susceptible only to those suggestions with which we are secretly in accord.   CARL GUSTAV JUNG

The ability to allow decisions to be discussed before committing the organization to follow them, represents the best method of pretesting ideas.   ANON

We often make self-defeating choices because we are unenlightened about our needs. We pick the opposite of what we really need because we don't know what we need.   LILA SWELL

Decisions, ideas, and directives lost much of their usefulness and vigor because of a delay.   E. J. THOMAS

Decided only to be undecided, resolved only to be irresolute, adamant for drift, solid for fluidity, all-powerful to be impotent.
                                           SIR WINSTON CHURCHILL

The fine art of executive decision consists in not deciding questions that are not now pertinent, in not deciding prematurely, in not making decisions that cannot be made effective, and in not making decisions that others should make.   CHESTER I. BARNARD

The objectives of the company can be subordinated to the aims and goals of its most aggressive and colorful personalities, each functional unit develops its own narrow perspective and decisions and made in terms of parochial intercept.   WILLIAM T. BRADY

When making a decision of a minor importance I have always found it advantageous to consider all the pros and cons. In vital matters, however, such as the choice of a mate or profession, the decision should come from the unconscious, from somewhere within ourselves. In important decisions of our personal life, we should be governed, I think, by the deep inner needs of our nature.   ROBERT L. HEILBRONER

Evaluate the situation in terms of its scope, your individual responsibility, the other people involved, and company policy.   *New York Adult Education Council*

At the last moment there is always a reason not existing before, namely, the impossibility of further vacillation.   GEORGE ELIOT

Hypotheses are only the pieces of scaffolding which are erected round a building during the course of construction, and which are taken away as soon as the edifice is completed.

JOHANN WOLFGANG von GOETHE

VI OPERATIONS

The Office

The office is a room
We get no luck without,
Unless the one to whom
We pass the buck is out.

The new electronic typewriters still can't spell.   ANON

If you work in any sort of office at all, chances are you'll spend at least
20 years of your life sitting down.   L. M. BOYD

Sometimes an executive who manages to keep his desk clear has a
couple of assistants who are buried under the stuff he's routed to them.
O. A. BATTISTA

Egos are affected most by the allocation of office space.   ANON

He and I had an office so tiny that an inch smaller and it would have
been adultery.   DOROTHY PARKER

The only difference between a secretary and a private secretary is that
one knows more and tells less.   EVAN ESAR

Only the bravest of stay-at-homes asks the ticklish question, 'Did
anybody ask where I was?'   HENRY S. HASKINS

In the office in which I work there are five people of whom I am afraid. Each of these five people is afraid of four people (excluding overlaps).
JOSEPH HELLER

I do most of my work sitting down: that's where I shine.
ROBERT BUSHBY

Office hours are from twelve to one with an hour off for lunch.
GEORGE S. KAUFMAN

A husband is someone who phones you from the office to ask you the number of his car (parked outside his office) and then says, "Thanks, son"!
PATRICIA STRANG

My secretary quit. She caught me kissing my wife.
LEOPOLD FECHTNER

If I can't spell the words in the first place how does he expect me to find them in the dictionary?
JACOB M. BRAUDE

Is the sibilant in Ms. any more disagreeable to the ear than the hiss in Miss?
CASEY MILLER and KATIE SWIFT

An office party is not, as is sometime supposed, the Managing Director's chance to kiss the tea-girl. It is the tea-girl's chance to kiss the Managing Director (however bizarre an ambition this may seem to anyone who has seen the Managing Director face on).
KATHERINE WHITEHORN

Why can't they move Sunday to the middle of the week so you could put it in the OUT tray on your desk.
RUSSELL HOBAN

Life is a series of yellow pads.
GEORGE STEVENS

A clever man is one who complains to his wife that his secretary doesn't understand him.
LEONARD LOUIS LEVINSON

The clear-desk system:
THOMAS MASARYK

A man who has no office to go to is a trial of which you can have no conception.
GEORGE BERNARD SHAW

Do you know that a ten-minute coffee break five days a week amounts to forty-three and one-third hours during a year—over a week's vacation in time?
HERBERT V. PROCHNOW

I think any man in business would be foolish to fool around with his secretary. If it's somebody else's secretary, fine!
SENATOR BARRY GOLDWATER

Our favourite desk motto reads: "Right now is a good time."
GERALD HORTON BATH

A man's secretary seldom has reason to be jealous of his wife.
EVAN ESAR

This Worker's demarcation-line business is making things tough. All offices now have to employ a full-time carpenter to sharpen pencils.
PETER CAGNEY

She hung her coat behind the office door and took her boss to the cleaners.
ANON

Offices are a tremendous waste of time for chief executives. I can be away from my office for three weeks, and things get done. But if I come in for one day, everything stops.
LAWRENCE A. APPLEY

A businessman needs three umbrellas—one to leave at the office, one to leave at home and one to leave on the train.
PAUL DICKSON

The best labor-saving device is a wastebasket.
ANON

Executive to personnel manager: "My secretary spells like a mathematician—she rounds off to the nearest letter of the alphabet."
ROBERT BRAULT

I yield to no one in my admiration for the office as a social center, but it's no place actually to get any work done.
KATHERINE WHITEHORN

Men rushing around the office with their paper cups of coffee like conscripts carrying their urine samples.
MALCOLM GLASK

I can always find plenty of women to sleep with, but the woman really hard for me to find is a typist who can read my writing.
THOMAS WOLFE

The busiest men have the fullest wastebaskets.   ANON

When you open the window yourself, you get fresh air. When someone
else opens it, you get a draught.   LUCILLE GOODYEAR

Electronic engineers have yet to devise a better interoffice communications system than the water cooler.   LEO ELLIS

A clean desk represents an empty mind.   FELIX FRANKFURTER

If a cluttered desk is a sign of a cluttered mind, we can't help wondering
what an empty desk indicates.   ANON

A secretary is not a thing
Wound by key, pulled by string.
Her pad is to write on,
And not spend the night in.   FRANK LOESSER

Not long after the famous admonition THINK was hung on our office
wall, some wit had added OR THWIM.   ANON

The corporation man sometimes emerges as much less than heroic to the
one person in a real position to know—his secretary, on whom he often
becomes markedly dependent.   MYRON BRENTON

Of all the damnable waste of human life that ever was invented, clerking
is the very worst.   GEORGE BERNARD SHAW

Probably, but for the introduction of the lady secretary into the business
man's office, the business man would have collapsed entirely by now.
She calls up the sacred fire in her and she communicates it to her boss.
He finds an added flow of energy and optimism, and business
flourishes.   DAVID HERBERT LAWRENCE

If President Nixon's secretary Rosemary Woods had been Moses'
secretary, there would be only eight commandments.
                                        ART BUCHWALD

An office is not a tea-bar, matrimonial bureau, betting shop, reading
room, fashion house or smoking lounge, but a place where paperwork
necessary to good management is originated and eventually filed.
                                   KEITH WATERHOUSE

Telemachines

When you find a machine to do
Half of your work for you,
I do not care
If it's not fair,
I should go right ahead and buy two.

Machines have less problems. I'd like to be a machine.
ANDY WARHOL

Why is the wrong telephone number never busy?　　　ANON

I don't mind being put on "hold" but I think they've got me on "ignore."
TROY GORDON

Well, if I called the wrong number, why did you answer the phone?
JAMES THURBER

I answer the phone "Dickerson here" because I'm Dickerson and I'm here. Now what the hell do you want, Martha?
CHARLES BARSOTTI

It is only when they go wrong that machines remind you how powerful they are.
CLIVE JAMES

Wives are people who think when the telephone rings, it's against the law not to answer it.
RING LARDNER

Secretary on telephone: "Our automatic answering device is away for repairs—this is a person speaking."
NORMAN WEED

The telephone is the greatest nuisance among conveniences, the greatest convenience among nuisances.
ROBERT LYND

"I wonder who this telegram is from?"
"Western Union. I recognize the handwriting."　　FRAN LEBOWITZ

A man never feels more important than when he receives a telegram containing more than ten words.
GEORGE ADE

Did you ever get the feeling that life has put you on hold?   ANON

There is something about saying "OK" and hanging up the receiver with a bang that kids a man into feeling that he has just pulled off a big deal, even if he has only called up central to find out the correct time.
ROBERT BENCHLEY

A Telex machine clattering up the office.   ANON

In the business world an executive knows something about everything, a technician knows everything about something—and the switchboard operator knows everything.   HAROLD COFFIN

Never answer the telephone if you are in the middle of something more important.   C. NORTHCOTE PARKINSON

The telephone is a device which does not ask questions but must be answered.   ANON

When a telephone rings, the average man settles deeper into his chair with the observation, "I wonder who that can be?"
MARCELENE COX

In heaven when the blessed use the telephone they will say what they have to say and not a word besides.
WILLIAM SOMERSET MAUGHAM

The telephone is a good way to talk to people without having to offer them a drink.   FRAN LEBOWITZ

Public telephones in Europe are like our pinball machines. They are primarily a form of entertainment and a test of skill rather than a means of communication.   MISS PIGGY

What do you mean, "This is a recording?" You phoned me!   ANON

"While I was out, did you take any messages?"
"No, sir, are there any missing?"   LEOPOLD FECHTNER

"Is that Russell, Linklater, Fitzgerald, Dolittle and Watson?"
"Yes, this is Russell, Linklater, Fitzgerald, Dolittle and Watson."
"I want to speak to Mr. Smith."   ANON

A woman is a person who reaches for a chair when she answers the telephone.   MILTON WRIGHT

The telephone is an invention of the devil which abrogates some of the advantages of making a disagreeable person keep his distance.
LEWIS and FAYE COPELAND

The answering-service operator has become the surrogate servant of the servantless society.   *Newsweek*

Never answer a telephone that rings before breakfast. It is sure to be one of three types of persons that is calling: a strange man in Minneapolis who has been up all night and is phoning collect; a salesman who wants to come over and demonstrate a new, patented combination Dictaphone and music box that also cleans rugs; or a woman out of one's past.
JAMES THURBER

Efficient people are always sending needless telegrams.
SYLVIA TOWNSEND WARNER

The telephone is of real use only to important businessmen or to women who have something to hide.   SIDONIE-GABRIELLE COLETTE

An urgently ringing telephone, pleading to be answered.
RICH GRAHAM

The Bell System is like a damn big dragon. You kick it in the tail, and two years later, it feels it in its head.   FREDERICK KAPPEL

In my country some 25 years ago, you could make a long distance call on a privately owned telephone system from San Francisco to New York for $28. For that same amount of money, you could send 1,376 letters. Today, you can make the same telephone call for two dollars and a half and for that amount you can only send 41 letters. So the government is investigating the Bell system!   RONALD REAGAN

The telephone is the most important single technological resource of later life.   ALEX COMFORT

One machine can do the work of 50 ordinary men, but no machine can do the work of one extraordinary man.   ELBERT HUBBARD

As machines get to be more and more like men, men will come to be more like machines.   JOSEPH WOOD KRUTCH

Computers

In spite of progress, there is no doubt,
Even though they've become much astuter,
As long as you can't get any more out
Than you put in—it's still a computer.

That arithmetic is the basest of all mental activities is proved by the fact that it is the only one that can be accomplished by a machine.
ARTHUR SCHOPENHAUER

The perfect computer has been developed. You just feed in your problems, and they never come out again.   AL GOODMAN

The computer is a moron.   PETER F. DRUCKER

We used to have lots of questions to which there were no answers. Now with the computer there are lots of answers to which we haven't thought up the question.   PETER USTINOV

The real danger is not that computers will begin to think like men, but that men will begin to think like computers.   SYDNEY J. HARRIS

It would take one hundred clerks working for one hundred years to make a mistake as monumental as a single computer can make in one thousandth of a second.   *Dental Economics*

In addition to hardware, which is the computer, and software, which is the program, computer scientists have lately begun talking about "wetware," which is the human brain.   LEE DEMBART

One good reason why computers can do more work than people is that they never have to stop to answer the telephone.   OLLIE M. JAMES

Machines from the Maxim gun to the computer are for the most part means by which a minority can keep free men in subjection.
LORD KENNETH CLARK

Had there been a computer in 1872, it would probably have predicted that by now there would be so many horse-drawn vehicles it would be almost impossible to clean up all the manure.
PROFESSOR K. WILLIAM KAPP

Like sex drives, card tricks and the weather, computers tend to be discussed in terms of results rather than processes, which makes them rather scary. MARTIN MAYER

In the future, you're going to get computers as prizes in breakfast cereals. You'll throw them out because your house will be littered with them. ROBERT LUCKY

A computer with as many vacuum tubes as a man has neurons in his head would require the Pentagon to house it, Niagara's power to run it, and Niagara's waters to cool it. WARREN S. McCULLOCH

To err is human; to really foul things up requires a computer.
BILL VAUGHAN

To err may become inhuman. LAURENCE J. PETER

There is no worse mess than a computer mess. IBM EXECUTIVE

The main impact of the computer has been the provision of unlimited jobs for clerks. PETER F. DRUCKER

I do not fear computers. I fear the lack of them. ISAAC ASIMOV

Technological man can't believe in anything that can't be measured, taped, put in a computer. CLARE BOOTHE LUCE

Computers can figure out all kinds of problems except the things in the world that just don't add up. JAMES MAGARY

A computer does not substitute for judgment any more than a pencil substitutes for literacy. But writing without a pencil is no particular advantage. ROBERT S. McNAMARA

All a computer does is tell a consistent story: a consistent truth or if the programmer's guesses are unlucky, a consistent fiction.
PAUL A. SAMUELSON

Scientists discovered a link between silicon and melba toast. After fifteen years of exposure to air, silicon turns into melba toast, according to a group of University of California researchers. The findings caused panic among computer makers and other businesses that rely on the silicon chip. However, makers of processed-cheese spreads were elated at the news. *Off the Wall Street Journal*

The first time a person gets a screwdriver, he's going to go around the house tightening all the screws, whether they need it or not. There's no reason a computer will not be similarly abused.

THEODORE K. RABB

Man is still the most extraordinary computer of all.

JOHN F. KENNEDY

I think there is a world market for about five computers.

THOMAS J. WATSON

Anyone who wishes to persuade a computer to work for him must explain his problem to the computer in precise detail. Before he can explain the problem, he must understand it thoroughly himself.   JOHN LEAR

If you put tomfoolery into a computer, nothing comes out but tomfoolery. But this tomfoolery having passed through a very expensive machine, is somehow ennobled and no one dares criticize it.   PIERRE GALLOIS

Paperwork

> *Paperwork's rotationary*
> *But I can disprove it;*
> *It always remains stationery,*
> *Whichever way you move it.*

Too often I find that the volume of paper expands to fill the available briefcases.   JERRY BROWN

It is estimated that far less than five per cent of paperwork that is filed away is ever looked at again.   ANON

Government employee to colleague: 'Here's something new in memos—it makes sense.'   LIGHTY and WAGNER

When the weight of the paperwork equals the weight of the equipment, the project is complete.   ENGINEERS' MAXIM

We can lick gravity, but sometimes the paperwork is overwhelming.
                                     WERNHER von BRAUN

The pencil sharpener is about as far as I have ever got in operating a
complicated piece of machinery with any success.
                                     ROBERT BENCHLEY

Why, a four-year-old child could understand this report. Run out and
find me a four-year-old child. I can't make head or tail out of it.
                                     GROUCHO MARX

He picked up a slip of paper and a blue pencil, intending to write the
word "Balls." But the pencil broke and as he sharpened it the gentleman
remembered where he was; he compromised, wrote "Round Objects,"
inserted the slip and pushed the file aside. Many weeks later, the file
came back to him with a note from the Director General which said:
"Who is Mr. Round and why does he object?"   GERALD KERSH

No inanimate thing will move from one place to another without a piece
of paper that goes along telling someone where to move it.
                                     GERALD E. WILSON

Twice as many people are engaged in clerical work as in 1940. Maybe we
are no more mixed up than ever, but we are getting it all down on paper.
                                     ANON

For most men life is a search for the proper manila envelope in which to
get themselves filed.   CLIFTON FADIMAN

Ms. A syllable which sounds like a bumblebee breaking wind.
                                     HORTENSE CALISHER

Office memos increasing by heaps and mounds.   DICK WEST

I can only assume that a "Do Not File" document is filed in a "Do Not
File" file.   SEN. FRANK CHURCH

A filing cabinet is a place where you can lose anything systematically.
                                     LEOPOLD FECHTNER

A memorandum is written not to inform the reader but to protect the
writer.   DEAN ACHESON

There are two kinds of reports. One says you can't do it. The other says it has been done. The first kind is no good. The second kind you don't need.   EDSON BLAIR

Busy people never write long winded reports.   ANON

Keep a diary and one day it'll keep you.   MAE WEST

Documentation has been simplified by switching over to red-tape recorders.   ANON

Manuscript: something submitted in haste and returned at leisure.
OLIVER HERFORD

Filing is concerned with the past; anything you actually need to see again has to do with the future.   KATHERINE WHITEHORN

Just get it down on paper, and then we'll see what to do with it.
MAXWELL PERKINS

More paperwork means less original thinking.   ANON

All papers that you save will never be needed until such time as they are disposed of, when they become essential.   JOHN CORCORAN

The man whose life is devoted to paperwork has lost the initiative. He is dealing with things that are brought to his notice, having ceased to notice anything for himself. He has been essentially defeated by his job.
C. NORTHCOTE PARKINSON

We have so many forms to fill in, and the excessive time spent on paper work means there is less time for prayer.   ABBOT LEO SMITH

"Try to handle each piece of paper only once." Every time you pick up a piece of paper needing your action, failing to act only means you'll have to double your time and energy spent on it by picking it up again.
MICHAEL LEBOEUF

Envelope, n. The coffin of a document; the scabbard of a bill; the husk of a remittance; the bed-gown of a love-letter.   AMBROSE BIERCE

Letters

Remember what's what,
If you want to impress;
We read quite a lot
From the sender's address.

That's not writing, that's typing.   TRUMAN CAPOTE

If a fellow wants to be a nobody in the business world, let him neglect
sending the mail man to somebody on his behalf.
                                              CHARLES F. KETTERING

If I don't get in touch with you in a couple of days please show me the
same consideration.   GERALD F. LIEBERMAN

Is it easy to understand?   E. J. THOMAS

I have made this letter longer than usual, only because I have not had the
time to make it shorter.   BLAISE PASCAL

Letters that should never have been written and ought immediately to be
destroyed are the only ones worth keeping.   SYDNEY TREMAYNE

Sydney Smith, or Napoleon or Marcus Aurelius (somebody about that
time) said that after ten days any letter would answer itself. You see what
he meant.   ALAN ALEXANDER MILNE

I'd rather sit down and write a letter than call someone up. I hate the
telephone.   HENRY MILLER

The test of a good letter is a very simple one. If one seems to hear the
other person talking as one reads, it is a good letter.
                                     ARTHUR CHRISTOPHER BENSON

If it takes her an hour to write a letter, how long will it take her to write
the alphabet?   ANON

The great secret in life is not to open your letters for a fortnight. At the
expiration of that period you will find that nearly all of them have
answered themselves.   ARTHUR BINSTEAD

You never have to change anything you got up in the middle of the night
to write.   SAUL BELLOW

This is my letter to the World
That never wrote to Me...   EMILY DICKINSON

It all begins and ends with the mailbox, and when they find a way to
remove mailboxes, much of our suffering will end.
                                        CHARLES BUKOWSKI

Never answer a letter while you are angry.   CHINESE PROVERB

Letters are largely written to get things out of your system.
                                          JOHN DOS PASSOS

I consider it a good rule for letter writing to leave unmentioned what the
recipient already knows, and instead tell him something new.
                                            SIGMUND FREUD

No man would set a word down on paper if he had the courage to live out
what he believed in.   HENRY MILLER

A letter shows the man it is written to as well as the man it is written by.
                                    EARL of CHESTERFIELD

The letter which merely answers another letter is no letter at all.
                                        MARK Van DOREN

Whenever you receive a letter from a creditor write fifty lines upon some
extraterrestrial subject, and you will be saved.
                                      CHARLES BAUDELAIRE

A good letter is an exercise of the ego, a modest letter writer a
contradiction in terms.   CLIFTON FADIMAN

An intention to write never turns into a letter. A letter must happen to
one like a surprise, and one may not know where in the day there was
room for it to come into being.   RAINER MARIA RILKE

Never confide your secets to paper; it is like throwing a stone in the air;
you do not know where it may fall.
                                    PEDRO CALDERON de la BARCA

Executives

Executives in the top bracket
Rarely make use of their jacket.
What they will use
Most are their shoes,
To survive in the corporate racket.

If a man has an office with a desk on which there is a buzzer, and if he can press that buzzer and have someone come dashing in response, then he's an executive. **ELMER ADAMS**

An executive is one who hires others to do what he is hired to do. **HERBERT V. PROCHNOW**

A molehill man is a pseudo-busy executive who comes to work at 9 am and finds a molehill on his desk. He has until 5 pm to make this molehill into a mountain. An accomplished molehill man will often have his mountain finished before lunch. **FRED ALLEN**

I don't want any yes-men around me. I want everyone to tell me the truth—even though it costs him his job. **SAMUEL GOLDWYN**

An executive is the man used to talk to visitors so that the others can get their work done. **ANON**

Yesterday's young hero who rode his bike "no hands" to impress his girl is today the executive submitting a 50-page proposal entitled "A Comprehensive Plan for Implementation of Participating Management with particular Attention to Line-Staff Interface." **WILLIAM N. PENZER**

Take the risk-bearing function out of an executive's job and his importance on the American scene would disappear overnight. **HARRY A. BULLIS**

This is my executive suite and this is my executive vice-president, Ralph Anderson, and my executive secretary, Adele Eades, and my executive desk and my executive carpet and my executive wastebasket and my executive ashtray and my executive pen set and my... **HENRY MARTIN**

The best executive is the one who has the most people with their shoulders to his wheel.   ANON

One who can always take off during the work-day for a game of golf with impunity.   EUGENE E. BRUSSELL

The executive exists to make sensible exceptions to general rules.
ELTING E. MORISON

The difference between a successful executive and an unsuccessful one is the difference between being right 55 percent of the time and being right only 49 percent of the time.   ANON

The executive's job is to get things done through other people.
J. C. PENNEY

A successful sales executive is a man who can keep both feet firmly implanted on the desk—and give the impression they belong there.
FRANKLIN DANE

An executive: A man who can make quick decisions and is sometimes right.   ELBERT HUBBARD

Executive ability is deciding quickly and getting somebody else to do the work.   J. G. POLLARD

It is an advantage to develop the ability to lose a point gracefully.
ANON

It was sad to reflect that if he had done it himself, he would have been able to do it right in 20 minutes but that, as things turned out, he himself spent two days trying to find out why it was that it had taken somebody else three weeks to do it wrong; yet such an idea would strike at the very foundation of the belief of all employees that an executive 'had nothing to do.'   F. F. BEIRNE

More frequently than not, an executive who gets along easily with others, who does not fight too hard for his position, who is willing to see the point of view of the other fellow, especially if the other fellow is his superior, gains a reputation of being constructive and cooperative. And that he is. The question remains, what else is he?   ELI GINZBERG

A good executive will concentrate on the best way to do something rather than the quickest way to finish.   ANON

An executive is by profession a decision maker. Uncertainty is his opponent. Overcoming it is his mission.   JOHN McDONALD

One of the greatest failings of today's executive is his inability to do what he's supposed to do.   MALCOLM KENT

It is more important for an executive to recognize and support ability than it is for him to have it himself.   ANON

The able executive is the man who can train assistants more capable than himself.   ANDREW CARNEGIE

Pessimists make poor executives, just as procrastinators never qualify.
          HARRY A. BULLIS

Many minor executives prefer a generous expense account to a raise in salary, which would be heavily taxed and more soberly spent. It is they who support the so-called expense account restaurants, places of exotic decor where patrons lunch in a darkness which is all but complete. They cannot see to read the prices on the menu, but these, in the special circumstances, are irrelevant.   C. NORTHCOTE PARKINSON

Communication is the means whereby management gets its job done. Without it an executive is as ineffectual as a violinist without his instrument. It is a skill of management; it is, however, essential to every other management skill.   LAWRENCE A. APPLEY

Being a director means you must submit to direction.
          RAYMOND QUENLEAU

A good executive can win without exulting and lose without moping.
          J. C. PENNEY

Absolutely no other communications can be as powerful as an executive's willingness to hear comments other than those he wants to hear.
          ANON

The occupational disease of a poor executive is inability to listen.
          DR. LYDIA GIBERSON

One roll of the executive is to eliminate from within the organization.
          PROFESSOR RAY E. BROWN

Damn the great executives, the men of measured merriment, damn the men with careful smiles, damn the men that run the shops, oh, damn their measured merriment.　　　　　　　　　　SINCLAIR LEWIS

The Boss

There's many who have a degree
And it may even be quite a hot one,
Yet, in spite of their biography,
They work for a boss who has not one.

By working faithfully eight hours a day, you may eventually get to be a boss and work twelve hours a day.　　　　　ROBERT FROST

BOSS spelt backwards is double S.O.B.　　　　　　　　　ANON

Boss: One who's late when you're early and early when you're late.
　　　　　　　　　　　　　　　　GERALD F. LIEBERMAN

Men who complain that the boss is dumb would be out of a job if he were any smarter.　　　　　　　　　　JACOB M. BRAUDE

The man in the crow's nest is often the last to hear of the hole in the hull.
　　　　　　　　　　　　　　　　ARTHUR WHITE

The boss is the one who watches the clock during the coffee break.
　　　　　　　　　　　　　　　　HUPP TREVIS

Reality is when you find out that the boss did overhear what you said about him.　　　　　　　　　　O. A. BATTISTA

How many rivers do we have to cross before we get to meet the boss.
　　　　　　　　　　　　　　　　BOB MARLEY

Tell the boss what you really think of him and the truth will set you free.
　　　　　　　　　　　　　　　　ANON

Dear, never forget one little point. It's my business. You just work here.
ELIZABETH ARDEN

Conviction is what the boss thinks. MICHAEL FARRING

If the boss cannot make you do something, he can make you wish you had. ANON

When the cat is away the mice will play. PROVERB

A good secretary can save her boss more time in a year than a business jet plane can. MALCOLM BALDRIGE

The first in a flock is still a sheep. BERNARD BERENSON

It is best for all bosses to realize that the ultimate master is the customer. ANON

The boss exists to make sensible exceptions to general rules.
ELTING E. MORISON

I am not bound by the rules, I make them. CHARLES DEDERICH

I never give them hell; I just tell the truth, and they think it's hell.
HARRY S. TRUMAN

The question "Who ought to be boss?" is like asking "Who ought to be the tenor in the quartet?" Obviously, the man who can sing tenor.
HENRY FORD

Please don't think of me as the boss. Think of me as a navigator on the Sea of Confusion. ROBERT ORBEN

He who pays the piper may call the tune. PROVERB

If you're the chief executive you get more blame than you deserve, and you also get more credit than you deserve. If you want one, you've got to accept the other, too. K. T. KELLER

The best way for a boss to save his company money is to fire his secretary. ANON

The eye of a master will do more work than both his hands.
BENJAMIN FRANKLIN

One eye of the master sees more than four of the servants. PROVERB

The aristocracy created by business rarely settles in the midst of the manufacturing population which it directs; the object is not to govern that population, but to use it.   COUNT ALEXIS de TOCQUEVILLE

The man who gives me employment, which I must have or suffer, that man is my master, let me call him what I will.   HENRY GEORGE

Few who reach the summit can be acquitted of vanity or conceit.
SIR JOHN COLVILLE

The days of the dictatorial, blustering boss are numbered; and that is a blessing. Your modern supervisor serves as a coordinator, an encourager, a smoother-outer of difficulties. Above all, he sees to it that all persons get a fair deal and that all questions from those working with him are viewed from a sympathetic stand-point. The first responsibilities of our supervisors are to build men and women, then medicine.
ELI LILLY

For peace of mind, resign as general manager of the universe.
LARRY EISENBERG

Hiring

If you're doing big things,
You attract big people.
If you're doing small things,
You attract small people.

Anythin' for a quiet life, as the man said when he took the situation at the lighthouse.   CHARLES DICKENS

Young men object that they can't get a job if their hair is long. They ought to see how tough it is to get one when the hair is sparse and grey.
BILL VAUGHAN

If you pay peanuts, you get monkeys.   SIR JAMES GOLDSMITH

Too many people quit looking for work when they find a job.   ANON

It is all one to me if a man comes from Sing Sing or Harvard. We hire a man, not his history.   HENRY FORD

Personnel officer to applicant: "Actually, we're looking for a Leo with a Scorpio ascendant."   BRENDA BURBANK

Brains will not come out at the top of an organization unless they are put in at the bottom.   CLARENCE B. RANDALL

Not sixteen per cent of the human race is, or ever has been engaged in any of the kinds of activity at which they excel.   PAUL MAIRET

Few great men could pass Personnel.   PAUL GOODMAN

I like your qualifications—you have the makings of a first-class underling.   GYLES BRANDRETH

The closest to perfection a person ever comes is when he fills out a job application form.   STANLEY J. RANDALL

Personnel manager to applicant: "What we're after is a man of vision; a man with drive, determination, fire; a man who never quits; a man who can inspire others; a man who can pull the company's bowling team out of last place!"   HERBERT V. PROCHNOW

When the Chairman retires, we hire an office boy.   ANON

The best minds are not in government. If any were, business would hire them away.   RONALD REAGAN

Never judge from appearances.   PROVERB

There's a great difference between someone looking for a job and one looking for work.   ANON

The employer generally gets the employee he deserves.
                                        SIR WALTER GILBEY

Most men would feel insulted if it were proposed to employ them in throwing stones over a wall, and then in throwing them back, merely that they might earn their wages. But many are no more worthily employed now.   HENRY DAVID THOREAU

Before recruitment it is vital to check all references fully.
PERSONNEL MAXIM

Anyone who is honestly seeking a job and can't find it, deserves the attention of the United States government, and the people.
JOHN F. KENNEDY

The company which always fills an important post by enticement from competitors reveals it's bankrupt in personnel policy.
CLARENCE B. RANDALL

Do you consider $10 a week enough for a longshoreman with a family to support?
If that's all he can get, and he takes it, I should say it's enough.
J. PIERPONT MORGAN

One can no more judge of a man by the actions of an hour than of the climate of a country by the temperature of the day.   J. PETIT-SENN

When white-collar people get jobs, they sell not only their time and energy but their personalities as well. They sell by week or month their smiles and their kindly gestures, and they must practice prompt repression of resentment and aggression.   C. WRIGHT MILLS

Since modern man experiences himself both as the seller and as the commodity to be sold on the market, his self-esteem depends on conditions beyond his control. If he is 'successful' he is valuable; if he is not, he is worthless.   ERICH FROMM

A man willing to work, and unable to find work, is perhaps the saddest sight that fortune's inequality exhibits under this sun.
THOMAS CARLYLE

To hire a man because he needs a job, rather than because the job needs him, is to assure him that he is useless. On the other side of the coin to help a man because it is in your own interest to help him is to treat him as an equal.   HENRY FORD

It is impossible to build a successful organization if the basic human material obtained is of limited potential.   ROBERT N. McMURRAY

S'pose you got a job a work an' there's jus' one fella wants the job. You got to pay 'im what he asts. But s'pose they's a hundred men wants that job. S'pose them men got kids an' them kids is hungry. S'pose a nickle'll bye leas' sompin for the kids. An' you got a hundred men. Jus' offer 'em a nickel—why, they'll kill each other fightin' for that nickel.

JOHN STEINBECK

The aim of the laborer should be, not to get his living, to get "a good job," but to perform well a certain work. Do not hire a man who does your work for money, but him who does it for love of it.

HENRY DAVID THOREAU

Firing

Admired,
Was hired.
Perspired
Got tired.
Expired
Was fired.

Tell me, how long have you been with us—not counting today.

DAVID FROST

Those not fired with enthusiasm will be fired with enthusiasm.

VINCE LOMBARDI

A company is known by the men it keeps losing.   ANON

It is much harder to find a job than to keep one.   JULES BECKER

It's only a suggestion and there's no need to do it—unless you want to keep your job!   ANON

If at first you don't succeed, you're fired.   JEAN GRAMAN

The big guns of business are often those who have never been fired.

IAN FERGUSON

Secretaries are fired for knowing too little or too much.   ANON

Are you really going to quit or are you just saying it to brighten my day?
LEOPOLD FECHTNER

People are too durable, that's their main trouble. They can do too much
to themselves, they last too long.   BERTOLT BRECHT

You can't help liking the managing director—if you don't, he fires you.
ANON

I just don't know what we'd do without you. But we're going to try.
DAVID FROST

We can't fire her. She's the only one who understands the filing system.
ANON

When more and more people are thrown out of work, unemployment
results.   CALVIN COOLIDGE

Human beings, unfortunately, tend to respond to negative incentives—
such as dismissal.   JOHN P. YOUNG

When two men in business always agree, one of them is unnecessary.
WILLIAM WRIGLEY

It seems that nothing ever gets to going good till there's a few
resignations.   FRANK McKINNEY HUBBARD

If the bird does like its cage, and does like its sugar, and will not leave
it, why keep the door so very carefully shut?   OLIVE SCHREINER

It is not fit that you should sit here any longer!... you shall now give
place to better men.   OLIVER CROMWELL

Despite all the suggestions I've made over the years, I've never been able
to fire you with enthusiasm. Until now.   DAVID FROST

My father worked for the same firm for twelve years. They fired him.
They replaced him with a tiny gadget this big. It does everything that my
father does, only much better. The depressing thing is my mother ran out
and bought one.   WOODY ALLEN

VII MEETINGS

Conferences

A lot of people like to lend a
Voice to most on the agenda;
So much time with much construing
Of what instead they should be doing.

A business conference is a meeting in which everyone says that there is no such thing as a free lunch—while eating one.   ANON

A conference is a gathering of important people who singly can do nothing, but together can decide that nothing can be done.
                                                          FRED ALLEN

Our conference table is twenty feet long, ten feet wide and sleeps fifteen.   ANON

After all is said and done, a hell of a lot more is said than done.
                                                    CLARK OLMSTEAD

A conference is convened to decide when the next meeting will take place.   ANON

The badge of the delegate shows you whom he is for, but it does not show you what he is after.   EVAN ESAR

A conference is a coffee break with real napkins. ANON

Oh for just one more conference regarding the eradication of all conferences! VLADIMIR MAYAKOVSKY

If there's one word that sums up everything that's gone wrong since the war, it's "workshop." KINGSLEY AMIS

Any order for a million that's signed with a swizzle stick is null and void. ANON

Gentlemen, I've been thinking. Bull times zero is bull. Bull divided by zero is infinity bull. And I'm sick and tired of the bull you've been feeding me. HAROLD S. GENEEN

A conference is just an admission that you want somebody to join you in your troubles. WILL ROGERS

This sales conference will now come to order—let's see if we can get our customers to do likewise. ANON

The hardest thing to stop is a temporary chairman.
FRANK McKINNEY HUBBARD

A straw vote only shows which way the hot air blows. O. HENRY

Where two or three are gathered together, that is about enough.
LESLIE MURRAY

In some organizations there is a pyramid structure, with the various subordinates arrayed in some kind of rank. Too often their conferences end in Nothing, because the low men on the totem poles say nothing, and the first lieutenants are wrangling about completely irrelevant subjects. They aren't trying to communicate any information but just to put on record that they are the smart people. And when they start attacking and defending ideas, they are simply showing off their brilliance.
PIERRE MARTINEAU

By God, Mr. Chairman, at this moment I stand astonished at my own moderation. ROBERT CLIVE

Trivial matters take up more time for discussion because some of us know more about them than we do about important matters.
THEODORE S. WEISS

Adjournment: And now, in the immortal words of Brigadier General George Armstrong Custer: "Let's get the hell out of here!"

ROBERT ORBEN

Open each session with a prayer and close it with a probe.

CLARENCE BROWN

In any assembly the simplest way to stop the transacting of business and split the ranks is to appeal to a principle.   JACQUES BARZUN

In the multitude of counsellors there is safety.   PROVERBS

Men are seldom more commonplace than on supreme occasions.

SAMUEL BUTLER

So long as there is any subject which men may not freely discuss, they are timid upon all subjects.   JOHN JAY CHAPMAN

Committees

The very best way
To get things done
Is to have final say
On a committee of one.

It isn't so much what's on the table that matters, as what's on the chairs.

WILLIAM S. GILBERT

Determination, tenacity, resolution, and strength can be the victims of a weak bladder.   LEONARD LOUIS LEVINSON

The ideal committee is one with me as chairman, and two other members in bed with flu.   LORD MILVERTON

The only meeting that ever started on time was held up for an hour while things were explained to people who came in late and didn't know what was going on.   DOUGLAS LARSON

A committee is a group of people each of whom thinks the others talk a lot of nonsense.   ANON

The Law of Triviality. Briefly stated, it means that the time spent on any item of the agenda will be in inverse proportion to the sum involved.
CYRIL NORTHCOTE PARKINSON

The usefulness of a meeting is in inverse proportion to the attendance.
LANE KIRKLAND

A camel is a horse designed by committee.   ANON

A committee is an animal with four back legs.   JOHN le CARRE

If rationality were the criterion for things being allowed to exist, the world would be one gigantic field of soya beans!   TOM STOPPARD

Meetings are indispensable when you don't want to do anything.
JOHN KENNETH GALBRAITH

A committee is appointed to find someone to do the work.   ANON

Committees have become so important nowadays that sub-committees have to be appointed to do the work.   LAURENCE J. PETER

If Columbus had had an advisory committee he would probably still be at the dock.   JUSTICE ARTHUR GOLDBERG

A yawn at a committee meeting may be bad manners, but it's an honest opinion.   HERBERT V. PROCHNOW

A committee will always take the longest and most difficult route to an obvious conclusion.   ANON

A decision is what a man makes when he can't get anybody to serve on a committee.   FLETCHER KNEBEL

A committee is a group of the unwilling picked from the unfit, to do something unnecessary.   RICHARD HARKNESS

A committee is a group of people who will talk for hours to produce a result called minutes.   ANON

I think a single man can accomplish in a day what a committee could accomplish in a month.   BILL LEAR

A committee is an arrangement enabling one to share the blame with others.   FRANKLIN JONES

A committee is any number of people, who cannot do in an hour what one person can do in a few minutes.   ANON

A committee is a cul de sac to which ideas are lured and then quickly strangled.   JOHN A. LINCOLN

Committees are to get everybody together and homogenize their thinking.   ART LINKLETTER

Quorum, n. A sufficient number of members of a deliberative body to have their own way and their own way of having it.
                                    AMBROSE BIERCE

Committee work is like a soft chair—easy to get into but hard to get out of.   KENNETH J. SHIVELY

A committee-of-five consists of a man who does the work, three others to pat him on the back, and one to bring in a minority report.   ANON

Our age will be known as the age of committees.
                                    SIR ERNEST BENN

When a committee flies the Atlantic, let me know.   ANON

If you ever live in a country run by a committee, be on the committee.
                                    WILLIAM GRAHAM SUMNER

I hate being placed on committees. They are always having meetings at which half are absent and the rest late.
                                    OLIVER WENDELL HOLMES

Voting magnifies mistrust more often than it creates confidence.
                                    ANON

You'll find in no park or city a monument to a committee.
                                    VICTORIA PASTERNAK

A candidate should not mean but be.   GORE VIDAL

We always carry out by committee anything in which any one of us alone would be too reasonable to persist. FRANK MOORE COLBY

Few people know how to hold a meeting. Even fewer know how to let it go. ANON

I said what is very true, that any committee is only as good as the most knowledgeable, determined and vigorous person on it. There must be somebody who provides the flame. LADY BIRD JOHNSON

Meetings that do not come off keep a character of their own. They stay as they were projected. ELIZABETH BOWEN

Living movements do not come of committees. CARDINAL JOHN HENRY NEWMAN

Meetings are rather like cocktail parties. You don't want to go, but you're cross not to be asked. JOHN KENNETH GALBRAITH

Skill at Meetings

You don't know what meetings are for,
Unless you are a grafter,
With preparation well before
And lots of action after.

To ensure your undivided attention, I'll announce at the end of the meeting who'll write the minutes. DALE McFEATTERS

Whenever you're wrong, admit it; whenever you're right, shut up. OGDEN NASH

I have never been hurt by anything I didn't say. CALVIN COOLIDGE

When everyone is against you, it means that you are absolutely wrong— or absolutely right. ALBERT GUINON

I was gratified to be able to answer promptly and I did. I said I didn't know. MARK TWAIN

Think before you think!   STANISLAW J. LEC

Having served on various committees, I have drawn up a list of rules.
Never arrive on time: this stamps you as a beginner. Don't say anything
until the meeting is half over: this stamps you as being wise. Be as vague
as possible; this avoids irritating the others. When in doubt, suggest that
a subcommittee be appointed. Be the first to move for adjournment: this
will make you popular; it's what everyone is waiting for.
                                                 HARRY CHAPMAN

The best way of answering a bad argument is to let it go on.
                                                 SYDNEY SMITH

A recount is when the chairman can't believe his eyes.
                                                 ROBERT ORBEN

My idea of an agreeable person, is a person who agrees with me.
                                                 HUGO BOHUN

Forewarned, forearmed.   PROVERB

The best way to say the right thing at the right time is to speak softly and
seldom.   ANON

Accentuate the positive,
Eliminate the negative,
Latch on to the affirmative,
Don't mess with Mr. In-Between.   JOHNNY MERCER

If one tells the truth, one is sure sooner or later to be found out.
                                                 OSCAR WILDE

A technical objection is the first refuge of a scoundrel.
                                                 HEYWOOD BROUN

There are times when silence is the best way to shout at the top of your
voice.   O. A. BATTISTA

The test of courage comes when we are in the minority; the test of
tolerance comes when we are in the majority.
                                                 REV. RALPH W. SOCKMAN

If you have an important point to make, don't try to be subtle or clever, use a pile-driver. Hit the point once. Then come back and hit it again. Then hit it a third time—a tremendous whack.
                                          SIR WINSTON CHURCHILL

Look wise, say nothing, and grunt. Speech was given to conceal thought.
                                              SIR WILLIAM OSLER

If you don't say anything, you won't be called on to repeat it.
                                                CALVIN COOLIDGE

The man who can make others laugh secures more votes for a measure than the man who forces them to think.   MALCOLM de CHAZAL

Genuinely good remarks surprise their author as well as his audience.
                                               JOSEPH JOUBET

Never make a defense or an apology until you are accused.
                                      CHARLES I, KING OF ENGLAND

It is wrong to be too right. To be too good is as bad—or nearly so—as to be too wicked.   SAMUEL BUTLER

During dinner, it may be necessary to excuse yourself for a telephone call. However, it is far preferable to have a phone brought to the table. As a general rule, white telephones go with fish and poultry, and black ones with anything else.   MISS PIGGY

One on God's side is a majority.   WENDELL PHILLIPS

Let your yea be yea; and your nay, nay.   *ST. JAMES*

Examine what is said, not him who speaks.   ARABIAN PROVERB

When in doubt, tell the truth.   MARK TWAIN

Never tell your resolution beforehand.   JOHN SELDEN

To ask the hard question is simple.   WYSTAN HUGH AUDEN

When you are right you cannot be too radical; when you are wrong, you cannot be too conservative.   DR. MARTIN LUTHER KING

Wrong must not win by technicalities.   AESCHYLUS

Three may keep counsel, if two be away.   JOHN HEYWOOD

Be brief, for no discourse can please when too long.
MIGUEL de CERVANTES

My method is to take the utmost trouble to find the right thing to say, and then to say it with the utmost levity.   GEORGE BERNARD SHAW

The only way to escape misrepresentation is never to commit oneself to any critical judgment that makes an impact—that is, never say anything.
F. R. LEAVIS

Whenever you commend, add your reasons for doing so; it is this which distinguishes the approbation of a man of sense from the flattery of sycophants and admiration of fools.   SIR RICHARD STEELE

There is a good deal to be said for blushing, if one can do it at the proper moment.   OSCAR WILDE

Pitfalls at Meetings

Every time you start to boast
You will wish that you had ceased,
Because the one who speaks the most
Is the one who says the least.

Open meetings often reveal a lot of closed minds.   JOE BROWNE

There is always time to add a word, never to withdraw one.
BALTASAR GRACIAN

He who thinks by the inch and talks by the yard deserves to be kicked by the foot.   LEOPOLD FECHTNER

When you say that you agree to a thing on principle, you mean that you have not the slightest intention of carrying it out in practice.
OTTO EDUARD LEOPOLD von BISMARCK

You are never more at risk than when you make chance remarks.
                                                              ANON

We always formulate opinions at a time when our judgment is at its
weakest.   GEORG CHRISTOPH LICHTENBERG

Don't talk about yourself; it will be done when you leave.
                                              ADDISON MIZNER

Any general statement is like a cheque drawn on a bank. Its value
depends on what is there to meet it.   EZRA POUND

We are growing serious and, let me tell you, that's the very next step to
being dull.   JOSEPH ADDISON

Steer clear of overviews. Those of us who have the situation in Lebanon
in perspective and know exactly how to plot a gay rights campaign are
usually morons.   CYNTHIA HEIMEL

He who slings mud, usually loses ground.   ADLAI STEVENSON

This man must be very ignorant, for he answers every question he is
asked.   FRANCOIS VOLTAIRE

The most likely place to have your idea pocket picked is at a meeting.
Here an idea becomes public property the moment it hits the air waves.
                                              JANE TRAHEY

All things to all men and to all men, nothing.   ANON

No matter what side of an argument you're on, you always find some
people on your side that you wish were on the other side.
                                          JASCHA HEIFETZ

There aren't any embarrassing questions—just embarrassing answers.
                                          CARL T. ROWAN

Confound the men who have made our remarks before us.   DONATUS

You're very foolish if you try to beat around the bush—you just meet
yourself coming around the bush the other way.   BETTY FORD

Whenever I indulge my sense of humour, it gets me into trouble.
                                          CALVIN COOLIDGE

Meetings should not be used as springboards for solo performances.
ANON

You can create a good impression on yourself by being right, but for creating a good impression on others, there's nothing to beat being totally and catastrophically wrong.   MICHAEL FRAYN

Generalizations are generally wrong.   MARY WORTLEY MONTAGU

The most silent people are generally those who think most highly of themselves.   WILLIAM HAZLITT

One always speaks badly when one has nothing to say.
FRANCOIS VOLTAIRE

Nodding the head does not row the boat.   IRISH PROVERB

Several excuses are always less convincing than one.
ALDOUS LEONARD HUXLEY

It is dangerous to be sincere unless you are also stupid.
GEORGE BERNARD SHAW

To say you get a vote of confidence would be to say you needed a vote of confidence.   ANDREW YOUNG

A little inaccuracy sometimes saves tons of explanation.   SAKI

I don't like these cold, precise, perfect people, who, in order not to speak wrong, never speak at all, and in order not to do wrong, never do anything.   HENRY WARD BEECHER

Do not take things by the point.   W. RANCE

To generalize is to be an idiot.   WILLIAM BLAKE

A word out of season may mar a whole lifetime.   AMBROSE BIERCE

The most sensible and intelligent nation in Europe lays down, as the Eleventh Commandment, the rule Never interrupt. Noise is the most impertinent of all forms of interruption.
ARTHUR SCHOPENHAUER

You have not converted a man because you have silenced him.
JOHN MORLEY

I was and I always shall be hampered by what I think other people will say.   VIOLETTE LEDUC

Hypothetical questions get hypothetical answers.   JOAN BAEZ

Those who exaggerate in their statements belittle themselves.
                                                    CHARLES SIMMONS

Those who never retract their opinions love themselves more than they love the truth.   JOSEPH JOUBERT

To give a reason for anything is to breed a doubt of it.
                                                    WILLIAM HAZLITT

I never gave away anything without wishing I'd kept it; nor kept it without wishing I had given it away.   LOUISE BROOKS

When the eagles are silent the parrots begin to jabber.
                                              SIR WINSTON CHURCHILL

Discussion

Discussion has three sides.
Learn this as a youth;
There is always my side,
Your side, and the truth.

Half the time when men think they are talking business, they are wasting time.   EDGAR WATSON HOWE

Discussion in America means dissent.   JAMES THURBER

Great minds discuss ideas, average minds discuss events, small minds discuss people.   ADMIRAL HYMAN G. RICKOVER

It's an odd thing that though we all disagree with each other, we are all of us in the right.   LOGAN PEARSALL SMITH

When a man tells me he's going to put all his cards on the table, I always look up his sleeve.   LORD HORE-BELISHA

Tolerance: the suspicion that the other fellow might be right.   ANON

It takes a rare person to want to hear what he doesn't want to hear.
DICK CAVETT

Never hold discussions with the monkey when the organ grinder is in the
room.   SIR WINSTON CHURCHILL

A difference of opinion is what makes horse racing and missionaries.
WILL ROGERS

Discussion is an exchange of intelligence. Argument is an exchange of
ignorance.   BILL GOLD

Wait for the question, before you give the answer.   ANON

We like a man to come right out and say what he thinks—if we agree
with him.   MARK TWAIN

There can be no worthwhile battle of ideas within the organization if the
reward is disfavor and ill will from the boss.
PROFESSOR RAY E. BROWN

A circle is the longest distance to the same point.   TOM STOPPARD

Self-restraint is feeling your oats without sowing them.
SHANNON FIFE

When a thing ceases to be a subject of controversy, it ceases to be a
subject of interest.   WILLIAM HAZLITT

Discussion: a method of confirming others in their errors.
AMBROSE BIERCE

We are more inclined to hate one another for points on which we differ
than to love one another for points on which we agree.
CHARLES CALEB COLTON

A little sincerity is a dangerous thing, and a great deal of it is absolutely
fatal.   OSCAR WILDE

My sad conviction is that people can only agree about what they're not
really interested in.   BERTRAND RUSSELL

I never discuss discussions.   DAG HAMMARSKJOLD

The point can become blunt, if you stick to it!   ANON

He not only closed the subject, he sat on the lid.   MARY RENAULT

The innocent is the person who explains nothing.   ALBERT CAMUS

I'll discuss anything—I like to go perhaps-ing around on all subjects.
ROBERT FROST

If is difficult to be emphatic when no one is emphatic on the other side.
CHARLES DUDLEY WARNER

A fanatic is one who can't change his mind and won't change the subject.
SIR WINSTON CHURCHILL

Don't agree with the boss until he says something.   ANON

Every man has a right to utter what he thinks truth, and every other man
has a right to knock him down for it.   SAMUEL JOHNSON

Partisanship is our great curse. We too readily assume that everything
has two sides and that it is our duty to be on one or the other.
JAMES HARVEY ROBINSON

Don't look at me in that tone of voice.   *Punch*

A disagreement may be the shortest cut between two minds.
KAHLIL GIBRAN

The right to be heard does not automatically include the right to be taken
seriously. To be taken seriously depends entirely upon what is being
said.   HUBERT H. HUMPHREY

One never discusses anything with anybody who can understand, one
discusses things with people who cannot understand.
GERTRUDE STEIN

When angry count four, when very angry, swear.   MARK TWAIN

Jaw-jaw is better than war-war.   SIR WINSTON CHURCHILL

Audi partem ulterum. (Hear the other side.)   SAINT AUGUSTINE

One of my favorite philosophical tenets is that people will agree with you only if they already agree with you. You do not change people's minds.
FRANK ZAPPA

Somebody has to have the last word. Otherwise, every reason can be met with another one and there would never be an end to it.
ALBERT CAMUS

We should have a great many fewer disputes in the world if words were taken for what they are, the signs of our ideas only, and not for things themselves.   JOHN LOCKE

You will find that the truth is often unpopular and the contest between agreeable fancy and disagreeable fact is unequal. For, in the vernacular we Americans are suckers for good news.   ADLAI STEVENSON

A soft answer turneth away wrath.   *Proverbs*

The mind of a bigot is like the pupil of the eye; the more light you pour upon it, the more it will contract.   OLIVER WENDELL HOLMES

Always be ready to speak your mind and a base man will avoid you.
WILLIAM BLAKE

Don't discuss yourself, for you are bound to lose; if you belittle yourself, you are believed; if you praise yourself, you are disbelieved.
MICHEL de MONTAIGNE

Argument

The way to win
A verbal fight
Is to begin
By being right.

The only way to get the best of an argument is to avoid it.
DALE CARNEGIE

Never argue with a fool—people might not know the difference.
                                        ARTHUR BLOCK

Keep raising the roof and people will think there's something wrong in
your attic.   FRANKLIN JONES

The moment you grab someone by the lapels, you're lost.
                                        BURT REYNOLDS

When a fellow says he agrees with you in principle, he's invariably
getting ready to argue with you.   ANON

Argument can do no more than clear the track; it cannot make the
engine move.   EDWYN BEVAN

Many people lose their tempers merely from seeing you keep yours.
                                    FRANK MOORE COLBY

You can make up a quarrel, but it will always show where it was patched.
                                    EDGAR WATSON HOWE

There is only one thing worse than a man who will argue over anything,
and that's a man who will argue over nothing.   ANON

I am righteously indignant:
You are annoyed;
He is making a fuss about nothing.   *New Statesman*

Never fight with a man who has nothing to lose.
                                    BALTASAR GRACIAN

In real life it takes only one to make a quarrel.   OGDEN NASH

The surest sign that you haven't any sense is to argue with one who
hasn't.   LAURENCE J. PETER

You cannot make a sound argument without a lot of noise.   ANON

The principal objection to a quarrel is that it interrupts an argument.
                                GILBERT KEITH CHESTERTON

Anyone who conducts an argument by appealing to authority is not using
his intelligence; he is just using his memory.
                                    LEONARDO da VINCI

Many a man's tongue broke his nose.   SEAMAS MACMANUS

Why does a heated argument create a chilly atmosphere?   ANON

When arguments fail, use a blackjack!
EDWARD 'SPIKE' O'DONNELL

I am not arguing with you—I am telling you.
EDWARD MORGAN FORSTER

There is no good arguing with the inevitable. The only argument available with an east wind is to put on your overcoat.
JAMES RUSSELL LOWELL

You may easily play a joke on a man who likes to argue—agree with him.   EDGAR WATSON HOWE

The best argument is that which seems merely an explanation.
DALE CARNEGIE

Deep-seated preferences cannot be argued about—you cannot argue a man into liking a glass of beer.   OLIVER WENDELL HOLMES

Keep your temper. Do not quarrel with an angry person, but give him a soft answer. It is commanded by the Holy Writ and, furthermore, it makes him madder than anything else you could say.   ANON

You raise your voice when you should reinforce your argument.
SAMUEL JOHNSON

When you have no basis for an argument, abuse the plaintiff.
CICERO

It is impossible to defeat an ignorant man in argument.
WILLIAM G. McADOO

When we quarrel how we wish we had been blameless.
RALPH WALDO EMERSON

An association of men who will not quarrel with one another is a thing which never yet existed from the greatest confederacy of nations down to a town meeting or a vestry.   THOMAS JEFFERSON

Your "If" is the only peacemaker; much virtue in "If."
WILLIAM SHAKESPEARE

The worst tempered people I've ever met were people who knew they
were wrong.   WILSON MIZNER

The pain of a dispute greatly outweighs its uses.   JOSEPH JOUBERT

It is not necessary to understand things in order to argue about them.
PIERRE AUGUSTIN CARON de BEAUMARCHAIS

It is only the intellectually lost who ever argue.   OSCAR WILDE

A half truth, like a half brick, is always more forcible as an argument
than a whole one. It carries better.   STEPHEN LEACOCK

I always get the better when I argue alone.   OLIVER GOLDSMITH

Soft words are hard arguments.   THOMAS FULLER

The difficult part of an argument is not to defend one's opinion but rather
to know it.   ANDRE MAUROIS

Sir, I have found you an argument; but I am not obliged to find you an
understanding.   SAMUEL JOHNSON

The most sensible people to be met with in society are men of business
and of the world, who argue from what they see and know, instead of
spinning cobweb distinctions of what things ought to be.
WILLIAM HAZLITT

Anger makes dull men witty, but it keeps them poor.
QUEEN ELIZABETH I

Compromise

A litte bit of good advice,
As wars will never cease,
That any peace at any price
Has rarely produced peace.

Better a handful of dry dates and content therewith than to own the Gate
of Peacocks and be kicked in the eye by a broody camel.
ARABIAN PROVERB

If you cannot catch a bird of paradise, better take a wet hen.
NIKITA KHRUSHCHEV

It is the weak man who urges compromise—never the strong man.
ELBERT HUBBARD

If you can't lick 'em—join 'em—.   PROVERB

An appeaser is one who feeds a crocodile hoping it will eat him last.
SIR WINSTON CHURCHILL

Life is a series of compromises.   CYRUS HEPPLEWAITE

A compromise is the art of dividing a cake in such a way that everyone
believes he has the biggest piece.   DR. LUDWIG ERHARD

When one divides, the other should have the right of first choice.
LEGAL MAXIM

The person who agrees to meet you halfway thinks they're standing on
the dividing line.   ANON

Compromise is but the sacrifice of one right or good in the hope of
retaining another, too often ending in the loss of both.
TYRON EDWARDS

Sometimes nothing is a real cool hand.   DONN PEARCE

Compromise used to mean that half a loaf was better than no bread. It
really seems to mean that half a loaf is better than a whole loaf.
GILBERT KEITH CHESTERTON

If you can't get half a loaf, take a whole one—a whole loaf is better than no bread.   JOSH BILLINGS

Sentiment has no cash value.   RONALD MACDOUGALL

Don't compromise yourself. You are all you've got.   JANIS JOPLIN

Many promising reconciliations have been broken down because, while both parties came prepared to forgive, neither party came prepared to be forgiven.   CHARLES WILLIAMS

The principle of give and The principle of give and take is the principle of diplomacy—give one and take ten.   MARK TWAIN

The only fellow who gets anywhere playing both ends against the middle is an accordian player.   O. A. BATTISTA

A lean compromise is better than a fat lawsuit.   PROVERB

Sometimes it's better to compromise—like giving a gunman your wallet without approving what he's doing.   FRANK A. CLARK

The one sure way to conciliate a tiger is to allow oneself to be devoured.   KONRAD ADENAUER

It's co-existence
Or no existence.   ANON

I had nothing to offer anybody except my own confusion.   JACK KEROUAC

He was so tolerant that he could have attended a lynching every day without becoming critical.   THORNE SMITH

I can promise to be sincere, but not to be impartial.   JOHANN WOLFGANG von GOETHE

To blow and swallow at the same moment is not easy.   TITUS MACCIUS PLAUTUS

Compromise makes a good umbrella but a poor roof; it is a temporary expedient.   JAMES RUSSELL LOWELL

I learned long ago, never to wrestle with a pig. You get dirty, and besides, the pig likes it.   CYRUS CHING

The concessions of the weak are the concessions of fear.
                                                    EDMUND BURKE

Right is more precious than peace.   WOODROW WILSON

The middle way is frequently taken by those who do not know where they
are going, and so find comfort in having company on both sides.
                                            PROF. F. A. HARPER

Once you say you're going to settle for second, that's what happens to you
in life, I find.   JOHN F. KENNEDY

Neutral men are the devil's allies.   EDWIN HUBBEL CHAPIN

The peak of tolerance is most readily achieved by those who are not
burdened with convictions.   ALEXANDER CHASE

To get others to come into our ways of thinking, we must go over to theirs
and it is necessary to follow, in order to lead.   WILLIAM HAZLITT

Neutrality, as a lasting principle, is an evidence of weakness.
                                                        KOSSUTH

I despise the pleasure of pleasing people whom I despise.
                                    LADY MARY WORTLEY MONTAGU

Adapt or perish, now as ever, is nature's inexorable imperative.
                                        HERBERT GEORGE WELLS

Every advantage has its tax.   RALPH WALDO EMERSON

A temporary compromise is a diplomatic act, but a permanent compromise is the abandonment of a goal.   LEON STEIN

There is nothing to which men, while they have food and drink, cannot
reconcile themselves.   GEORGE SANTAYANA

One's first step in wisdom is to question everything—and one's last is to
come to terms with everything.
                            GEORG CHRISTOPH LICHTENBERG

Living apart and at peace with myself, I came to realize more vividly the
meaning of the doctrine of acceptance. To refrain from giving advice, to
refrain from meddling in the affairs of others, to refrain, even though the

motives be the highest, from tampering with another's way of life—so simple, yet so difficult for an active spirit! Hands off!

HENRY MILLER

Silence

The best way I've seen
To keep your nose clean
Is to do nothing but
Keep your mouth shut.

Silence is the best substitute for brains ever invented.

SENATOR HENRY F. ASHURST

Better to remain silent and be thought a fool than to speak out and remove all doubt.   ABRAHAM LINCOLN

Few men have ever repented of silence.   PATRICK HENRY

Monkeys, who very sensibly refrain from speech, lest they should be set to earn their livings.   KENNETH GRAHAME

If a man keeps his trap shut, the world will beat a path to his door.

FRANKLIN P. ADAMS

Silence makes legends.   PETER GRANT

A closed mouth catcheth no flies.   PROVERB

An ounce of keeping your mouth shut is worth a pound of explanation.

EVAN ESAR

The best time to hold your tongue is the time you feel like you must say something or bust.   JOSH BILLINGS

Some people talk simply because they think sound is more manageable than silence.   MARGARET HALSEY

If nobody ever said anything unless he knew what he was talking about, a ghastly hush would descend upon the world.   SIR ALAN HERBERT

Blessed are they who have nothing to say, and who cannot be persuaded to say it.   JAMES RUSSELL LOWELL

Silence is the unbearable repartee.   OLIVER HERFORD

A man is a fool to put anything in writing if he knows how to talk, and he shouldn't talk if he is able to nod or shake his head.
                                    MARTIN LOMASNEY

Didn't you hear me keeping still?   SAMUEL GOLDWYN

Once the toothpaste is out of the tube, it's hard to get it back in.
                                    H. R. HALDEMAN

Better silent than stupid.   GERMAN PROVERB

He who does not understand your silence will probably not understand your words.   ELBERT HUBBARD

The silent man is the best to listen to.   JAPANESE PROVERB

The thoughtless are rarely wordless.   HOWARD W. NEWTON

Do not the most moving moments of our lives find us without words?
                                    MARCEL MARCEAU

An inability to stay quiet is one of the most conspicuous failings of mankind.   WALTER BAGEHOT

Speech is the small change of silence.   GEORGE MEREDITH

Silence is one of the hardest arguments to refute.   JOSH BILLINGS

We need a reason to speak, but none to keep silent.
                                    PIERRE NICOLE

Deep rivers move in silence, shallow brooks are noisy.
                                    ENGLISH PROVERB

Fools live to regret their words, wise men to regret their silence.
                                    WILL HENRY

Silence gives consent.   PROVERB

Let a fool hold his tongue and he will pass for a sage.
                                        PUBLILIUS SYRUS

It is never more difficult to speak well than when we are ashamed of
keeping silent.   FRANCOIS DUC de la ROCHEFOUCAULD

The silent bear no witness against themselves.
                              ALDOUS LEONARD HUXLEY

Men of few words are the best men.   WILLIAM SHAKESPEARE

Silence is the most perfect expression of scorn.
                              GEORGE BERNARD SHAW

Speech may sometimes do harm; but so may silence, and a worse harm
at that. No offered insult ever caused so deep a wound as a tenderness
expected and withheld; and no spoken indiscretion was ever so bitterly
regretted as the words that one did not speak.   JAN STRUTHER

VII PEOPLE

Internal Communications

The grapevine's full of twattle
That they will never throttle.
It's just fine
To drink the wine
But never buy the bottle.

It's all about people!   ANON

The big trouble with communication today is the short supply of those
willing to be communicated with.   DON FRASER

Armies and corporations alike have ways of sweetening the news as it
ascends the hierarchy of command.   ROBERT L. HEILBRONER

All simple statements are wrong.   FRANK KNIGHT

Communication without purpose is artistic masturbation.
                                                    ROD STEIGER

Just because a rumor is idle doesn't mean it isn't working.
                                              MAURICE SEITTER

Good communication is as stimulating as black coffee, and just as hard
to sleep after.   ANNE MORROW LINDBERGH

The most common note in the suggestion box is where you can put it!
ANON

Science may never come up with a better office communication system than the tea break. EARL WILSON

Bulletin: A can of pressed beef. PETER CAGNEY

The bad news should be broadcast as well as the good.
E. J. THOMAS

For years employee communications meant bowling scores, personal items, and similar information not related to the company's business situation. Then somebody had the good sense to ask the employees what they really wanted, and they overwhelmingly said they wanted to be informed on developments of all types around the company.
DON G. MITCHELL

Often there is a middle man in the organization who is a block to effective communication. He is oriented to the top, and he sees to it that no communication gets through to top management unless it is agreeable. PIERRE MARTINEAU

The genius of communication is the ability to be both totally honest and totally kind at the same time. JOHN POWELL

Stop the transmission belt which conveys the company's policies and goals to its workers, shareholders, and customers, and the company will eventually stagnate and die. LAWRENCE A. APPLEY

Until Image Words came along, "communication" meant "sharing"—but the communication division doesn't want any backtalk. It wants to dish it out, not take it in, so it "municates" instead. ARTHUR HERZOG

Corporations have at different times been so far unable to distinguish freedom of speech from freedom of lying that their freedom has to be curbed. CARL BECKER

Despite the great amount of unanimity as to the importance of effective communications within a company, much of it has been left to chance and taken for granted. The problem seems always to be in someone else's backyard. "Our men always know what's going on... We're a small outfit; communication with us is no problem." And so forth. It was while working in one of these "no problem" companies that a salesman discovered, after being on the road for five weeks, that for the last three weeks his plant had been closed down two days out of each week. And who told him? Right—a customer.   WALTER E. BRUNAUER

Communications should be a continuous process and not emphasized only when there is trouble in the air or new developments to publicize.
E. J. THOMAS

The communicator is the person who can make himself clear to himself first.   LEO ROSTEN

If management cannot communicate with the owners of the business, how can it communicate effectively with the organization. The answer is that it usually doesn't, because poor communications with one major group usually means poor communications with another.
DON G. MITCHELL

Problems that reach the top level of the organization usually carry with them the troubled ponderings of those involved along the line of ascent.
PROFESSOR RAY E. BROWN

Effective communication is not propaganda used to brainwash employees or mislead the public.   ANON

It is no secret that communication can be effective only in an atmosphere of truth.   LAWRENCE A. APPLEY

Precision of communication is important, more important than ever, in our era of hair-trigger balances, when a false, or misunderstood word may create as much disaster as a sudden thoughtless act.
JAMES THURBER

People may change their minds as often as their coats, and new sets of rules of conduct may be written every week.   LAMMOT duPONT

If the trade thinks the product is poor, if employee morale is low, if the organization is loaded with incompetents, all these unpleasant realities are often carefully screened from those in the top echelons.
PIERRE MARTINEAU

The only occasion when news need not be communicated is when disclosure would damage your competitive position.   E. J. THOMAS

How many communicators really understand the basic underlying principle of communication? How many well-conceived, well-planned programs of communication really consist of a one-way stream of information that inundates, and frustrates, and frequently irritates the poor individual on the receiving end? Remember, unless you are receiving as well as transmitting—unless you are getting a playback—you really aren't communicating at all.   DON G. MITCHELL

Communication is and should be hell fire and sparks as well as sweetness and light.   AMAN VIVIAN RAKOFF

Personal Communications

Listening and reading
are more important than
Talking and writing.

Doors were invented for the simple purpose of permitting discriminate entry.   PROFESSOR RAY E. BROWN

Nobody tells me anything.   JOHN GALSWORTHY

It was hard to communicate with you. You were always communicating with yourself—the line was busy.   JEAN KERR

I hate to look another human being in the eye and say, "No comment!"   ANDREW YOUNG

I don't want to be quoted, and don't quote me that I don't want to be quoted.   WINSTON BURDETT

Dr. Paul Rankin of Ohio State University undertook to find out how much time the average person spends in communications. He concluded: About 9 per cent in writing, 16 per cent in reading, 30 per cent in speaking and 45 per cent in listening. When I told the Ladyfriend she could save 30 per cent of her time by not talking, she said, 'Why bother? I already save 45 per cent by not listening.'   L. M. BOYD

The art of effective listening is essential to clear communication, and clear communication is necessary to management success. Since the biggest part of your job as an executive consists in getting things done through people, it will pay you to learn how to become a good listener if you aren't one already.   J. C. PENNEY

The best communicators are those who have managed to retain their infantile directness and resisted the crippling effects of education.
                                                      LEO ROSTEN

While enormous strides have been made in communications in recent years, there's still a lot to be said for the smile.   FRANKLIN JONES

Informal lines of communication are just as important as formal lines.
                                                      E. J. THOMAS

Extremists think "communication" means agreeing with them.
                                                      LEO ROSTEN

With three or more people there is something bold in the air: direct things get said which would frighten two people alone and conscious of each inch of their nearness to one another. To be three is to be in public—you feel safe.   ELIZABETH BOWEN

Reprove thy friend privately; commend him publicly.   SOLON

Have no friends equal to yourself.   CONFUCIUS

Let us have a care not to disclose our hearts to those who shut up theirs against us.   FRANCIS BEAUMONT

There is, indeed, no wild beast more to be dreaded than a communicative man having nothing to communicate. If you are civil to the voluble, they will abuse your patience; if brusque, your character.
                                                      JONATHAN SWIFT

Industrial Relations

If they "close the shop,"
It could be tit for tat;
The Company can stop
And then where are they at?

Industrial relations are like sexual relations. It's better between two consenting parties.   VIC FEATHER

No tin hat brigade of goose-stepping vigilantes or Bible babbling mob of blackguarding and corporation-paid scoundrels will prevent the onward march of labor.   JOHN L. LEWIS

The state of the Union depends largely on the state of the unions. ANON

Labor unions are the worst thing that ever struck the earth because they take away a man's independence.   HENRY FORD

Another fact of life that will not have escaped you is that, in this country, the twenty-four hour strike is like the twenty-four hour flu. You have to reckon on it lasting at least five days.   DENIS NORDEN

The unions have never forgiven God for recommending a 6-day week.
                                        ANON

Prophecy today is hardly the romantic business that it used to be. The old tools of the trade, like the sword, the hair shirt, and the long fast in the wilderness, have given way to more contemporary, mundane instruments of doom—the book, the picket, the petition, and the sit-in.
                                        JANE KRAMER

Collective bargaining is where management bargains and labor collects.
                                        ANON

I'm going to my cake-decorating class. I don't really want to, but we're electing a new secretary and it's like everything else: if the rank and file don't go, the militants take over.   ALAN BENNETT

Labor: One of the processes by which A acquires property of B.
                                        AMBROSE BIERCE

A red is any son of a bitch who wants thirty cents when we're paying
twenty-five.   JOHN STEINBECK

Everybody wants shorter hours. What's wrong with sixty minutes?
                                                           ANON

Unionism seldom, if ever, uses such power as it has to insure better
work: almost always it devotes a large part of that power to safeguarding
bad work.   HENRY LOUIS MENCKEN

Those that want a four-day week are not too conscientious about a five-
day week.   ANON

Always run from a knife and rush a gun.   JIMMY HOFFA

You can't mine coal without machine guns.   RICHARD MELLON

There is strength in union and even more strength in unions.   ANON

The workers have nothing to lose but their chains. They have a world to
gain. Workers of the world, unite.   KARL MARX

A steam shovel was digging an excavation when a union official stomped
in. He said: "A hundred men could be doing that job with shovels!" The
contractor agreed but added: "Why not a thousand men with tea-
spoons?"   ROBERT ORBEN

Strikes are contagious.   ANON

Automation and unions have led to a continuously shortened day for men
but the work day of housewives with children has remained constant.
                                               BEVERLY JONES

After God had finished the rattlesnake, the toad, the vampire, He had
some awful substance left with which He made a scab. JACK LONDON

Unions run by workers are like alcoholic homes run by alcoholics, a sure
recipe for tyranny.   ROY KERRIDGE

One of the chief arguments used in support of the policy of an open shop
is that every man has an inalienable and constitutional right to work. I
never found that in the Constitution. If a man has a constitutional right to

work, he ought to have a constitutional right to a job. A man has a right to work only if he can get a job, and he has also a right not to work.
CLARENCE DARROW

One way to avoid having industrial troubles is to avoid having industries.   DONALD ROBERT PERRY MARQUIS

I should like to see our country unionized to the hilt.
FRANK LLOYD WRIGHT

Before you can get action, you've got to have a crisis. And in any crisis, someone's nerve has got to crack. I always bet that I can hold out longer than the government or the operators.   JOHN L. LEWIS

Liberty is conforming to the majority.   HUGH SCANLON

There is no right to strike against the public safety by anybody, anywhere, anytime.   CALVIN COOLIDGE

There must be a division not only of profits, but a division also of responsibilities. We must insist upon labor sharing the responsibilities for the result of the business.   JUSTICE LOUIS D. BRANDEIS

In the first place, trade unions are about individuals, and the right of a man to answer back to his boss.   LEN MURRAY

Show me the country in which there are no strikes and I'll show you that country in which there is no liberty.   HEYWOOD BROUN

The growth of unions means far more than the substitution of collective bargaining for individual bargaining. It means that the United States is gradually shifting from a capitalistic community to a laboristic one— that is, to a community in which employees rather than business men are the strongest single influence.   SUMNER H. SLICHTER

It is essential that there should be organizations of labor. This is an era of organization. Capital organizes and therefore labor must organize.
THEODORE ROOSEVELT

Nobody wins a strike against schoolchildren, or against the sick, or against bus or subwayriders. We can avoid such strikes. The challenge is to improve collective bargaining—not to replace it.
THEODORE W. KNEEL

It is one of the characteristics of a free and democratic modern nation that it have free and independent labor unions.

FRANKLIN D. ROOSEVELT

With all their faults, trade unions have done more for humanity than any other organization of men that ever existed. They have done more for decency, for honesty, for education, for the betterment of the race, for the developing of character in man, than any other association of men.

CLARENCE DARROW

I believe in the dignity of labor, whether with head or hand; that the world owes no man a living, but that it owes every man an opportunity to make a living.   JOHN D. ROCKEFELLER

A U.S. labor leader of an earlier generation summed up labor's philosophy in one four-letter word: "More." Nowadays the philosophy might be summed up in two four-letter words: "Much more." At times, indeed, organized labor seems to be chasing the delusion that a society can consume more than it produces, and that everybody can prosper by beggaring his neighbor. But wage increases in excess of productivity or output per man-hour are inevitably followed by unemployment or price increases or both. And it is the unorganized, the unemployed and the aged who pay.   GILBERT BURCK

The idea which is popular with rich men, that industrial disputes would disappear if only the output of wealth were doubled, and every one were twice as well off, not only is refuted by all practical experience, but is in its very nature founded upon an illusion. For the question is not one of amounts but of proportions.   R. H. TAWNEY

If the managers of industry can develop some universal plan which will make labor not only well paid but happy in doing the work itself, one of the greatest possible boons to mankind will have been realized.

CHARLES M. SCHWAB

We demand that big business give the people a square deal; in return we must insist that when anyone engages in big business honestly endeavours to do right, he shall himself be given a square deal.

THEODORE ROOSEVELT

Despite our demonstrated capacity for cooperative teamwork, some among us seem to accept the shibboleth of an unbridgeable gap between those who hire and those who are employed... that for one side to profit, the other must be depressed. Such distorted doctrine is false and foreign to the American scene.   DWIGHT D. EISENHOWER

Our capitalism in the 80's and 90's was a buccaneer capitalism, and our labor leaders during the formative years of the American Federation of Labor were primitive tribal chieftains, each craft a tribe, who fought back with desperate guerrilla tactics.   BENJAMIN STOLBERG

There are the Trade-Unionists, once the oppressed, now the tyrants, whose selfish and sectional pretensions need to be bravely opposed.
JOHN MAYNARD KEYNES

If capitalism is fair, then unionism must be. If men have a right to capitalize their ideas and the resources of their country, then that implies the right of men to capitalize their labor.
FRANK LLOYD WRIGHT

We will have to distinguish more sharply, and especially in collective bargaining, between genuine questions of principle and matters which are really just questions of advantage. We should not wrap ourselves in a banner of so-called principle when we are really concerned only with economic advantage. And we should be prepared, on questions of genuine principle, to stand firm against the heaviest economic pressure.
JOHN L. McCAFFREY

The socialist or anarchist who seeks to overturn present conditions is to be regarded as attacking the foundation upon which civilization itself rests.... One who studies this subject will soon be brought face-to-face with the conclusion that upon the sacredness of property, civilization itself depends—the right of the laborer to his hundred dollars in the savings bank, and equally the legal right of the millionaire to his millions.   ANDREW CARNEGIE

Democratic capitalism, combined with industrial democracy, is unquestionably the best way of life for mankind.   DAVID J. McDONALD

Wealthy owners and all masters of labor should be mindful of this—that to exercise pressure upon the indigent and the destitute for the sake of gain, and to gather one's profit out of the need of another, is condemned by all laws, human and divine.   POPE LEO XIII

Both business and labor have fostered the notion that any form of mandatory settlement will inhibit genuine efforts to reach agreement through bargaining. Yet it is difficult to see why the prospect of arbitration should stymie fruitful bargaining any more than the prospect of formal resolution of any other area of human disagreement would stymie voluntary settlement. Why not say that outlawing of duels inhibits private settlement of personal disputes?   O. GLENN STAHL

Human Relations

People are the corporation,
* Not machinery and plant;*
But there is one complication,
* Some you lead and some you can't.*

The best guide to human relations is in the Bible—the Sermon on the Mount.   J. C. PENNEY

There is always an easy solution to every human problem—neat, plausible and wrong.   HENRY LOUIS MENCKEN

Good Human Relations are the best form of Industrial Relations. ANON

It's not the hundred-and-one problems of production and distribution that keep executives awake at night trying to solve them; it's the problems of working with people, the human problems of their jobs.
                                        THEODORE V. HOUSER

Behaviourism is a kind of flat-earth view of the mind.
                                        ARTHUR KOESTLER

The secret principle of human nature is the craving to be appreciated.
                                        WILLIAM JAMES

The rules of fair play require that a person be told where he stands and why.   ANON

I have a dream that one day this nation will rise up, live out the true meaning of its creed: we hold these truths to be self-evident, that all men are created equal.   REV. MARTIN LUTHER KING

The executive is expected to serve as a social worker but to abhor paternalism. ANON

Sociology is the science with the greatest number of methods and the least results. J. H. POINCARÉ

Rome owed much of her patriotism to her many festivals.
JEAN PAUL RICHTER

Personal relations are the important thing for ever and ever, and not this outer life of telegrams and anger. EDWARD MORGAN FORSTER

Any man who thinks he is going to be happy and prosperous by letting the Government take care of him should take a close look at the American Indian. ANON

If you improve workers' morale and strengthen their sense of belonging, you create a cooperative spirit that results in better work. E. J. THOMAS

I thought my group insurance plan was fine until I found out I couldn't collect unless the whole group is sick. LEOPOLD FECHTNER

Man is still the most inexpensive, nonlinear, all purpose computing system that is capable of being mass-produced by unskilled labor.
ANON

Almost all of our relationships begin, and most of them continue, as forms of mutual exploitation, a mental or physical barter, to be terminated when one or both parties run out of goods.
WYSTAN HUGH AUDEN

The employer puts his money into business and the workman his life. The one has as much right as the other to regulate that business.
CLARENCE S. DARROW

You can be social minded without being a socialist.
CHARLES E. WILSON

If the worker has a feeling of belonging, he will be much more content with his work. ANON

There's nothing so exhausting as the management of men, except the management of women. BENJAMIN DISRAELI

Nothing shakes the morale of an organization as much as the sudden lowering of the boom on an individual without prior notice to improve his deficiencies.   PROFESSOR RAY E. BROWN

It is important that employees identify with the company, that they are made to feel part of it and not just a number.   ANON

The voice of dissent must be heard.   HENRY FORD

There is little friendship in the world, and least of all between equals.
                                    SIR FRANCIS BACON

It is essential to have stated policies of recognition for jobs well done, rewards for ideas, a policy of promotion from within and news publicity for accomplishments.   HERMAN W. STEINKRAUS

God and the devil are an effort after specialization and division of labor.
                                    SAMUEL BUTLER

An unfulfilled vocation drains the colour from a man's entire existence.
                                    HONORE de BALZAC

Behaviourism has substituted for the erstwhile anthropomorphic view of the rat, a ratomorphic view of man.   ARTHUR KOESTLER

Contrary to the belief that workers are not interested in their company, most employees want more information relating to their role in the company.   E. J. THOMAS

A sense of duty is useful in work, but offensive in personal relations. People wish to be liked, not be endured with patient resignation.
                                    BERTRAND RUSSELL

I believe in the supreme worth of the individual, and in his right to life, liberty, and the pursuit of happiness.   JOHN D. ROCKEFELLER

The executive is supposed to play Freud but respect the privacy and dignity of the individual.   PROFESSOR RAY E. BROWN

Office and plant morale should be a continuous state. It should not be turned on and off from day to day according to the boss's mood. When a mere smile and a nod from the boss cause an unaccustomed ripple of happiness to flow over an office, that's a bad sign. It's a sign that up to that moment, the people had been tense, harassed, fearful, nervous, worried.   CHARLES S. DAVIS

Every manufacturer ought to remember that his fortune was not achieved by himself alone but by the cooperation of his workmen. He should acknowledge their rights to share the benefits of that which could not exist without their faithful performance of duty. Not until the capitalist is just enough to recognize this truth can he ever join a group of workmen and feel himself among his friends.   PETER COOPER

Human relations can be described as the integration of people into groups that can work together harmoniously and positively for the economic benefit and social satisfaction of all.
                                         HERMAN W. STEINKRAUS

What makes men happy is loving to do what they have to do. This is a principle on which society is founded.   HELVETIUS

The effort of boredom on a large scale in history is underestimated. It is a main cause of revolutions, and would soon bring to an end all the static Utopias and the farmyard civilization of the Fabians.
                                     DEAN WILLIAM RALPH INGE

In the field of modern business, so rich in opportunity for the exercise of man's finest and most varied mental faculties and moral qualities, mere money-making cannot be regarded as the legitimate end... since with the conduct of business human happiness or misery is inextricably interwoven.   JUSTICE LOUIS D. BRANDEIS

Make your people feel more important by taking a serious, personal interest in their work. Let them know that the measure of their success is also the measure of success of their company or department.
                                         THEODORE V. HOUSER

The fact is that the possession of a highly sensitive social conscience about large-scale issues is no guarantee whatever of reasonable conduct in private relations.   LEWIS HASTINGS

Advice

As long as you live,
   Advice, you'll perceive,
Is much better to give
   Than have to receive.

Advice is a drug in the market: the supply always exceeds the demand.
                                                    JOSH BILLINGS

A word of advice: don't give it!   ANON

Advice is what we ask for when we already know the answer but wish we
didn't.   ERICA JONG

Ask the young: they know everything!   JOSEPH JOUBERT

A good scare is worth more to a man than good advice.
                                          EDGAR WATSON HOWE

When we ask advice we are usually looking for an accomplice.
                                          MARQUIS de la GRANGE

Never take the advice of someone who has not had your kind of trouble.
                                              SIDNEY J. HARRIS

I realize that advice is worth what it costs—that is, nothing.
                                          DOUGLAS MacARTHUR

If someone gives you so-called good advice, do the opposite. You can be
sure it will be the right thing nine out of ten times.
                                          ANSELM FEUERBACH

How happily some people would live if they would only mind other
people's business as little as they mind their own!
                                  GEORG CHRISTOPH LICHTENBERG

Why must the phrase "It is none of my business" always be followed by
the word "but"?   ANON

I give myself sometimes admirable advice, but I am incapable of taking it.   LADY MARY WORTLEY MONTAGU

There are exceptions to all rules, but it seldom answers to follow the advice of an opponent.   BENJAMIN DISRAELI

It is always a silly thing to give advice, but to give good advice is absolutely fatal.   OSCAR WILDE

No vice is so bad as advice.   MARIE DRESSLER

Never trust the advice of a man in difficulties.   AESOP

People who are sensible enough to give good advice are usually sensible enough to give none.   EDEN PHILLPOTTS

The best way to find out if a man has done something is to advise him to do it. He will not be able to resist boasting that he has done it without being advised.   COMTESSE DIANE

Never give advice unless asked.   GERMAN PROVERB

Ask your neighbor only about things you know better. His advice might be valuable.   KARL KRAUS

Less advice and more hands.   GERMAN PROVERB

If a man loves to give advice, it is a sure sign that he himself wants it.   LORD HALIFAX

Nobody can give you wiser advice than yourself.   CICERO

Advice is not disliked because it is advice; but because so few people know how to give it.   LEIGH HUNT

It was a high counsel that I once heard given to a young person, "Always do what you are afraid to do."   RALPH WALDO EMERSON

In giving advice, seek to help, not please, your friend.   SOLON

We may give advice, but we can never prompt behavior.
                    FRANCOIS DUC de la ROCHEFOUCAULD

This is the gist of what I know:
Give advice and buy a foe.   PHYLLIS McGINLEY

As a grown up man you should know better than to go round advising
people.   BERTOLT BRECHT

Good advice is one of those injuries which a good man ought, if possible,
to forgive, but at all events to forget at once.   HORACE SMITH

Advice is always a confession.   ANDRE MAUROIS

We ask advice, but we mean approbation. CHARLES CALEB COLTON

Just as I do not ask advice, I rarely give it. If my advice is not often
called for, still less is it followed. I know of no public or private business
which it has corrected or bettered.   MICHEL de MONTAIGNE

Before giving advice we must have secured its acceptance, or rather,
have made it desired.   FREDERIC AMIEL

Your ears will always lead you right, but you must know why.
                                              ANTON von WEBERN

The advice of friends must be received with a judicious reserve; we must
not give ourselves up to it and follow it blindly, whether right or wrong.
                                              PIERRE CHARRON

There are some men who turn a deaf ear to reason and good advice, and
wilfully go wrong for fear of being controlled. JEAN de la BRUYERE

Understanding People

Again
I finds
Ten men
Ten minds.

People have one thing in common: they are all different.
                                              ROBERT ZEND

Most men are like eggs, too full of themselves to hold anything else.
                                                        JOSH BILLINGS

Monkeys are superior to men in this: when a monkey looks into a mirror,
he sees a monkey.   MALCOLM de CHAZAL

An unlearned carpenter of my acquaintance once said in my hearing:
"There is very little difference between one man and another, but what
there is is very important.   WILLIAM JAMES

There's a wonderful family called Stein,
There's Gert, and there's Epp and there's Ein:
Gert's poems are bunk,
Epp's statues are junk,
And no one can understand Ein.   ANON

Some folk are wise, and some are otherwise.
                                        TOBIAS GEORGE SMOLLETT

We do not learn to know men through their coming to us. To find out what
sort of persons they are, we must go to them.
                                        JOHANN WOLFGANG von GOETHE

It seems a pity that psychology should have destroyed all our knowledge
of human nature.   GILBERT KEITH CHESTERTON

There are two kinds of people: those who don't do what they want to do,
so they write down in a diary about what they haven't done, and those
who haven't time to write about it because they're out doing it.
                        RICHARD FLOURNOY and LEWIS R. FOSTER

The trouble with business is it's full of people. A machine will never go
off in a corner and sulk—but people will. A machine will never make a
mistake—but people will. A machine will never show up late for work,
take time off, leave early or argue with the boss—but people do.
                                                JOHN McCAFFERY

There are people who are too stupid to have prejudices.
                                                EGON FRIEDELL

Some people seem as if they can never have been children, and others
seem as if they could never be anything else.
                                        GEORGE DENNISON PRENTICE

Almost every person, if you will believe himself, holds quite a different theory of life from the one on which he is patently acting.

ROBERT LOUIS STEVENSON

People don't change, they only become more so.

JOHN BRIGHT-HOLMES

If you choose to represent the various parts in life by holes upon a table, of different shapes—some circular, some triangular, some square, some oblong—and the persons acting these parts by bits of wood of similar shapes, we shall generally find that the triangular person has got into the square hole, the oblong into the triangular, and a square person has squeezed himself into the round hole.   SYDNEY SMITH

Men have a trick of coming up to what is expected of them, good or bad.

JACOB RIIS

It is only when we are misunderstood by others that we really understand ourselves.   VAN WYCK BROOKS

People only see what they are prepared to see.

RALPH WALDO EMERSON

It is always safe to assume that people are more subtle and less sensitive than they seem.   ERIC HOFFER

Fools and wise men are equally harmless. It is the half-fools and the half-wise that are dangerous.   JOHANN WOLFGANG von GOETHE

It is only in the country that we can get to know a person or a book.

CYRIL CONNOLLY

Emperors, kings, artisans, peasants, big people, little people, at bottom we are all alike and all the same; all just alike on the inside, and when our clothes are off, nobody can tell which of us is which. MARK TWAIN

It is no wonder that people were so horrible when they started life as children.   KINGSLEY AMIS

In the study of Man it is easier to understand the species than the individual.   FRANCOIS DUC de la ROCHEFOUCAULD

Friendship is like money, easier made than kept. SAMUEL BUTLER

Gratitude preserves old friendships and procures new.
                                        THOMAS FULLER

Keep strong, if possible. In any case, keep cool. Have unlimited
patience. Never corner an opponent, and always assist him to save his
face. Put yourself in his shoes—so as to see things through his eyes.
Avoid self-righteousness like the devil—nothing is so self-blinding.
                                        B. H. LIDDELL HART

The man who desires to improve a human being must begin by
appreciating him.   ROMANO GUARDINI

A real superior man is like a bell. If you ring it, it rings, and if you don't,
it don't, as the saying is.   BERTOLT BRECHT

Most people are hidden most of the time, their appearances are brief and
controlled, their movements secret, the outlines of their lives obscured.
                                        JONATHAN RABAN

People are always sincere. They change sincerities, that's all.
                                        TRISTAN BERNARD

Each of us really understands in others only those feelings he is capable
of producing himself.   ANDRE GIDE

If you do not understand a man you cannot crush him. And if you do
understand him, very probably you will not.
                                        GILBERT KEITH CHESTERTON

Few men are of one plain, decided color; most are mixed, shaded and
blended, and vary as much, from different situations, as changeable
silks do from different lights.   EARL of CHESTERFIELD

We would know mankind better if we were not so anxious to resemble
one another.   JOHANN WOLFGANG von GOETHE

People are made alarming by one's dread of their unremitting, purposeful continuity.   ELIZABETH ARDEN

For Jack's good life to certify,
Nor friends, nor strangers can be got:
Those who don't know him, know not why;
Those who do know him, I know why not.   EDMUND FULLER

To observe a man, observe how he wins his object, rather than how he loses it; for when we fail our pride supports us, when we succeed, it betrays us.   CHARLES CALEB COLTON

A child-like man is not a man whose development has been arrested; on the contrary, he is a man who has given himself a chance of continuing to develop long after most adults have muffled themselves in the cocoon of middle-aged habit and convention.   ALDOUS LEONARD HUXLEY

Teach me to feel another's woe,
To hide the fault I see;
That mercy I to others show,
That mercy show to me.   ALEXANDER POPE

Working with People

> If you do to others
>   What you would like them
>   To do to you,
>   Do not expect others
>   To do to you
>   What you do to them.

Working with people is difficult, but not impossible.
                                        PETER F. DRUCKER

There are people whom one should like very well to drop, but would not wish to be dropped by.   SAMUEL JOHNSON

All men are equal—all men, that is to say, who possess umbrellas.
                                        EDWARD MORGAN FOSTER

I am free of all prejudices. I hate everyone equally.   W. C. FIELDS

People are too durable, that's their main trouble. They can do too much to themselves, they last too long.   BERTOLT BRECHT

It is less dangerous to treat most man badly than to treat them too well.
                              FRANCOIS DUC de la ROCHEFOUCAULD

Nothing between human beings is one to three. In fact, I long ago came
to the conclusion that all life is six to five against. DAMON RUNYON

Don't judge any man until you have walked two moons in his moccasins.
                                                     INDIAN PROVERB

You can't have everything in one person.   ANON

That all men are equal is a proposition which, at ordinary times, no sane
individual has ever given this assent. ALDOUS LEONARD HUXLEY

There are four sorts of men:
He who knows not and knows not he knows not:
    He is a fool—shun him;
He who knows not and knows he knows not:
    He is simple—teach him.
He who knows and knows not he knows:
    He is asleep —wake him.
He who knows and knows he knows:
    He is wise—follow him.   LADY BURTON

It is so pleasant to come across people more stupid than ourselves. We
love them at once for being so.   JEROME K. JEROME

No matter how much work a man can do, no matter how engaging his
personality may be, he will not advance far in business if he cannot work
through others.   JOHN CRAIG

Almost all of our relationships begin and most of them continue as forms
of mutual exploitation, a mental or physical barter, to be terminated
when one or both parties run out of goods. WYSTAN HUGH AUDEN

I don't believe in the goodness of disagreeable people.
                                                    ORVILLE DEWEY

Not all of those to whom we do good love us, neither do all those to whom
we do evil hate us.   JOSEPH ROUX

You never know till you try to reach them how accessible men are, but
you must approach each man by the right door.
                                          HENRY WARD BEECHER

He who thinks he can find in himself the means of doing without others is much mistaken; but he who thinks that others cannot do without him is still more mistaken.   FRANCOIS DUC de la ROCHEFOUCAULD

Therefore all things whatsoever ye would that men should do to you, do ye even to to them.   *ST. MATTHEW*

Judge a person by the way he treats somebody who can be of no use to him.   ANON

Grieve not that men do not know you: grieve that you do not know men.
                                                            CONFUCIUS

Draw from others the lesson that may profit yourself.   TERENCE

When one is helping another, both are strong.   GERMAN PROVERB

The man who can put himself in place of the other man, who can understand the working of other minds, need never worry about what the future has in store for him.   OWEN D. YOUNG

To get the best out of our associates, we must know their problems and aspirations and take a genuine interest in them.
                                                 LAWRENCE A. APPLEY

Jam today, and men aren't at their most exciting: Jam tomorrow, and one often sees them at their noblest.   CHARLES PERCY SNOW

The greatness of a man can nearly always be measured by his willingness to be kind.   ANON

Among giants, try and be a dwarf; among dwarfs, try and be a giant, but among equals, try and be an equal.   STANISLAW J. LEC

Alienation from one's self not only arrests one's growth as a person; it also tends to make a farce out of one's relationship with people.
                                                    SIDNEY JOURARD

If your body were to be put at the disposal of a stranger you would certainly be indignant. Then aren't you ashamed of putting your mind at the disposal of chance acquaintance by allowing yourself to be upset if he happens to abuse you.   EPICTETUS

I will believe in anything rather than any man's consistency.
MICHEL DE MONTAIGNE

No one of you is a believer until he desires for his brother that which he desires for himself. SUNNAH MOHAMMEDAN LAW

When you have found out the prevailing passion of any man, remember never to trust him where that passion is concerned.
EARL of CHESTERFIELD

The bonds that unite another person to ourself exist only in our mind.
MARCEL PROUST

The vain man hates his like, the exceptional man seeks out his.
JEAN PAUL RICHTER

Everybody, my friend, everybody lives for something better to come. That's why we want to be considerate of every man. Who knows what's in him, why he was born and what he can do. MAXIM GORKY

Speak the truth by all means; be bold and fearless in your rebuke of error, and in your keener rebuke of wrongdoing; but be human, and loving, and gentle, and brotherly, the while. W. N. PUNSHON

It is axiomatic that we should all think of ourselves as being more sensitive than other people because, when we are insensitive in our dealings with others, we cannot be aware of it at the time: conscious insensitivity is a self-contradiction. WYSTAN HUGH AUDEN

It is safer to offend certain men than it is to oblige them; for as proof that they owe you nothing, they seek recourse in hatred.
LUCIUS ANNAEUS SENECA

Believe nothing against another but on good authority; and never report what may hurt another, unless it be a greater hurt to some other to conceal it. WILLIAM PENN

When we come to judge others it is not by ourselves as we really are that we judge them, but by an image that we have formed of ourselves from which we have left out everything that offends our vanity or would discredit us in the eyes of the world.
WILLIAM SOMERSET MAUGHAM

Selection

If they look bad,
They are.
If they look good,
They may be.

Anyone can pick a loser.   ANON

Always verify your references.   MARTIN JOSEPH ROUTH

You don't set a fox to watching the chickens just because he has a lot of experience in the hen house.   HARRY S. TRUMAN

Vote for the man who promises least—he'll be the least disappointing.
BERNARD BARUCH

We should all be obliged to appear before a board every five years, and justify our existence to its satisfaction on pain of liquidation.
GEORGE BERNARD SHAW

Battle fatigue in business could be the result of the right man in the wrong job, but more likely the wrong man in the right job and most often the wrong man in the wrong job.   ROBERT N. McMURPHY

As I grow older, I pay less attention to what men say—I just watch what they do.   ANDREW CARNEGIE

Rotten wood cannot be saved.   CHINESE PROVERB

It is easier to make a businessman out of a musician than a musician out of a businessman.   GODDARD LIEBERSON

Many top businessmen would be out of a job if they had to take personality and capability tests given applicants for employment or promotion in their own companies.   SAMUEL FEINBERG

When a top executive is selecting his key associates, there are only two qualities for which he should be willing to pay almost any price—taste and judgment. Almost everything else can be bought by the yard.
JOHN GARDNER

A good way to judge a man is by what he says, a better way is by what he does, and the best way is by what he gives.   EVAN ESAR

When you send a clerk on business to a distant province, a man of rigid morals is not your best choice.   IHARA SAIKUKU

You can't always tell what makes a man tick until you meet his wife. She may be the works.   FRANKLIN P. JONES

There's small choice in rotten apples.   WILLIAM SHAKESPEARE

Judge a man by his questions rather than his answers.
           FRANCOIS VOLTAIRE

What they have done is of more interest than what they have been.
           JEAN RACINE

O give us the man who sings at his work!   THOMAS CARLYLE

The person selected must always be the best available and a decision on friendship is wrong.   ANON

I choose the likely man in preference to the rich man; I want a man without money rather than money without a man.   THEMISTOCLES

No duty the Executive had to perform was so trying as to put the right man in the right place.   THOMAS JEFFERSON

We ought not to judge of men's merits by their qualifications, but by the use they make of them.   PIERRE CHARRON

In a professional once engaged, the performance of the job comes first.
           GARSON KANIN

It is an article of faith in my creed to pick the man who does not take himself seriously, but does take his work seriously.
           MICHAEL C. CAHILL

Give us men to match our mountains,
Give us men to match our plains:
Men with empires in their purpose
And new eras in their brains.
           H. T. MILLER

Recognizing Personal Traits

A diagnosis
Pathogenic:
That two in one is
Schizophrenic.

There may be said to be two classes of people in the world: those who constantly divide the people of the world into two classes, and those who do not.   ROBERT BENCHLEY

People who are much older than they look seldom have much intelligence.   GEORG CHRISTOPH LICHTENBERG

Just when you're beginning to think pretty well of people, you run across somebody who puts sugar on sliced tomatoes.   WILL CUPPY

Experience teaches you that the man who looks you straight in the eye, particularly if he adds a firm handshake, is hiding something.
                    CLIFTON FADIMAN

Those who talk of the mine, the mill, the factory as if they were inherently inhuman and horrible are those who never have known the miner, the weaver, or the steel or iron worker.   IDA TARBELL

Some people fall for everything and stand for nothing.   ANON

Men their rights and nothing more; women their rights and nothing less.
                    SUSAN B. ANTHONY

The higher the voice, the smaller the intellect.   ERNEST NEWMAN

If a young or middle-aged man, when leaving a company, does not recollect where he laid his hat, it is nothing; but if the same inattention is discovered in an old man, people will shrug their shoulders, and say, 'His memory is going.'   SAMUEL JOHNSON

A great big good-for-nothing is a great big good-for-nothing—but he does not constitute a species.   DENIS DIDEROT

One man's Mede is another man's Persian.   GEORGE S. KAUFMAN

The idealist walks on his toes, the materialist on his talons.
MALCOLM de CHAZAL

Some men are born mediocre, some men achieve mediocrity, and some men have mediocrity thrust upon them. With Major Major it has been all three.   JOSEPH HELLER

Lovers of "Humanity" generally hate people and children and keep parrots or puppy dogs.   ROY CAMPBELL

He's a modest little man with much to be modest about.
SIR WINSTON CHURCHILL

There are, I have discovered, two kinds of people in this world: those who long to be understood and those who long to be misunderstood. It is the irony of life that neither is gratified.   CARL van VECHTEN

The goodness of some people is the worst thing about them.
EDGAR WATSON HOWE

There are no uninteresting things, there are only uninterested people.
GILBERT KEITH CHESTERTON

Men may be divided almost any way we please, but I have found the most useful distinction to be made between those who devote their lives to conjugating the verb "to be" and those who spend their lives conjugating the verb "to have."   SIDNEY J. HARRIS

Humanity, I love you cause when you're hard up, you pawn your intelligence to buy a drink.   EDWARD ESTLIN CUMMINGS

Men's natures are alike; it is their habits that carry them far apart.
CONFUCIUS

I don't think being well rounded is particularly important. I would rather see people with a cutting edge on them.   BARNABY KEENEY

Men who are "orthodox" when they are young are in danger of being middle-aged all their lives.   WALTER LIPPMAN

People, like boats, toot loudest when they're in a fog.   ANON

Men of cold passions have quick eyes.   NATHANIEL HAWTHORNE

An idealist believes the short run doesn't count. A cynic believes the long run doesn't matter. A realist believes that what is done or left undone in the short run determines the long run. SYDNEY HARRIS

I will have nothing to do with a man who can blow hot and cold with the same breath.   AESOP

A person I knew used to divide human beings into three categories: those who prefer having nothing to hide rather than being obliged to lie, those who prefer lying to having nothing to hide, and finally those who like both lying and the hidden.   ALBERT CAMUS

An intelligent person often talks with his eyes; a shallow man often swallows with his ears.   MR. TUT-TUT

Tell me what you brag about and I'll tell you what you lack.   SPANISH
                                                            PROVERB

Watch out for the one who removes a loose hair from your clothes. ANON

He did not know that a keeper is only a poacher turned outside in, and a poacher is a keeper turned inside out.   CHARLES KINGSLEY

Humanity is composed but of two categories, the invalids and the nurses.   WALTER SICKERT

There are persons who, when they cease to shock us, cease to interest us.   FRANCIS HERBERT BRADLEY

Let the world beware of the man who hates himself, for he will perpetually revenge himself upon his neighbors. DAVID L. NORTON

Half of us are blind, few of us feel, and we are all deaf.
                                                      WILLIAM OSLER

It is fair to judge peoples by the rights they will sacrifice most for.
                                                      CLARENCE DAY

What the superior man seeks is in himself. What the mean man seeks is in others.   CONFUCIUS

A man who is sure to cause injuries to be done to him wherever he goes is almost as great an evil and inconvenience as if he were himself the wrongdoer.   SIR HENRY TAYLOR

The obstinacy of human beings is exceeded only by the obstinacy of
inanimate objects.   ALEXANDER CHASE

You see, I always divide people into two groups. Those who live by what
they know to be a lie, and those who live by what they believe, falsely, to
be the truth.   CHRISTOPHER HAMPTON

There is a freemasonry among the dull by which they recognize and are
sociable with the dull, as surely as a correspondent tact in men of
genius.   RALPH WALDO EMERSON

Watch what people are cynical about, and one can often discover what
they lack.   HARRY EMERSON FOSDICK

The fact remains that human nature has not changed and does not
change, that inherent human beliefs stay the same, that fundamental
rules of human conduct continue to hold.   LAMMOT duPONT

IX BACKGROUND

Commuting

Those who're behind
In the hierarch
Never can find
A good place to park.

I can't even enjoy a blade of grass unless I know there's a subway handy.
FRANK O'HARA

It's really great, sitting in your car listening to them saying: "Traffic is light and moving freely"—and you haven't had your foot off the brake in fifteen minutes!... For him up at 1,800 feet, it's moving freely. For you, it's a parking lot with tolls!
ROBERT ORBEN

What is known as congestion on the underground is called atmosphere in a nightclub.
ANON

Walking isn't a lost art—one must, by some means, get to the garage.
EVAN ESAR

The suburbs are merely vast dormitories, where a man may sleep in comparatively pure air while his office is being washed.
WILLIAM McFEE

Many people advocate mass transit for the other person so they themselves will be able to enjoy riding on congestion-free expressways.
ERIC SEVAREID

Rough-hour traffic.   ANON

A commuter is one who never knows how a show comes out because he has to leave early to catch a train to get him back to the country in time to catch a train to bring him back to the city.   OGDEN NASH

It is easier to find a travelling companion than to get rid of one.
ART BUCHWALD

A man's home is his wife's castle.   ALEXANDER CHASE

The only way of catching a train is to miss the one before.
GILBERT KEITH CHESTERTON

The crisis in human dignity.... I've been spat on, vomited on, pushed and shoved, delayed three hours in a fire, and wound up on a D train which became an F train in midflight.   HAROLD M. PROSHANSKY

It costs you the same to live in the city as it does outside. What you save on carfare you spend on locks.   ANON

Suburbs are things to come into the city from.   ART LINKLETTER

There's one nice thing about driving a train. No one's gonna put a gun at your head and say, "Havana."   E. B. SELOVER

A million lemmings can't be wrong.   ANON

He who hesitates loses the place to park his car.
HERBERT V. PROCHNOW

If you can do four years on the New Haven, you won't even notice it when you crack up.   ANON

If you take off your right-hand glove in very cold weather, the key will be in your left-hand pocket.   MARTIN QUIGLEY

Most commuters are as untalkative as native Vermonters. You have your paper, and he has his. I remember a short story about a commuter who used to admire the girl who took the same train as his for twelve years, but never picked her up.   MAX LERNER

Think about all those people in automobiles, driving about with their debts.   ELIZABETH HARDWICK

When you ride the subway twice a day, it's difficult to think of the immortal soul.   ANON

Genius cried the commuter,
As he ran for the 8.13,
Consists of an infinite capacity
For catching trains.   CHRISTOPHER MORLEY

To me the outdoors is what you must pass through in order to get from your apartment into a taxicab.   FRAN LEBOWITZ

There are two classes of travel—first class and with children.
                        ROBERT BENCHLEY

Mass transportation is doomed to failure in North America because a person's car is the only place where he can be alone and think.
                        MARSHALL McLUHAN

Once a man would spend a week patiently waiting if he missed a stage coach, but now he rages if he misses the first section of a revolving door.
                        SIMEON STRUNSKY

Very few can keep their hands in their pockets while giving directions.
                        ANON

One look at the rush-hour jam in the subway and you know why no one rides it any more.   JOHN CIARDI

The man who tips a quarter every time he stops for gasoline is giving away annually the cost of lubricating his car.   J. PAUL GETTY

I figure three more helicopters and we'll need cars on the ground advising them!   ROBERT ORBEN

Commuter—one who spends his life

In riding to and from his wife;
A man who shaves and takes a train
And then rides back to shave again.   ELWYN BROOKS WHITE

In a subway you not only learn to think on your feet but on other people's.
                                                              ANON

There are men in New York who ride the subways but do not want it
generally known. The impulse is that the subways are for proles and the
people of status travel only by cab, or perhaps once in a while by bus.
                                                          TOM WOLFE

The other line always moves faster.   BARBARA ETTORE

Jet lag affects you less when you fly west than when you fly east, and less
than either when you fly north or south.   ANON

You always bump into someone you haven't seen for an age when you are
looking your worst.   FIONA PUREFOY

Home is the place where, when you have to go there, they have to take
you in.   ROBERT FROST

On the evening bus, the tense pinched faces of young file clerks and
elderly secretaries tell us more than we care to know. STUDS TERKEL

They stand like infantry at dawn waiting to be shipped to the front.
                                              ALEX SHOUMATOFF

Every year it takes less time to fly across the Atlantic, and more time to
drive to the office.   ANON

Commuters give the city its tidal restlessness; natives give it solidity and
continuity, but the settlers give it passion. ELWYN BROOKS WHITE

The alarm clock rings and to life's lofty duel I rise like a rocket—just out
of fuel.   ANON

Father, dear Father, come home with me now!
The clock on the steeple strikes one.
You said you were coming right home from the shop
As soon as your day's work was done.   HENRY CLAY WORK

It is incredible what a difference it makes to one's feelings towards the
whole human race when one is treated with politeness and kindness in
buses, trains, trams, subways, ferries, stores, shops, and streets.

                                        JOHN COWPER POWYS

Environment

The relationship may end,
When you do business with a friend;
The true atmosphere of trade
Is with strangers better made.

People of the same trade seldom meet together, even for merriment and
diversion, but the conversation ends in a conspiracy against the public,
or in some contrivance to raise prices.   ADAM SMITH

Job enrichment has been around for sixty years. It's been successful
every time it has been tried, but industry is not interested.

                                        PETER DRUCKER

Future archeologists specializing in our culture will divide the twentieth
century into two groups called Beercan Culture I (tin) and II (alumi-
num).   LUCIEN BRUSH

If living conditions don't stop improving in this country, we're going to
run out of humble beginnings for our great men. RUSSELL P. ASKUE

If we do more with less, our resources will be adequate to take care of
everybody.   R. BUCKMINSTER FULLER

This will never be a civilized country until we expend more money for
books than we do for chewing gum.   ELBERT HUBBARD

You say you haven't got a club, young feller? Where the devil do you
relieve yourself, then?   LAURENCE MEYNELL

If the energy crisis forces us to diminish automobile use in the cities,
stops us from building highways and covering the country with concrete

and asphalt, forces us to rehabilitate the railroads, causes us to invest in mass transportation and limits the waste of electrical energy, one can only assume that the Arab nations and the big oil companies have united to save the American republic.   JOHN KENNETH GALBRAITH

That's what show business is—sincere insincerity.   BENNY HILL

It is bad economy to bring a man through a quarter of a century of training and then when his chance comes have him added to the casualties listed in the next Heart Fund campaign merely because he was not given working conditions suited to his responsibility.
CLARENCE B. RANDALL

A cocktail party is a device for paying off obligations to people you don't want to invite to dinner.   CHARLES MERRILL SMITH

The more the citizen is trained in the consumption of packaged goods and services, the less effective he seems to become in shaping his environment.   IVAN ILLICH

One of the most pleasurable moments in air travel is the one when you arrive at the baggage claim location and spot your luggage.
O. A. BATTISTA

The business schools in the United States Universities, set up less than half a century ago, have been preparing well trained clerks.
PETER F. DRUCKER

Two of a trade seldom agree.   *Ray's Oriverbs*

The businessman is coming to realize that education is to business what fertilizer is to farming.   W. H. PILLSBURY

Pollution is nothing but resources we're not harvesting.
R. BUCKMINSTER FULLER

The young men of today seem mostly to be interested in the manner rather than the matter.   ALICE B. TOKLAS

How happy some people would be if they troubled themselves as little about other people's business as they do about their own.
GEORG CHRISTOPH LICHTENBERG

You are not here merely to make a living. You are here in order to enable the world to live more amply, with greater vision, with a finer spirit of hope and achievement. You are here to enrich the world, and you impoverish yourself if you forget the errand.   WOODROW WILSON

Industrial mankind can be likened to irresponsible tenants in a rented house. We've been burning up the furniture, woodwork and food supplies to keep the place warm because we've been too irresponsible, and lazy to figure out how to work the central heating.
                                        HENRY KING STANFORD

I am not quite sure what the advantage is in having a few more dollars to spend if the air is too dirty to breathe, the water too polluted to drink, the commuters are losing out in the struggle to get in and out of the city, the streets are filthy, and the schools so bad that the young perhaps stay away, and the hoodlums roll citizens for some of the dollars they saved in the tax out   JOHN KENNETH GALBRAITH

Except during the nine months before he draws his first breath, no man manages his affairs as well as a tree does. GEORGE BERNARD SHAW

Small rooms discipline the mind; large ones distract it.
                                        LEONARDO DA VINCI

The great companies did not know that the line between hunger and anger is a thin line.   JOHN STEINBECK

Take the so-called standard of living. What do most people mean by "living"? They don't mean living. They mean the latest and closest plural approximation to singular prenatal passivity which science, in its finite but unbounded wisdom, has succeeded in selling their wives.
                                    EDWARD ESTLIN CUMMINGS

A man in business must put up many affronts if he loves his own quiet.
                                        WILLIAM PENN

Live together like brothers and do business like strangers.
                                        ARABIC PROVERB

Industrialism is the systematic exploitation of wasting assets . . . progress is merely an acceleration in the rate of that exploitation. Such prosperity as we have known up to the present is the consequence of rapidly spending the planet's irreplaceable capital.
                                    ALDOUS LEONARD HUXLEY

Bucking the Trend

Bucking the trend
Is just not allowed,
If you want to spend
Your life with the crowd.

I'd much rather have that fellow inside my tent pissing out, than outside my tent pissing in. **LYNDON BAINES JOHNSON**

They tell me I often go out on a limb. Well that's where I like to be.
HENRY J. KAISER

The minority is always right. **HENRIK IBSEN**

If you feed people just with revolutionary slogans they will listen today, they will listen tomorrow, they will listen the day after tomorrow, but on the fourth day they will say "To hell with you!" **NIKITA KHRUSHCHEV**

Don't be so inde-goddam-pendent. **BILL ROPER**

I'm the one that's got to die when it's time for me to die, so let me live my life the way I want to. **JIMI HENDRIX**

I think it is better to be one-sided than no-sided. **A. C. BENSON**

All reactionaries are paper tigers. **MAO TSE-TUNG**

And the only way to avoid playing the game is never to belong to a club, class, set, or trade union. As soon as you do, you're accepting someone else's rules, and as soon as you do that, you start looking down on the other chap with different rules. **CHARLOTTE BINGHAM**

A radical is a person whose left hand does not know what his other left hand is doing. **BERNARD ROSENBERG**

God is the only one who is perfectly independent. **NOAH WEBSTER**

One revolution is like one cocktail, it just gets you organized for the next. **WILL ROGERS**

Don't just stand there—undo something.   MURRAY WEIDENBAUM

I think Dostoevsky was right, that every human being must have a point at which he stands against the culture, where he says, this is me and the damned world can go to hell.   ROLLO MAY

The individual is always mistaken.   RALPH WALDO EMERSON

When a man makes up his mind to become a rascal he should examine himself closely and see if he isn't better constructed for a fool.
                    JOSH BILLINGS

People are much too solemn about things. I'm all for sticking pins into episcopal behinds.   ALDOUS LEONARD HUXLEY

A radical is a man with both feet firmly planted in the air.
                    FRANKLIN ROOSEVELT

The man who threatens the world is always ridiculous: for the world can easily go on without him, and, in a short time, it will cease to miss him.
                    SAMUEL JOHNSON

We might define an eccentric as a man who is a law unto himself, and a crank as one who, having determined what the law is, insists on laying it down for others.   LOUIS KRONENBERGER

He who imagines he can do without the world deceives himself much; but he who fancies the world cannot do without him is still more mistaken.   FRANCOIS DUC de la ROCHEFOUCAULD

No one can go on being a rebel too long without turning into an autocrat.
                    LAWRENCE DURRELL

There is not enough darkness in all the world to put out the light of even one small candle.   ROBERT ALDEN

The nail that sticks out is hammered down.   JAPANESE PROVERB

If a man is a minority of one, we lock him up.
                    OLIVER WENDELL HOLMES

Every generation revolts against its fathers and makes friends with its grandfathers.   LEWIS MUMFORD

All unusual actions are liable to sinister interpretation.
MICHEL de MONTAIGNE

Commonplace people have an answer for everything and nothing ever surprises them.　FERDINAND VICTOR EUGENE DELACROIX

How glorious it is—and also how painful—to be an exception.
ALFRED de MUSSETT

The simple man everywhere is apt to see whatever differs from himself as an affront, a challenge and a menace.　　W. J. CASH

We never reflect how pleasant it is to ask for nothing.
LUCIUS ANNAEUS SENECA

If you act in your own interest, others will respect you more and your own self-esteem will be higher than if you do other people's bidding and see yourself trapped or coerced.　　ARNOLD LAZARUS

Follow your own bent, no matter what people say.　　KARL MARX

Whatever little we have gained, we have gained by agitation, while we have uniformly lost by moderation.　　DANIEL O'CONNELL

Insolent ones are never without wounds.　　TURKISH PROVERB

It is a bad cause, that none dares speak in.　　EDMUND FULLER

We are less hurt by the contempt of fools than by the lukewarm approval of men of intelligence.　　MARQUIS de VAUVENARGUES

The downright fanatic is nearer to the heart of things than the cool and slippery disputant.　　EDWIN HUBBELL CHAPIN

It is possible for a single individual to defy the whole might of an unjust empire to save his honour, his religion his soul, and lay the foundation for that empire's fall or its regeneration.　　MAHATMA GANDHI

Let all your views in life be directed to a solid, however moderate, independence: without it no man can be happy nor even honest. JUNIUS

Praise

There's one type of praise
You feel in the gut;
It ends with a phrase
That starts with a "but."

Some fellows pay a compliment like they expect a receipt.
                              FRANK McKINNEY HUBBARD

So long as men praise you, you can only be sure that you are not yet on
your own true path but on someone else's.
                              FRIEDRICH WILHELM NIETZSCHE

The movies are the only business where you can go out front and applaud
yourself.   WILL ROGERS

Kind words will never die—neither will they buy groceries.
                              EDGAR WILSON NYE

The advantage of doing one's praising for oneself is that one can lay it on
so thick and exactly in the right places.   SAMUEL BUTLER

Once in a century a man may be ruined, or made insufferable by praise.
But surely once in a minute something generous dies for want of it.
                              JOHN MASEFIELD

Do not trust to the cheering, for those very persons would shout as much
if you and I were going to be hanged.   OLIVER CROMWELL

I have always said that if I were a rich man I would employ a professional
praiser.   SIR OSBERT SITWELL

I will praise any man that will praise me. WILLIAM SHAKESPEARE

Praise makes good men better and bad men worse. THOMAS FULLER

The trouble with most of us is that we would rather be ruined by praise
than saved by criticism.   REV. NORMAN VINCENT PEALE

He who praises you for what you lack wishes to take from you what you have. DON JUAN MANUEL

It's more than magnificent—it's mediocre. SAMUEL GOLDWYN

When we admire somebody we like to hear him praised by others—but not too much. GERALD BRENNAN

The best thing to do behind a person's back is pat it. FRANKLIN P. JONES

He who praises everybody praises nobody. SAMUEL JOHNSON

There's no praise to beat the sort you can put in your pocket. JEAN BAPTISTE MOLIERE

Encouragement after censure is as the sun after a shower. JOHANN WOLFGANG von GOETHE

An industrial worker would sooner have a 5 note but a countryman must have praise. RONALD BLYTHE

Soldiers usually win the battles, and generals get the credit for them. NAPOLEON BONAPARTE

Financial rewards are one of the most concrete ways there are to praise a person and show him you mean what you say. THEODORE V. HOUSER

Praise should be directed at the performance and not to the person. ANON

As the Greek said, any men know how to flatter; few know how to praise. WENDELL PHILLIPS

Among the smaller duties of life I hardly know any one more important than that of not praising where praise is not due. SYDNEY SMITH

Generally we praise only to be praised. FRANCOIS DUC de la ROCHEFOUCAULD

Praise to the face
Is open disgrace. V. S. LEAN

Some praise at morning what they blame at night. ALEXANDER POPE

What is the sign of a proud man? He never praises anyone. *THE ZOHAR*

When you cannot get a compliment in any other way, pay yourself one.
                                        AMBROSE BIERCE

Approval for a job well done is as important as disapproval for faulty
performance.   ANON

There is not a person we employ who does not, like ourselves, desire
recognition, praise, gentleness, forbearance, patience.
                                    HENRY WARD BEECHER

Be moderate in praising a man when he is present, but give him full
credit when he is absent.   *The Talmud*

Merit unregarded is a very troublesome thing both to itself and others.
                                                  ANON

Almost every man wastes part of his life in attempts to display qualities
which he does not possess, and to gain applause which he cannot keep.
                                        SAMUEL JOHNSON

With faint praises one another damn.   WILLIAM WYCHERLEY

We begin to praise when we begin to see a thing needs our assistance.
                                    HENRY DAVID THOREAU

It's a sure sign of mediocrity always to be moderate with praise.
                                    MARQUIS de VAUVENARGUES

From none but self expect applause.   ROBERT BURTON

We refuse praise from a desire to be praised twice.
                        FRANCOIS DUC de la ROCHEFOUCAULD

He too serves a certain purpose who only stands and cheers.
                                            HENRY ADAMS

Modesty is the only sure bait when you angle for praise.
                                    EARL of CHESTERFIELD

A continual feast of commendation is only to be attained by merit or by wealth. SAMUEL JOHNSON

All charming people have something to conceal, usually their total dependence on the appreciation of others. CYRIL CONNOLLY

Encouragement after censure is like the sun after a shower. ANON

He who loves praise loves temptation. THOMAS WILSON

He who gladly does without the praise of the crowd will not miss the opportunity of becoming his own fan. KARL KRAUS

If you call a thing bad you do little, if you call a thing good you do much. JOHANN WOLFGANG von GOETHE

Praises from an enemy imply real merit. THOMAS FULLER

It would seldom be a bad bargain to disclaim all praise on condition of receiving no blame. FRANCOIS DUC de la ROCHEFOUCAULD

You will only offend men by praise which suggests the limit of their worth. MARQUIS de VAUVENARGUES

To speak ill of others is a dishonest way of praising ourselves. WILL DURANT

Applause is the spur of noble minds, the end and aim of weak ones. CHARLES CALEB COLTON

To approve is more difficult than to admire. HUGO von HOFMANNSTHAL

It is not he that searches for praise that finds it. COMTE de RIVAROL

When someone does something good, applaud! You will make two people happy. SAMUEL GOLDWYN

Praise, like gold and diamonds, owes its value only to its scarcity. It becomes cheap as it becomes vulgar, and will no longer raise expectation or animate enterprise. SAMUEL JOHNSON

Never accept flattery as though it were a compliment, and never treat a compliment as though it were mere flattery. RUSSELL LYNES

Good men hate those who praise them too much. EURIPIDES

The applause of a single human being is of great consequence. SAMUEL JOHNSON

A medal glitters, but it also casts a shadow. SIR WINSTON CHURCHILL

Sincerity is the highest compliment you can pay. RALPH WALDO EMERSON

Praises for our past triumphs are as feathers to a dead bird. PAUL ELDRIDGE

Praise the bridge that carried you over. GEORGE COLMAN, THE YOUNGER

A man desires praise that he may be reassured, that he may be quit of his doubting of himself; he is indifferent to applause when he is confident of success. ALEC WAUGH

Expect not praise without envy until you are dead. CHARLES CALEB COLTON

It is as great a spite to be praised in the wrong place, and by a wrong person, as can be done to a noble nature. BEN JONSON

Criticism

Any fool can criticize
And many of them do.
Watch that they don't recognize
The same faults about you.

Critics are like eunuchs in a harem: they know how it's done, they've seen it done every day, but they're unable to do it themselves.
BRENDAN BEHAN

Never speak ill of yourself; your friends will always say enough on that subject.
CHARLES M. de TALLEYRAND-PERIGORD

It had only one fault. It was kind of lousy.
JAMES THURBER

Critics can't even make music by rubbing their back legs together.
MEL BROOKS

I can take any amount of criticism, so long as it is unqualified praise.
NOEL COWARD

People ask you for criticism, but they only want praise.
WILLIAM SOMERSET MAUGHAM

Backbite: To speak of a man as you find him, when he can't find you.
AMBROSE BIERCE

The best way to learn how to do it yourself is to criticize the way the committee is doing it.
ROBERT ORBEN

To escape criticism—do nothing, say nothing, be nothing.
ELBERT HUBBARD

Never join with your friend when he abuses his horse or his wife unless the one is to be sold, and the other to be buried.
CHARLES CALEB COLTON

No one so thoroughly appreciates the value of constructive criticism as the one who's giving it.
HAL CHADWICK

I don't care how unkind the things people say about me are so long as they don't say them to my face.   OGDEN NASH

Criticism is what you get when you have everything else.   ANON

In reviling, it is not necessary to prepare a preliminary draft.
                                                        CHINESE PROVERB

A critic is a man who knows the way but can't drive the car.
                                                        KENNETH TYNAN

Show me the man who insists that he welcomes criticism if only it is "constructive," and I will show you a man who does not want any criticism at all.   HAROLD L. ICKES

Criticism is the disapproval of people, not for having faults, but for having faults different from our own.   ANON

Criticism is a study by which men grow important and formidable at very small expense.   SAMUEL JOHNSON

There is luxury in self-reproach. When we blame ourselves we feel that no one else has the right to blame us.   OSCAR WILDE

A critic is a legless man who teaches running. CHANNING POLLOCK

I have never found that criticism is ever inhibited by ignorance.
                                                        HAROLD MACMILLAN

Two pats on the back, before one kick up the arse.   ANON

We all think we are exceptional and are surprised to find ourselves criticized just like anyone else.   COMTESSE DIANE

Criticism is like champagne: nothing more execrable if bad, nothing more excellent if good.   CHARLES CALEB COLTON

Nobody wants constructive criticism. It's all we can do to put up with constructive praise.   MIGNON McLAUGHLIN

Taking to pieces is the trade of those who cannot construct.
                                                        RALPH WALDO EMERSON

It is much easier to be critical than to be correct.

BENJAMIN DISRAELI

If you're out to beat a dog, you're sure to find a stick.

YIDDISH PROVERB

Don't abuse your friends and expect them to consider it criticism.

EDGAR WATSON HOWE

Criticism is fundamental to improvement.

PROFESSOR RAY E. BROWN

Rebuke with soft words and hard arguments.   PROVERB

They have a right to censure that have a heart to help. WILLIAM PENN

Criticism may not be agreeable, but it is necessary. It fulfills the same function as pain in the human body, it calls attention to an unhealthy state of things.   SIR WINSTON CHURCHILL

Qui s'accuse s'excuse.   CHRISTOPHER RICKS

It is ridiculous for any man to criticize the works of another if he has not distinguished himself by his own performance.   JOSEPH ADDISON

A man must serve his time to every trade
Save censure—critics are all ready made.

LORD GEORGE GORDON NOEL BYRON

I like criticism when it is constructive; then it helps me. But when someone is critical just to be mean or tear something down, I must go away from that person. It depresses me.   SOPHIA LOREN

Hate no one; hate their vices, not themselves.   J. G. C. BRAINARD

Correct people's mistakes without humiliating them.   ANON

It is salutary to train oneself to be no more affected by censure than by praise.   W. SOMERSET MAUGHAM

We resent all criticism which denies us anything that lies in our line of advance.   RALPH WALDO EMERSON

We every day and every hour say things of another that we might more properly say of ourselves could we but apply our observations to our own concerns.   MICHEL de MONTAIGNE

It is discouragement, belittling and faultfinding that produce conceit.
                                                              ANON

Whatever you condemn, you have done yourself. GEORGE GRODDECK

There should be a dash of the amateur in criticism. For the amateur is a man of enthusiasm, who has not settled down and is not habit-bound.
                                        JUSTIN BROOKS ATKINSON

You may scold a carpenter who has made you a bad table, though you cannot make a table. It is not your trade to make tables.
                                                SAMUEL JOHNSON

Having been a little chastised, they shall be greatly rewarded.
                                              Wisdom of Solomon

It is folly to censure him whom all the world adores. PUBLILIUS SYRUS

Censure pardons the raven but rebukes the doves.   LATIN PROVERB

We are apt to be very pert at censuring others, where we will not endure advice ourselves.   WILLIAM PENN

Discouragement serves no possible purpose; it is simply the despair of wounded self-love.   FRANCOIS de FENELON

For constructive criticism use the Sandwich method; slip the "meat" of your criticism between two layers of praise and recognition.
                                                THEODORE V. HOUSER

I am sorry to think that you do not get a man's most effective criticism until you provoke him.   HENRY DAVID THOREAU

Never mind whom you praise, but be very careful whom you blame.
                                                EDMUND GOSSE

The rule in carving holds good as to criticism; never cut with a knife what you can cut with a spoon.   CHARLES BUXTON

I like criticism, but it must be my way.   MARK TWAIN

Privilege

Number One
  On the management chart
Seldom plays
  In the principal part.

The longer the title, the less important the job. GEORGE McGOVERN

Those who insist on the dignity of their office, show they have not deserved it. BALTASAR GRACIAN

A right is not what someone gives you; it's what no one can take from you. RAMSEY CLARK

There is no settling the point of precedency between a louse and a flea. SAMUEL JOHNSON

It's always easy to tell your station in life. Sooner or later someone tells you where to get off. HERB DANIELS

It is the high and mighty who have the longest distance to fall. ARNOLD LOBEL

What men prize most is a privilege even if it be that of chief mourner at a funeral. JAMES RUSSELL LOWELL

Rights that do not flow from duty well performed are not worth having. MOHANDAS K. GANDHI

IBM is making top corporate positions hereditary. The sweeping change is designed to take advantage of new estate tax laws and stimulate child production among the right people.

Off the Wall Street Journal

People who value their privileges above their principles soon lose both. DWIGHT D. EISENHOWER

Privilege is privilege, whether it is due to money or intellect or whether you have six toes. PHILIP, DUKE of EDINBURGH

Men are like numbers, they acquire their importance from their
position.   NAPOLEON BONAPARTE

In the United States "First" and "Second" class can't be painted on
railroad cars, for all passengers being Americans, are equal and it
would be "unAmerican." But paint "Pullman" on a car and everyone is
satisfied.   OWEN WISTER

Privilege is the greatest enemy of right.
                                    MARIE EBNER von ESCHENBACH

People of privilege will always risk their complete destruction rather
than surrender any material part of their advantage.
                                         JOHN KENNETH GALBRAITH

Prestige is the shadow cast by power.   DEAN ACHESON

Man is used to having convictions, so there we are. We can none of us do
without our hangers-on, though we despise them at the bottom of our
souls.   LEO SHESTOV

No man was ever endowed with a right without being at the same time
saddled with a responsibility.   GERALD W. JOHNSON

If we cannot secure all our rights, let us secure what we can.
                                             THOMAS JEFFERSON

There is no worse heresy than that the office sanctifies the holder of it.
                                                     LORD ACTON

Silence never won rights. They were not handed down from above; they
are forced by pressures from below.   ROGER BALDWIN

They that stand high have many blasts to shake them.
                                          WILLIAM SHAKESPEARE

If it were ever allowable to forget what is due to superiority of rank, it
would be when the privileged themselves remembered it.
                                           MADAME SWETCHINE

It is sure that those are most desirous of honor or glory who cry out
loudest of its abuse and the vanity of the world. BARUCH SPINOZA

Status

Status symbols are
Not left on the shelf,
They're things like the car
We give to ourself.

There is merit without rank, but there is no rank without some merit.
                    FRANCOIS DUC de la ROCHEFOUCAULD

We laugh at the savages who take a tribal pride in the size of their totem
poles, but we ourselves judge the status of a citizen by the number and
length of the cars in his driveway.   SYDNEY J. HARRIS

No really great man ever thought himself so.   WILLIAM HAZLITT

My father always told me that if you saw a man in a Rolls Royce you
could be sure he was not a gentleman unless he was the chauffeur.
                                        EARL of ARRAN

We salute the uniform, not the man.   JEAN de la FONTAINE

A man of stature has no need of status.   ANON

It is always possible for anyone to judge the financial status of his host by
the distance of the table tops and chair seats from the floor. The higher
the income bracket the lower the furniture.   QUENTIN CRISP

A throne is only a bench covered with velvet.
                                  NAPOLEON BONAPARTE

A thing is important if anyone thinks it important. WILLIAM JAMES

Gadgets are objects which cost more to maintain than their initial cost.
                              HYMAN MAXWELL BERSTON

Perched on the loftiest throne in the world, we are still sitting on our own
behind.   MICHEL de MONTAIGNE

The longer you live, the less importance you attach to things, and the less importance you also attach to importance.   JEAN ROSTAND

It is an interesting question how far men would retain their relative rank if they were divested of their clothes.   HENRY DAVID THOREAU

Don't take action because of a name! A name is an uncertain thing, you can't count on it.   BERTOLT BRECHT

Being put on a pedestal has disadvantages which you're apt to discover the first time you fail to watch your step.   FRANKLIN JONES

The boss's room bristles with weapons. The apparent comfort that disarms those entering is in reality a hidden arsenal.
WALTER BENJAMIN

Rank is to merit what dress is to a pretty woman.
FRANCOIS DUC de la ROCHEFOUCAULD

And you cannot tell by the way a party looks or how he lives in this town, if he has any scratch, because many a party who is around in automobiles, and wearing good clothes, and chucking quite a swell is nothing but a phonus bolonus and does not have any real scratch whatever.   DAMON RUNYON

If the cap fits, wear it.   PROVERB

The keeping of an idle woman is a badge of superior social status.
DOROTHY L. SAYERS

Men and statues that are admired in an elevated situation, have a very different effect on us when we approach them; the first appear less than we imagined them, the last bigger.   LORD GREVILLE

There are no persons more solicitous about the preservation of rank, than those who have no rank at all.   WILLIAM SHAKESPEARE

To be vain of one's rank or place, is to show that one is below it.
LESZINSKI STANISLAUS

Tolerably early in life I discovered that one of the unpardonable sins, in the eyes of most people, is for a man to go about unlabelled. The world regards such a person as the police do an unmuzzled dog.
THOMAS HENRY HUXLEY

If two people ride the same horse, one must ride behind.
BISHOP FOWLER

The frog tried to look as big as the elephant, and burst.
AFRICAN PROVERB

The sparrow is sorry for the peacock at the burden of its tail.
RABINDRANATH TAGORE

People who are arrogant on account of their wealth are about equal to the Laplanders, who measure a man's worth by the number of his reindeer.
FREDERICKA BREMER

I would rather sit on a pumpkin, and have it all to myself, than to be crowded on a velvet cushion. HENRY DAVID THOREAU

A wise man looks upon men as he does on horses; all their comparisons of title, wealth, and place, he considers but as harness.
RICHARD CEVIL

High seats are never but uneasy, and crowns are always stuffed with thorns. JAMES GORDON BROOKS

Titles distinguish the mediocre, embarrass the superior, and are disgraced by the inferior. GEORGE BERNARD SHAW

Distinction of rank is necessary for the economy of the world, and was never called in question, but by barbarians and enthusiasts. ROWE

Persons require to possess a title, or some other badge of rank, or of the consideration of people of rank, to be able to indulge somewhat in the luxury of doing as they like without detriment to their estimation.
JOHN STUART MILL

Quality and title have such allurements that hundreds are ready to give up all their own importance to cringe, to flatter, to look little, and to pall every pleasure in constraint, merely to be among the great, though without the least hopes of improving by their understanding or sharing their generosity: they might be happy among their equals, but those are despised for company where they are despised in turn.
OLIVER GOLDSMITH

The megalomaniac differs from the narcissist by the fact that he wishes to be powerful rather than charming, and seeks to be feared rather than loved. To this type belong many lunatics and most of the great men of history. BERTRAND RUSSELL

Opinions

When you're right,
Nobody shows.
When you're wrong,
Everyone knows.

When I want your opinion I'll give it to you. LAURENCE J. PETER

Broad-minded is just another way of saying a fellow's too lazy to form an opinion. WILL ROGERS

When some folks agree with my opinions I begin to suspect I'm wrong. FRANK McKINNEY HUBBARD

I have heard your views. They do not harmonize with mine. The decision is taken unanimously. CHARLES de GAULLE

The average man's opinions are much less foolish than they would be if he thought for himself. BERTRAND RUSSELL

You've no idea what a poor opinion I have of myself—and how little I deserve it. WILLIAM SCHWENCK GILBERT

When half the people believe one thing, and the other half another, it is usually safe to accept either opinion. EDGAR WATSON HOWE

A prejudice is a vagrant opinion without visible means of support. AMBROSE BIERCE

If everyone agrees with you, they probably don't mean it. ANON

Men get opinions as boys learn to spell. By reiteration chiefly. ELIZABETH BARRETT BROWNING

It is often easier as well as more advantageous to conform to other men's opinions than to bring them over to ours.   JEAN de la BRUYERE

Seeing ourselves as others see us wouldn't do much good. We wouldn't believe it.   JACOB M. BRAUDE

Prejudice saves a lot of time, because you can form an opinion without the facts.   ANON

Opinion is that exercise of the human will which helps us to make a decision without information.   JOHN ERSKINE

The difference between a conviction and a prejudice is that you can explain a conviction without getting angry.   ANON

It is not that I don't have opinions, rather that I'm paid not to think aloud.
          PRESIDENT YITZHAK NAVON of ISRAEL

In all matters of opinion our adversaries are insane.   MARK TWAIN

When the man you like switches from what he said a year ago, or four years ago, he is a broadminded person who has courage enough to change his mind with changing conditions. When a man you don't like does it, he is a liar who has broken his promise. FRANKLIN P. ADAMS

A flatterer is a man that tells you your opinion and not his own. ANON

A man's opinions are generally of much more value than his arguments.
          OLIVER WENDELL HOLMES

Do not speak for other men; speak for yourself.
          HENRY DAVID THOREAU

Accustom yourself to not knowing what your opinions are till you have blurted them out, and thus find out what they are.
          JOHN JAY CHAPMAN

Lidian says that the only sin which people never forgive in each other is a difference of opinion.   RALPH WALDO EMERSON

What you see is news, what you know is background, what you feel is opinion.   LESTER MARKEL

There is more safety in men's good opinion than in money.
                                        LATIN PROVERB

One often contradicts an opinion when it is really only the tone in which
it has been presented that is unsympathetic.
                        FRIEDRICH WILHELM NIETZSCHE

We think very few people sensible, except those who are of our opinion.
                        FRANCOIS DUC de la ROCHEFOUCAULD

All empty souls tend to extreme opinion. WILLIAM BUTLER YEATS

Most of our personal opinions lie on the board like iron filings. But pass
the magnet of a strong emotion over them and they will change overnight
and point in the opposite direction   GERALD BRENNAN

Opinions cannot survive if one has no chance to fight for them.
                                        THOMAS MANN

I often marvel how it is thought each man loves himself beyond all else,
he should yet value his own opinion of himself less than that of others.
                                        MARCUS AURELIUS

The moment we want to believe something, we suddenly see all the
arguments for it, and become blind to the arguments against it.
                        GEORGE BERNARD SHAW

At eighteen our convictions are hills from which we look; at forty-five
they are caves in which we hide.   F. SCOTT FITZGERALD

We are not certain, we never are certain. If we were we could reach some
conclusions, and we could, at least, make others take us seriously.
                                        ALBERT CAMUS

The man who never alters his opinion is like standing water, and breeds
reptiles of the mind.   WILLIAM BLAKE

Man is a gregarious animal, and much more so in his mind than in his
body. He may like to go alone for a walk, but he hates to stand alone in
his opinions.   GEORGE SANTAYANA

Ask no opinion but your own.   FLACCUS AULUS PERSIUS

We tolerate differences of opinion in people who are familiar to us. But differences of opinion in people we do not know sound like heresy or plots. BROOKS ATKINSON

There is no greater mistake than the hasty conclusion that opinions are worthless because they are badly argued. THOMAS HENRY HUXLEY

It is a golden rule not to judge men by their opinions but rather by what their opinions make of them. GEORG CHRISTOPH LICHTENBERG

The people who are most bigoted are those who have no conviction at all. GILBERT KEITH CHESTERTON

I could never divide myself from any man upon the difference of an opinion, or be angry with his judgment for not agreeing with me in that from which perhaps within a few days I should dissent myself. SIR THOMAS BROWNE

Do not think of knocking out another person's brains because he differs in opinion from you. It would be as rational to knock yourself on the head because you differ from yourself ten years ago. HORACE MANN

There never were two opinions alike in all the world, no more than two hours or two grains: the most universal quality in diversity. MICHEL de MONTAIGNE

Every man should periodically be compelled to listen to opinions which are infuriating to him. To hear nothing but what is pleasing to one is to make a pillow of the mind. ST. JOHN ERVINE

The ambitious man grasps at opinion as necessary to his designs; the vain man sues for it as a testimony to his merit; the honest man demands it as his due; and most men consider it as necessary to their existence. CESARE B. BECCARIA

Our opinions are less important than the spirit and temper with which they possess us, and even good opinions are worth very little unless we hold them in a broad, intelligent, and spacious way. JOHN MORLEY

The chief effect of talk on any subject is to strengthen one's own opinions, and, in fact, one never knows exactly what he does believe until he is warmed into conviction by the heat of attack and defence. CHARLES DUDLEY WARNER

Nothing so obstinately stands in the way of all sorts of progress, as pride of opinion; while nothing is so foolish and baseless.

JOSIAH GILBERT HOLLAND

The more unpopular an opinion is, the more necessary is it that the holder should be somewhat punctillious in his observance of conventionalities generally.   SAMUEL BUTLER

If you pay nervous attention to other people's opinions, maneuver to obtain their indulgence and to stand high in their esteem, you will be whisked about in their winds and you will lose yourself. You know how you ought to behave, and that is the way to behave regardless of the subjective views of anyone else.   JO COUDERT

We should be eternally vigilant against attempts to check the expression of opinions that we loathe.   OLIVER WENDELL HOLMES

X DANGERS

Worry

If you're always in a hurry,
  Who are you trying to overtake?
For the more you tend to worry,
  It may be you they undertake!

You probably wouldn't worry about what people think of you if you could know how seldom they do.   OLIN MILLER

Today is the tomorrow you worried about yesterday. JACOB M. BRAUDE

Don't despair, not even over the fact that you don't despair.
                                        FRANZ KAFKA

Gentlemen, in the little moment that remains to us between the crisis and the catastrophe, we might as well take a glass of champagne.
                                        PAUL CLAUDEL

Cheer up, the worst is yet to come.   PHILANDER JOHNSON

Do you think every sole meuniere comes to you untouched by suffering?
                                        TOM STOPPARD

I've got so many things on my mind that if something else happens today it'll be 10 days before I can get round to worrying about it!   ANON

Show me a man who keeps his two feet on the ground and I'll show you a man who can't get his pants off.   JAMES MICHENER

There are two days in the week on which I never worry; one is yesterday and the other is tomorrow.
                                           ROBERT JONES BURDETTE

The only man in the world with clenched hair.   NEIL SIMON

The clever man often worries; the loyal person is often overworked.
                                                      MR. TUT-TUT

I'm so nervous, yesterday I got a fingernail transplant.
                                                    ROBERT ORBEN

Each person is worrying about himself, no one is worrying about you.
                                                      JO COUDERT

One has two duties—to be worried, and not to be worried.
                                                    E. M. FORSTER

Those who worry most about the future are often those who are doing least to prepare for it.   ANON

Why hoard your troubles? They have no market value, so just throw them away.   ANN SCHADE

It's a long time between drinks.   J. M. MOREHEAD

Worry: It ain't no use putting up your umbrella till it rains.
                                                 ALICE HEGAN RICE

Many a man's profanity has saved him from a nervous breakdown. ANON

Blessed is the person who is too busy to worry in the day-time, and too sleepy to worry at night.   LEO AIKMAN

Worries go down better with soup than without.   JEWISH PROVERB

We have the term "paranoia" for someone who feels he's persecuted when he isn't. But there's no term for someone who doesn't feel persecuted when he really is. And that's much more the normal state of affairs these days.   R. D. LAING

The best cure for worry, depression, melancholy, brooding, is to go deliberately forth and try to lift with one's sympathy the gloom of somebody else. ARNOLD BENNETT

Everybody knows better than anybody. FRENCH PROVERB

One of the symptoms of approaching nervous breakdown is the belief that one's work is terribly important. If I were a medical man, I should prescribe a holiday to any patient who considered his work important. BERTRAND RUSSELL

It is not work that kills men; it is worry. Work is healthy, and you can hardly put more upon a man than he can bear; but worry is rust upon the blade. It is not the revolution that destroys the machinery, it is the friction. HENRY WARD BEECHER

The worst thing you can possibly do is worrying and thinking about what you could have done. GEORG CHRISTOPH LICHTENBERG

When I've had a rough day, before I go to sleep I ask myself if there's anything more I can do right now. If there isn't, I sleep sound. L. L. COLBERT

Worry a little bit every day and in a lifetime you will lose a couple of years. If something is wrong, fix it if you can. But train yourself not to worry. Worry never fixes anything. MARY HEMINGWAY

Worrying helps you some. It seems as if you are doing something when you're worrying. LUCY MAUD MONTGOMERY

Don't let your sorrow come higher than your knees. SWEDISH PROVERB

Everyone constructs their own bed of nails. D. SUTTEN

Do not anticipate trouble, or worry about what may never happen. Keep in the sunlight. BENJAMIN FRANKLIN

Don't try to do two or more things at once. Set priorities so that you are not worrying about something else while you are attending to the task at hand. Arrange your work space so that your eyes aren't drawn to other jobs that need to be done. The time you invest to organize your space will be paid back with improved efficiency. Don't put unreasonable demands on your attention span. Even if you are under pressure, time spent taking a regular break will increase your overall productivity. But make it a real break; don't just switch to another demanding task... Lack of sleep is a major reason for poor concentration. Learn to take catnaps or use a meditation technique instead of a drug to help you to keep going until you get a good night's rest.

WILLIAM BENNETT, M.D.

Beware lest in your anxiety to avoid war you obtain a master.

DEMOSTHENES

Laziness

If you ever should try to stand still
And let your own world go downhill,
You can be sure
Of nothing more,
Not that it might, but it will.

My only hobby is laziness, which naturally rules out all the others.

GRANNI NAZZANO

You can tell a workman by his hands—they're always in his pockets.

GRAFFITO

It is better to have loafed and lost than never to have loafed at all.

JAMES THURBER

The world is full of willing people; some willing to work, the rest willing to let them.   ROBERT FROST

The way to be nothing is to do nothing.   EDGAR WATSON HOWE

I have often been struck by the fact that the symptoms of laziness and fatigue are practically identical.   FREDERICK LEWIS ALLEN

Lazy people have no spare time.   JAPANESE PROVERB

A loafer always has the correct time. FRANK McKINNEY HUBBARD

Laziness travels so slowly that poverty soon overtakes him.
BENJAMIN FRANKLIN

Lazy folks' stomachs don't git tired. JOEL C. HARRIS

I've found a great way to start the day—I go straight back to bed! ANON

In the contest between ease and liberty, the first hath generally
prevailed. MARQUIS of HALIFAX

Better to idle well than to work badly. SPANISH PROVERB

Every night I make up my mind to rise early the next morning, but every
morning I make up my body to lie still. ANON

He slept beneath the moon;
He basked beneath the sun;
He lived a life of going-to-do
And died with nothing done. JAMES ALBERY

I have enough money to get by. I'm not independently wealthy, just
independently lazy, I suppose. MONTGOMERY CLIFF

Good luck is a lazy man's estimate of a worker's success. ANON

The reason American cities are prosperous is that there is no place to sit
down. A. J. TALLEY

Loafing needs no explanation and is its own excuse.
CHRISTOPHER MORLEY

He who rises late may trot all day, and not overtake his business at night.
BENJAMIN FRANKLIN

I prefer rogues to imbeciles, because they sometimes take a rest.
ALEXANDER DUMAS

Laziness could be an overwhelming longing for physical calm. ANON

The lazy are always wanting to do something.
MARQUIS de VAUVENARGUES

In the "social order" one is the worker, and nine are idlers.
V. V. ROZINOV

He is without strict doubt a Hoorah Henry, and he is generally figured as nothing but a lob as far as doing anything useful in this world is concerned.   DAMON RUNYON

The laziest man I ever met put popcorn in his pancakes so they would turn over by themselves.   W. C. FIELDS

As a boy, he swallowed a teaspoon. And he hasn't stirred since. ANON

Rust wastes more than use.   FRENCH PROVERB

Some folks can look so busy doing nothin' that they seem indispensable.
FRANK McKINNEY HUBBARD

The first external revelations of the dry-rot in men is a tendency to lurk and lounge; to be at street corners without intelligible reason; to be going anywhere when met; to be about many places rather than any; to do nothing tangible but to have an intention of performing a number of tangible duties tomorrow or the day after.   CHARLES DICKENS

Time deals gently only with those who take it gently.
ANATOLE FRANCE

Sloth makes all things difficult, but industry all things easy.
BENJAMIN FRANKLIN

Stretched on the rack of a too easy chair.   ALEXANDER POPE

Better to be eaten to death with a rust then to be scoured to nothing with perpetual motion.   WILLIAM SHAKESPEARE

Expect poison from standing water.   WILLIAM BLAKE

Laziness grows on people: it begins in cobwebs and ends in iron chains. The more business a man has to do the more he is able to accomplish, for he learns to economize his time.   SIR M. HALE

People with lazy minds feast on their own thoughts when they are alone.
PLATO

No one knows what is in him till he tries; and many would never try if they were not forced to.   BASIL W. MATURIN

By too much sitting still the body becomes unhealthy, and soon the mind.   HENRY WADSWORTH LONGFELLOW

Go to the Ant, thou sluggard,
Consider her ways and be wise.   PROVERB

Sloth, like rust, consumes faster than labor wears, while the used key is always bright.   BENJAMIN FRANKLIN

Enemies

Always forgive them
That kick in the crutch;
Nothing annoys them
Quite half as much.

Instead of loving your enemies, treat your friends a little better.
          EDGAR WATSON HOWE

Ashes to ashes, and clay to clay, if the enemy doesn't get you, your own folks may.   JAMES THURBER

All wars are popular for the first thirty days.
          ARTHUR SCHLESINGER

Don't tell me peace has broken out.   BERTOLT BRECHT

When the news of Napoleon's death came, before the King had been informed of it by his Ministers, Sir E. Nagle, anxious to communicate the welcome tidings, said to him, "Sir, your bitterest enemy is dead." "Is she, by God!" said the tender husband.   HENRY EDWARD FOX

The best weapon against an enemy is another enemy.
          FRIEDRICH WILHELM NIETZSCHE

Forgive your enemies—if you can't get back at them any other way.
                                                      FRANKLIN JONES

The bigger they come, the harder they fall.   ROBERT FITZSIMMONS

If you have no enemies, you are apt to be in the same predicament in
regard to friends.   ELBERT HUBBARD

I'm sick of war for many reasons,
Three of them will do:
It's 1815,
I am French
And this is Waterloo.   MEL BROOKS

Use your enemy's hand to catch a snake.   PERSIAN PROVERB

Your enemies are not those who dislike you, but those whom you dislike.
                                                              ANON

Do not throw the arrow which will return against you.
                                                  KURDISH PROVERB

To have a good enemy, choose a friend: he knows where to strike.
                                                DIANE de POITIERS

He hasn't an enemy in the world—but all his friends hate him.
                                                    EDDIE CANTOR

If you wish to make a man your enemy, tell him simply, "Your are
wrong." This method works every time.   HENRY G. LINK

It's far easier to forgive an enemy after you've got even with him.
                                                    OLIN MILLER

The wars of the people will be more terrible than those of kings.
                                              SIR WINSTON CHURCHILL

I love an opposition that has enemies.   FREDERICK THE GREAT

Enemies to me are the "sauce piquante" to my dish of life.
                                                    ELSA MAXWELL

Friends may come and go, but enemies accumulate.   ANON

I see many enemies around and mighty few friends. BILLY THE KID

A man cannot be too careful in the choice of his enemies.
OSCAR WILDE

War hath no fury like a noncombatant.
CHARLES EDWARD MONTAGUE

No enemy is stronger than one who does not know he is beaten.
J. MIDDLETON MURRY

The only people I would permit to fight duels would be priests and lawyers.   ADOLF HITLER

Today's friend may be tomorrow's foe.   SOPHOCLES

A moderate is a fellow who makes enemies left and right.   ANON

The enemy of my enemy is my friend.   ARAB PROVERB

We make more enemies by what we say than friends by what we do.
CHURTON COLLINS

Answer violence with violence.   JUAN PERON

Speak well of your enemies, sir, you made them.   OREN ARNOLD

The tree of Russian liberty is watered with the blood of Russian martyrs.
EMMA GOLDMAN

If you would keep your secret from an enemy, tell it not to a friend.
BENJAMIN FRANKLIN

You can discover what your enemy fears most by observing the means he uses to frighten you.   ERIC HOFFER

Peace with a cudgel in hand is war.   PORTUGESE PROVERB

We should support whatever the enemy opposes and oppose whatever the enemy supports.   MAO TSE-TUNG

And the battle ended through lack of combatants.
PIERRE CORNEILLE

Great God, let me walk three weeks in the footsteps of my enemy, carry the same burden, have the same trials and temptations as he, before I say one word to criticize him. **AN INDIAN CHIEF'S PRAYER**

Jealousy is no more than feeling alone among smiling enemies.
ELIZABETH BOWEN

It is far more necessary to forgive ourselves than to forgive our enemies.
JO COUDERT

None but yourself who are your greatest foe.
HENRY WADSWORTH LONGFELLOW

There is no finer revenge than that which others inflict on your enemy. Moreover, it has the advantage of leaving you the role of a generous man.
CESARE PAVESE

Our enemies' opinion of us comes closer to the truth than our own.
FRANCOIS DUC de la ROCHEFOUCAULD

He makes no friend who never made a foe.
ALFRED LORD TENNYSON

Be thine enemy an ant, see in him an elephant. **TURKISH PROVERB**

In taking revenge, a man is but even with his enemy; but in passing it over, he is superior. **FRANCIS BACON**

A common danger unites even the bitterest enemies. **ARISTOTLE**

If you have no enemies, then fortune passed you by.
PORTUGESE PROVERB

Our friends may be the undoing of us; in the end it is our enemies who save us. **HENRY HAVELOCK ELLIS**

Every effect that one produces gives one an enemy. To be popular one must be a mediocrity. **OSCAR WILDE**

However rich or powerful a man may be it is the height of folly to make personal enemies for one unguarded moment may yield you to the revenge of the most despicable of mankind. **LORD LYTTLETON**

Opposition

Your opponents are probably hopin'
That you'll follow your usual tack;
But why always attack in the open,
When you can get them around the back?

I suppose nobody has ever been struck a direct blow by a rabbit. At least, not deliberately. CASSANDRA

Your arms are too short to box with God. ALEX BRADFORD

If you ever get belted and see three fighters through the haze, go after the one in the middle. That's what ruined me—I went after the two guys on the end. MAX BAER

Why inflict pain on oneself, when so many others are ready to save us the trouble? GEORGE W. PACAUD

I hate victims who respect their executioners. JEAN-PAUL-SARTRE

Whoever is not against us is with us. JANOS KADAR

Never fight fair with a stranger, boy. You'll never get out of the jungle that way. ARTHUR MILLER

A thousand curses never tore a shirt. ARABIAN PROVERB

If you start throwing hedgehogs under me, I shall throw two porcupines under you. NIKITA KHRUSHCHEV

The Porcupine, whom one must handle gloved,
May be respected, but is never loved. ARTHUR GUITERMAN

Nobody ever forgets where he buried a hatchet.
FRANK McKINNEY HUBBARD

I don't care anything about formations or new offenses or tricks on defense. You block and tackle better than the team you're playing, you win. VINCE LOMBARDI

When a fellow is kicking, he has only one leg to stand on.
                                          LYMAN ROCKEY

I shoot the Hippopotamus
With bullets made of platinum,
Because if I use the leaden ones,
His hide is sure to flatten 'em.   HILAIRE BELLOC

To take away all animosity from a rivalry is like playing whist for love.
                                          SAMUEL BUTLER

The kind of smile a victorious boxer gives the loser.
                                          WILLIAM McILVANNEY

It is only cold-blooded animals whose bite is poisonous.
                                          ARTHUR SCHOPENHAUER

Never ascribe to an opponent motives meaner than your own.
                                          SIR JAMES BARRIE

Who draws his sword against the prince must throw away the scabbard.
                                          ENGLISH PROVERB

What on earth would a man do with himself if something did not stand in
his way?   HERBERT GEORGE WELLS

What is sauce for the goose is sauce for the gander.   PROVERB

Revenge, the longer it is delayed, the crueller it grows.
                                          THOMAS FULLER

Meekness, n. Uncommon patience in planning a revenge that is worth
while.   AMBROSE BIERCE

No revenge is more honorable than the one not taken.
                                          SPANISH PROVERB

Revenge is a dish that should be eaten cold.   ENGLISH PROVERB

Revenge is a luscious fruit which you must leave to ripen.
                                          EMILE GABORIAU

Revenge never repairs an injury.   THOMAS FULLER

Admission of error is one of the best means of taking the fight out of the opposition. PROFESSOR RAY E. BROWN

Pope Leo used to cite his father, Lorenzo de Medici, who often said, "Remember that those who speak ill of us don't love us." FRANCESCO GUICCIARDINI

Any man can stand up to his opponents; give me the man who can stand up to his friends. WILLIAM GLADSTONE

There are exceptions to all rules, but it seldom answers to follow the advice of an opponent. BENJAMIN DISRAELI

"Here, young man, you shouldn't hit a boy when he's down."
"G'wan! Wat d'yer think I tuk all dat trouble ter git 'm down fer?" JACOB M. BRAUDE

He that does you a very ill turn will never forgive you. ENGLISH PROVERB

Never befriend the oppressed unless you are prepared to take on the oppressor. OGDEN NASH

My adversaries... applied the one means that wins the easiest victory over reason: terror and force. ADOLF HITLER

Go hang thyself in thine own heir-apparent garters! WILLIAM SHAKESPEARE

If you kick a man, he kicks you back again. Therefore never be too eager to combat injustice. BERTOLT BRECHT

Ugly deeds are taught by ugly deeds. SOPHOCLES

Whoever frightens monsters should see to it that in the process he does not become a monster. FRIEDRICH WILHELM NIETZSCHE

He that flings dirt at another dirtieth himself most. THOMAS FULLER

If you succeed in life, you must do it in spite of the efforts of others to pull you down. There is nothing in the idea that people are willing to help those who help themselves. People are willing to help a man who

can't help himself, but as soon as a man is able to help himself, and does it, they join in making his life as uncomfortable as possible.
EDWARD HOWE

Opposition brings concord. Out of discord comes the fairest harmony.
HERACLITUS

The effects of opposition are wonderful. There are men who rise refreshed on hearing of a threat—men to whom a crisis which intimidates and paralyses the majority, comes graceful and beloved as a bride.   RALPH WALDO EMERSON

If you hate a person, you hate something in him that is part of yourself. What isn't part of ourselves doesn't disturb us.   HERMANN HESSE

A man can be destroyed but not defeated.   ERNEST HEMINGWAY

It is human nature to hate the man whom you have hurt.
CORNELUIS TACITUS

They had tails like unto scorpions, and there were stings in their tails.
The Book of Revelations

While it is true that an inherently free and scrupulous person may be destroyed, such an individual can never be enslaved or used as a blind fool.   ALBERT EINSTEIN

Adversity

For prosperity
  You need a teacher.
For adversity
  You need a preacher.

The times are not so bad as they seem; they couldn't be.
JAY FRANKLIN

One day as I sat musing, sad and lonely, and without a friend, a voice came to me from out of the dark saying, "Cheer up, things could be worse." So I cheered up, and sure enough, things got worse.   ANON

When it comes to a knockdown struggle with adversity, it is a question of how many last gasps we can gasp.   HENRY S. HASKINS

Adversity reminds men of religion.   TITUS LIVY

Adversity has the same effect on a man that severe training has on the pugilist—it reduces him to his fighting weight.   JOSH BILLINGS

The lowest ebb is the turn of the tide.
HENRY WADSWORTH LONGFELLOW

The world breaks everyone, and afterwards many are strong in the broken places.   ERNEST HEMINGWAY

God gives almonds to those who have no teeth.   SPANISH PROVERB

By trying we can easily learn to endure adversity. Another man's, I mean.   MARK TWAIN

Things are going to get a lot worse before they get worse. LILY TOMLIN

If you're feeling low...Do something!
If you've been doing something...Do something different!   ANON

There is nothing more disappointing than failing to accomplish a thing, unless it is to see somebody else accomplish it. HENRY S. HASKINS

Prosperity makes friends, adversity tries them.   PUBLILIUS SYRUS

God brings men into deep waters, not to drown them but to cleanse them.
THOMAS AUGHEY

He knows not his own strength that hath not met adversity.
BEN JONSON

Calamities are of two kinds: misfortune to ourselves, and good fortune to others.   AMBROSE BIERCE

Adversity introduces a man to himself.   ANON

When the going gets tough, the tough get going.   JOHN MITCHELL

Sadness is almost never anything but a form of fatigue. ANDRE GIDE

Do not lay things too much to heart. No one is really beaten unless he is
discouraged.   LORD AVEBURY

In the day of prosperity, adversity is forgotten and in the day of adversity,
prosperity is not remembered.   *Ecclesiastes*

In prosperity friends do not leave you unless desired, whereas in
adversity, they stay away of their own accord.
                              DEMETRIUS of PHALERUM

There is no one less fortunate than he whom adversity neglects; he has
no chance to prove himself.   ANON

In adversity a man is saved by hope.   MENANDER

The toad beneath the harrow knows
Exactly where each tooth-point goes.
The butterfly upon the road
Preaches contentment to that toad.   RUDYARD KIPLING

Fire is the test of gold; adversity of strong men.
                              LUCIUS ANNAEUS SENECA

He that can't endure the bad, will not live to see the good.
                                          YIDDISH PROVERB

There is no man so low down that the cure for his condition does not lie
strictly with himself.   THOMAS L. MASSON

Adversity is the state in which a man most easily becomes acquainted
with himself, being especially free from admirers then.
                                          SAMUEL JOHNSON

Nothing is harder to direct than a man in prosperity; nothing more easily
managed than one in adversity.   PLUTARCH

Constant success shows us but one side of the world; adversity brings out
the reverse of the picture.   CHARLES CALEB COLTON

Into each life some rain must fall,
Some days must be dark and dreary.
HENRY WADSWORTH LONGFELLOW

Prosperity has no power over adversity.   PUBLILIUS SYRUS

The good things which belong to prosperity are to be wished, but the good things that belong to adversity are to be admired.
LUCIUS ANNAEUS SENECA

In victory even the cowardly like to boast, while in adverse times even the brave are discredited.   GAIUS VALERIUS SALLUST

In the day of prosperity be joyful, but in the day of adversity consider.
Ecclesiastes

The virtue of prosperity is temperance; the virtue of adversity is fortitude.   FRANCIS BACON

Problems

Most every man
Knows long
The drill;
If anything can
Go wrong,
It will.

No problem is so big or so complicated that it can't be run away from.
ANON

The more directives you issue to solve a problem the worse it gets.
HACK ROBERTSON

The real problem is what to do with the problem-solvers after the problems are solved.   GAY TALESE

Many a problem will solve itself if you'll forget it and go fishing.
OLIN MILLER

If you continue to apply yesterday's solution to tomorrow's problem, you may discover that the problem has disappeared with the job.   ANON

Rowe's Rule: The odds are six to five that the light at the end of the tunnel is the headlight of an oncoming train.   PAUL DICKSON

It isn't the incompetent who destroy an organization. The incompetent never get in a position to destroy it. It is those who have achieved something and want to rest upon their achievements who are forever clogging things up.   CHARLES SORENSON

Freedom from the desire for an answer is essential to the understanding of a problem.   J. KRISHNAMURTI

I have yet to see any problem, however complicated, which, when you looked at it in the right way, did not become still more complicated.
POUL ANDERSON

The most delicate component will be the one to drop. ARTHUR BLOCH

The crisis of yesterday is the joke of tomorrow.
HERBERT GEORGE WELLS

If there's a harder way of doing something, someone will find it.
RALPH E. ROOS

Today our problem is not making miracles—but managing them.
LYNDON BAINES JOHNSON

It isn't that they can't see the solution. It is that they can't see the problem.   GILBERT KEITH CHESTERTON

I become the problem instead of the solution to the problem.
NELSON ROCKEFELLER

We only think when we are confronted with a problem. JOHN DEWEY

Our troubles will continue as long as we train people to locate problems instead of solve them.   ANON

If you have a job without aggravations, you don't have a job.
MALCOLM S. FORBES

The course of true anything never does run smooth. SAMUEL BUTLER

The 'crisis' technique is used to obscure more serious situations. ANON

Problems are only opportunities in work clothes. HENRY J. KAISER

Only the man who finds everything wrong and expects it to get worse is
thought to have a clear brain. JOHN KENNETH GALBRAITH

A great many people, maybe most people, confronted by a difficult
situation, one in which they don't know what to do, get nowhere because
they are so busy pointing out that the situation should be remade so they
will know what to do. JAMES GOULD COZZENS

It's so much easier to suggest solutions when you don't know too much to
solve it. BRENDAN FRANCIS

If it ain't broke, don't fix it. BERT LANCE

Those who are fond of setting things to rights, have no great objection to
seeing them wrong. WILLIAM HAZLITT

In every important problem, be sure to allow additional time by way of a
safety margin before your deadline. HARRY A. BULLIS

I do not believe in final solutions. Even if you solve some problem, the
solution will always give rise to another problem. ISAIAH BERLIN

It requires a very unusual mind to undertake the analysis of the obvious.
ALFRED NORTH WHITEHEAD

Most people spend more time and energy in going around problems than
in trying to solve them. HENRY FORD

The critical factor of a problem is the element that has to be changed
before anything else can be changed. PETER F. DRUCKER

Where everything is bad it must be good to know the worst.
FRANCIS HERBERT BRADLEY

There are no hopeless situations; there are only men who have grown hopeless about them.   CLARE BOOTHE LUCE

Some very able and conscientious people never make effective executives because their approach to difficult problems is judicial in its quality rather than dynamic.   CLARENCE B. RANDALL

Executives can be tempted to rationalize their distaste for facing up to problems by holding out for the perfect solution.
PROFESSOR RAY E. BROWN

Every solution of a problem is a new problem.
JOHANN WOLFGANG von GOETHE

When things come to the worst, they generally mend.
SUSANNA MOODIE

When you've got a problem with swine, you've got to call in the pigs.
S I. HAYAKAWA

It's not the size of the ship, it's the size of the waves.
LITTLE RICHARD

There are plenty of people to whom the crucial problems of their lives never get presented in terms that they can understand.
JOHN JAY CHAPMAN

Whenever you are too selfishly looking out for your own interest, you have only one person working for you—yourself. When you help a dozen other people with their problems, you have a dozen people working with you.   WILLIAM B. GIVEN

But it is doubtless impossible to approach any human problem with a mind free from bias.   SIMONE de BEAUVOIR

Cleanse the fountain if you would purify the streams.
A. BRONSON ALCOTT

All problems become smaller if you don't dodge them but confront them. Touch a thistle timidly, and it pricks you, grasp it boldly, and its spines crumble.   WILLIAM S. HALSEY

Everything has two handles, one by which it may be borne, another by which it cannot.   EPICTETUS

Mistakes

The mistakes of a beginner
Are known by everyone but him.
The mistakes of a true winner
Are known by no one else but him.

The fellow who never makes a mistake takes his orders from one who does. HERBERT V. PROCHNOW

Too many companies over-penalize the mistake and undercredit the fresh and new. WILLIAM T. BRADY

Lord, deliver me from the man who never makes a mistake, and also from the man who makes the same mistake twice. DR. WILLIAM J. MAYO

The greatest temptation is to have an alibi. GEORGE ABBOTT

There is no mistake so great as that of being always right.
SAMUEL BUTLER

The business system is blessed with a built-in corrective, namely, that one executive's mistakes become his competitor's assets. LEO CHERNE

There's many a mistake made on purpose. THOMAS C. HALIBURTON

Mistakes are always initial. CESARE PAVESE

Learn from the mistakes of others. You can't live long enough to make them all yourself. MARTIN VANBEE

The man who makes no mistakes does not usually make anything.
EDWARD JOHN PHELPS

My only regret is I did it my way. JAMES STEVENSON

The only people who make no mistakes are dead people. I saw a man last week who has not made a mistake for four thousand years. He was a mummy in the Egyptian department of the British Museum.
HERMAN LINCOLN WAYLAND

All the mistakes I ever made were when I wanted to say "No" and said
"Yes."   MOSS HART

Even when the experts all agree, they may well be mistaken.
                                        BERTRAND RUSSELL

Mistakes are a fact of life.
It is the response to the error that counts.   NIKKI GIOVANNI

When you have saved someone from the possiblity of making a mistake,
you have also prevented them from developing initiative.
                                            JACOB M. BRAUDE

Don't go to visit your friend in the hour of his disgrace.
                            RABBI SIMEON BEN ELEAZAR

Never give a man up until he has failed at something he likes.
                                            LEWIS E. LAWES

The greatest mistake is trying to be more agreeable than you can be.
                                            WALTER BAGEHOT

I don't care a damn for your loyal service when you think I am right;
when I really want it most is when you think I am wrong.
                                GENERAL SIR JOHN MONASH

There is glory in a great mistake.   NATHALIA CRANE

I never made a mistake in my life; at least, never one that I couldn't
explain away afterward.   RUDYARD KIPLING

There is nothing final about a mistake, except its being taken as final.
                                            PHYLLIS BOTTOME

Only he who does nothing makes a mistake.   FRENCH PROVERB

To err is human,
To forgive takes restraint;
To forget you forgave
Is the mark of a saint.   SUZANNE DOUGLASS

The best brewers sometimes make bad beer.   GERMAN PROVERB

It is very easy to forgive others their mistakes. It takes more gut and gumption to forgive them for having witnessed your own.

JESSAMYN WEST

It is hard to realize why almost a paralyzing fear of error curbs the initiative of so many men in management. This fear of error is one of the main reasons for costly red tape and controls that are established to insure against errors which, if made, could not cost anywhere near as much as the controls do. It is this intolerance of mistakes that curbs decentralization of responsibility and authority. It is unreasonableness of this kind that causes able men to keep their noses clean and their mouths shut. LAURENCE A. APPLEY

All the mistakes I make arise from forsaking my own station and trying to see the object from another person's point of view.

RALPH WALDO EMERSON

The follies which a man regrets most in his life are those which he didn't commit when he had the opportunity. HELEN ROWLAND

If only one could have two lives: the first in which to make one's mistakes, which seem as if they have to be made; and the second in which to profit by them. DAVID HERBERT LAWRENCE

Nowadays most people die of a sort of creeping common sense, and then discover when it is too late that the only things one never regrets are one's mistakes. OSCAR WILDE

A clever man commits no minor blunders.

JOHANN WOLFGANG von GOETHE

There is no mistake; there has been no mistake; and there shall be no mistake. DUKE of WELLINGTON

Frustration

Those without gain
Always complain,
But there's no need
When you succeed.

No matter what the job is, it ain't final. You can always quit.
                                        PETER F. DRUCKER

The difference between this place and a hedgehog is that a hedgehog has
all the pricks on the outside.   GRAFFITO

I was born below par to the extent of two whiskies.
                                        CHARLES E. MONTAGUE

What have we done that the American people want us to stop?
                                        SITTING BULL

Once a job is fouled up, anything done to improve it only makes it worse.
                                        ARTHUR BLOCK

It's a curious world: you upset the applecart only to find you've spilled
the beans.   FRANKLIN JONES

Custom reconciles us to everything.   EDMUND BURKE

The man who is always trying to create a sensation will soon find that he
can't even create a disturbance.   JOSH BILLINGS

Life is divided into the horrible and the miserable.
                        WOODY ALLEN & MARSHALL BRICKMAN

I tell you there is such a thing as creative hate!   WILLA CATHER

Don't believe the world owes you a living; the world owes you nothing—it
was here first.   ROBERT J. BURDETTE

The rule is, jam tomorrow and jam yesterday—but never jam today.
                                        LEWIS CARROLL

One of the heaviest burdens a person can carry is a chip on his shoulder.
OLIN MILLER

Why should a worm turn? It's probably just the same on the other side.
IRVIN COBB

All men are created equal but only in the eyes of God.   ANON

Life, as it is called, is for most of us one long postponement.
HENRY MILLER

A variety of nothing is better than a monotony of something.
JEAN PAUL RICHTER

Few men ever drop dead from overwork, but many quietly curl up and die
because of undersatisfaction.   SYDNEY J. HARRIS

Being frustrated is disagreeable, but the real disasters in life begin
when you get what you want.   IRVING KRISTOL

The more things change, the more they are the same.
ALPHONSE KARR

Nothing is as good as it seems beforehand.   GEORGE ELIOT

Forgive, O Lord, my little jokes on Thee
and I'll forgive Thy great big one on me.   ROBERT FROST

When your cup of happiness is full, somebody always jogs your elbow.
ANON

The one who complains the loudest is generally he who contributes the
least.   A. G. SERTILLANGES

Don't despair, not even over the fact that you don't despair.
FRANZ KAFKA

If not actually disgruntled, he was far from being gruntled.
PELHAM GRENVILLE WODEHOUSE

To have a grievance is to have a purpose in life.   ERIC HOFFER

Those who do not complain are never pitied.   JANE AUSTEN

All the animals except man know that the principal business of life is to enjoy it.   SAMUEL BUTLER

We are all serving a life sentence in the dungeon of self.
                                                CYRIL CONNOLLY

I admit I may have seen better days, but I am still not to be had for the price of a cocktail—like a salted peanut.   JOSEPH L. MANKIEWICZ

Oh, wouldn't the world seem dull and flat with nothing whatever to grumble at?   WILLIAM SCHWENCK GILBERT

When we sing everybody hears us: when we sigh nobody hears us.
                                                RUSSIAN PROVERB

Let us swear while we may, for in heaven it will not be allowed.
                                                MARK TWAIN

My theory is to enjoy life, but the practice is against it.
                                                CHARLES LAMB

Those who cannot live fully often become destroyers of life. ANAIS NIN

I don't care what becomes of me so long as it's a change for the better.
                                                WILLIAM FEATHER

There are two kinds of discontent in this world: the discontent that works, and the discontent that wrings its hands. The first gets what it wants, and the second loses what it has. There's no cure for the first but success; and there's no cure at all for the second. GORDON GRAHAM

Our business in this world is not to succeed, but to continue to fail, in good spirits.   ROBERT LOUIS STEVENSON

People will endure their tyrants for years, but they tear their deliverers to pieces if a millennium is not created immediately.
                                                THOMAS WOODROW WILSON

Man is the only animal that laughs and weeps; for he is the only animal that is struck with the difference between what things are, and what they ought to be.   WILLIAM HAZLITT

The dogs bark, but the caravan moves on.   ARABIAN PROVERB